# China and the Global Economy

## Also by Peter Nolan

*Inequality: India and China Compared, 1950–1970* (with T. J. Byres). Milton Keynes: Open University Press, 1976.

*Growth Processes and Distributional Change in a South Chinese Province: The Case of Guangdong*. London University: Contemporary China Institute, 1983.

*The Political Economy of Collective Farms: An Analysis of China's Post-Mao Rural Economic Reforms*. Cambridge: Polity Press, 1988.

*State and Market in the Chinese Economy: Essays on Controversial Issues*. Basingstoke, UK: Macmillan, 1993.

*China's Rise, Russia's Fall: Politics and Economics in the Transition from Stalinism*. Basingstoke, UK: Macmillan, 1995.

*Indigenous Large Firms in China's Economic Reform: The Case of Shougang Iron and Steel Corporation*. London University: Contemporary China Institute, 1998.

*Strategic Reorganisation* (with Wang Xiaoqiang, in Chinese). Shanghai: Wenhui Publishers, 1999.

*Coca-Cola and the Global Business Revolution*. Cambridge: The Judge Institute of Management Studies, 1999.

*China and the Global Business Revolution*. Basingstoke, UK: Palgrave, 2001.

*The Transformation of the Communist Economies: Against the Mainstream* (ed. with Ha-Joon Chang). Basingstoke, UK: Macmillan, 1994.

*China's Economic Reforms in the 1980s: the Costs and Benefits of Incrementalism* (ed. with Fan Qimiao). Basingstoke, UK: Macmillan, 1994.

*The Chinese Economy and its Future* (ed. with Dong Fureng). Cambridge: Polity Press, 1990.

*Market Forces in China: Competition and Small Business, the Wenzhou Debate* (ed. with Dong Fureng), London: Zed Books, 1989.

*Re-Thinking Socialist Economics* (ed. with S Paine). Cambridge: Polity Press, 1986.

# CHINA AND THE GLOBAL ECONOMY

**National Champions, Industrial Policy and the Big Business Revolution**

*Peter Nolan*

palgrave

First published 2001 by
PALGRAVE
Houndmills, Basingstoke, Hampshire RG21 6XS and
175 Fifth Avenue, New York, N.Y. 10010
Companies and representatives throughout the world

PALGRAVE is the new global academic imprint of
St. Martin's Press LLC Scholarly and Reference Division and
Palgrave Publishers Ltd (formerly Macmillan Press Ltd).

ISBN 0–333–94565–4

This book is printed on paper suitable for recycling and made
from fully managed and sustained forest sources.

A catalogue record for this book is available from the British Library.

Library of Congress Cataloging-in-Publication Data

Nolan, Peter, 1949–
    China and the global economy : national champions, industrial
policy, and the big business revolution / Peter Nolan.
        p. cm.
    Includes bibliographical references and index.
    ISBN 0–333–94565–4
        1. China—Economic conditions—1976– 2. China—Economic
policy—1976– 3. International economic relations. I. Title.
    HC427.92 .N64 2001
    337.51—dc21

                                                            2001021736

Formatted by The Ascenders Partnership, Basingstoke

10  9  8  7  6  5  4  3  2  1
10  09 08 07 06 05 04 03 02 01

Printed and bound in Great Britain by
Creative Print and Design (Wales),
Ebbw Vale

*For Dermot and Maeve*

# Contents

# List of Tables

# Preface

From 1994 to 1999 I carried out a series of case studies of large Chinese enterprises. These were undertaken together with Dr. Wang Xiaoqiang. A key part of the Chinese government programme of industrial reform was the use of industrial policies to nurture a group of large, modern corporations that could compete with the world's leading firms based in the high-income economies. These enterprises were members of the so-called 'national team'. It rapidly became obvious that a simultaneous business system revolution was under way in the advanced economies. We shifted the focus of our research. We attempted to combine our analysis of the evolution of large Chinese firms with an analysis of the simultaneous revolutionary 'restructuring' of capitalist big businesses headquartered in the advanced economies. The incredible speed and depth of the global business revolution presented a massive challenge to China's attempt to 'catch up' at the level of the large firm. China's large firms face a far greater challenge than faced those of any previous 'late-comer' country, including Japan. The theme of this book is the interaction between China's internal large enterprise system restructuring and the global business revolution.

The results of this research were published by both myself and Dr Wang, individually and together in various forms both inside and outside China. The entire set of case studies is published in *China and the Global Business Revolution* by Peter Nolan (Palgrave, 2001). This book is a synthesis of the key ideas in *China and the Global Business Revolution*. These books are the product of innumerable discussions between Dr. Wang and myself over the past few years.

We were helped in our research by numerous people. I wish especially to thank the following: Liu Yan, Wang Xuejia, Yang Ying, Zhang Jin, Godfrey Yeung, Dylan Sutherland, Wu Qing, Zhang Xinchuan, Lu Yansun, Jiang Xiaoming, Qin Xiao, Kang Dian, Elizabeth Briggs, and Felicity Pugh.

Our research formed the focal point of the *China Big Business Programme* in the Judge Institute of Management Studies. I am indebted to Liu Xingli and Matthew Bullock for their crucial roles in enabling this Programme to come into existence. The Programme uses the case studies as the basis for interactive meetings between senior Chinese and Western company officers and government officials. I am most grateful to the participating companies, both in China and in the UK, for allowing Dr. Wang and me to conduct in-depth research within their organizations. The Programme and the research that forms its core was made possible by the generous financial support of the following companies and institutions: British Aerospace (now BAe Systems), Rolls-Royce, Shell, BP Amoco, Rio Tinto, Barclays Capital, SBC Warburg, The Foreign and Commonwealth Office (UK), and the Department of Trade and Industry (UK).

Responsibility for the views expressed in this book rests entirely with me.

Peter Nolan
*Cambridge, 2001*

# Part I

# China's Ambitions: Building the 'National Team'

## Introduction

From the late 1970s to the late 1990s, the Chinese government used a wide array of industrial policies to support the growth of a 'national team' of large firms that could compete with the world's leading corporations. The foundations of this effort were the large industrial plants inherited from the former command economy. This approach to economic policy directly challenged the prevailing trend of globalization and liberalization. It was radically different from that advocated by the free market orthodoxy of mainstream economics and from the policies advanced by the international institutions of the 'Washington Consensus', notably the IMF and the World Bank. It differed comprehensively from the industrial reform policies pursued in the former Soviet Union and in Eastern Europe. The attempt raised deep questions about the role of the state in promoting national economic development and about the nature of capitalism itself. It involved fundamental questions concerning China's international relations in the early twenty-first century, namely the terms under which it will interact with the high-income countries in general, and, in particular, with the global superpower, the United States.

# 1.1   Lessons from historical experience

## Industrial structure and economic development: the neoclassical view

The debate about the transition from the Communist system of political economy has been intense. Industrial reform was at the centre of this debate. The approach adopted by the mainstream 'Washington Consensus' was built around the notion that large enterprises should mostly be closed down and replaced with a sea of new, small and medium-scale enterprises. Throughout the literature on the 'transition' in the industrial sector, attention was focused on the privatization of individual plants. In many industrial sectors under communist planning, China and the former USSR each had a small number of relatively large plants. The Washington Consensus gave no attention at all to the desirability of merging these plants within any given sector, in order to produce large, globally competitive multi-plant firms. 'Industrial policy' focused simply on ways of privatizing individual plants. In its interpretation of China's economic success since the 1970s, the World Bank has placed great emphasis on the growth of small and medium enterprises as the 'foundation for economic growth'.

It is certainly the case that small firms were neglected within the traditional planned economies. It was to be expected that the growth of market forces would lead to a greatly increased role for small firms. Many of these would arise from the demerging of segments of large vertically integrated state enterprises. However, this does not mean that large indigenous firms could have no significant role to play in the transition from Communist planning. The approach toward industrial reform that was adopted in the former USSR and Eastern Europe was guided by the powerful influence of the mainstream traditions of neoclassical economic theory. It had a highly idealized view of the workings of advanced capitalism, which emphasized the contribution of small firms and downplayed that of large firms.

Views which emphasize the importance of small firms over large firms have a long tradition in neoclassical economics. The mainstream approach is deeply suspicious of departures from perfect competition, under which there are large numbers of anonymous firms, none of which can exert any influence on the market. The neoclassical approach emphasizes the importance of competition among small firms as the explanation for the prosperity of the advanced economies. Despite the numerous assumptions necessary for the perfectly competitive model to operate, the influence of the model remains deeply embedded in the minds of mainstream economists. In the neoclassical view, the central task of microeconomics is to regulate the industrial structure so as to prevent a high degree of industrial concentration.

The neoclassical view of the 'East Asian miracle' regards the reason for their success as the fact that they allegedly conformed to the principle of comparative advantage and were guided by free trade in resource allocation:

> South Korea, Singapore, Hong Kong and Taiwan are examples of economies which
> have achieved fast and stable economic growth through exploiting their resources'
> comparative advantages … They relied on the function of the market. Market-
> determined relative prices reflected their relative scarcities or factor endowments. With
> the guidance of relative prices, they developed the sectors that could exploit their
> comparative advantages. These economies achieved unexpectedly rapid economic
> growth and became the rising stars of economic development.
>
> JUSTIN LIN

The neoclassical economists argue that China needs to be closely integrated
with the world economy in order to send the right 'undistorted' price signals to
enterprises, which will in turn enable maximum efficiency in resource use. The
argument is identical to that which Adam Smith made in his passionate criticism
of protection in Britain in the late eighteenth century. It underpinned Adam
Smith's famous proposition (1776) that the US would be much poorer under a
protectionist regime than with free trade:

> Were the Americans, either by combination or by any other sort of violence, to stop the
> importation of European manufactures, and by thus giving a monopoly to such of their
> own countrymen as could manufacture the like goods, divert any considerable part of
> their capital into this employment, they would retard instead of accelerating the further
> increase in the value of their annual produce, and would obstruct instead of promoting
> the progress of their country towards real wealth and greatness.

There is a close connection between the neoclassical economists' perspective
on international trade and their view of industrial structure. In simplistic
neoclassical theory, developing countries are argued to be capital-scarce and
labour-abundant. Developing countries are argued to have a comparative
advantage in labour-intensive goods but not in capital-intensive ones:

> The utilization of comparative advantage in an economy is a process of selecting the
> economy's industrial structure. Because different goods require different combinations
> of factor inputs, each country should choose the most advantageous industrial structure
> based on its resource endowment…At the early stage of a country's development,
> capital in general is extremely scarce and is a bottleneck for development; *therefore, the
> country must develop the clothing industry instead of the automobile industry.*
>
> JUSTIN LIN

The neoclassical economists argue that developing countries should go through
a 'normal' sequence of development of their industrial structure. In the early
stages of their development, which China is argued still to be in, they maintain
that China's growth should be based on small-scale, labour-intensive light
industries, rather than the use of industrial policy to support the growth of large-
scale, capital-intensive and technology-intensive industries. Taiwan is held up as
the best example for China to follow: 'Taiwan relied on the development of

labour-intensive and low-technology industries to push forward the industrialization of the whole economy. Because its industrial structure reflected the comparative advantage of its resource endowment, Taiwan's economy was very competitive in the world economy'. The neoclassical economists believe that the key to understanding China's rapid growth during the reform years is the fact that China has moved towards an industrial structure that reflects its comparative advantage. The most dynamic element in this growth is argued to be the small and medium-sized enterprises, especially the so-called township and village enterprises (TVEs). A great deal of neoclassical literature on the Chinese reforms has for this reason focused on the growth of TVEs: 'The TVEs' important role can be explained by the fact that they are well-placed to exploit the comparative advantages of relatively abundant labour resources ...TVEs are concentrated in low capital-intensive industries'.

In his classic article on the nature of the firm, Ronald Coase (1937) investigated the determinants of producing goods and services within the firm as opposed to purchasing them through market transactions. The global business revolution has brought drastic changes in the range of activities that firms wish to undertake within the firm as opposed to purchase through the market. A major factor in this process has been the extraordinary developments in information technology. These have reduced drastically the costs involved in undertaking transactions with other firms. Since the early 1980s, large firms have, on a widespread basis, outsourced service functions. Extensive outsourcing of components production has taken place throughout the manufacturing sector. Increasingly, 'outsourcing' has extended to R&D activities and to manufacturing large sub-units of complex products. Systems integrators are less and less involved in the direct manufacture of goods.

Many neoclassical analysts believe that the large corporation has become progressively less important. Current trends in industrial structure are seen to mark the end of the large corporation, and herald the beginning of a world of virtual corporations based around small firms, even perhaps the end of the firm in conventional terms: 'While big companies control ever larger flows of cash, they are exerting less and less direct control over business activity. They are, you might say, growing hollow'.

## Industrial structure and economic development: the unorthodox view

The reality of business history has been quite different from the neoclassical view. Instead of being an occasional deviation, oligopoly, barriers to entry and imperfect competition have been the normal path of capitalist development. Industrial policy in China has drawn its inspiration from non-mainstream economic theory, and from empirical evidence about the policies pursued in late-industrializing countries as well as from considerations of national pride and power.

## The tendency to concentration

From the earliest stages in the development of modern capitalism, there were economists who recognized the tendency towards concentration of industrial power. Marx, in *Capital*, Vol. 1, published in 1867, argued that there was a 'law of centralisation of capital' or the 'attraction of capital by capital'. The driving force of concentration was competition itself, which pressured firms to cheapen the cost of production by investing ever larger amounts of capital in new means of production and in 'the technological application of science', which in turn creates barriers to entry:

> The battle of competition is fought by cheapening commodities. The cheapness of commodities depends, *ceteris paribus*, on the productiveness of labour, and this again on the scale of production. Therefore the larger capital beats the smaller ...Everywhere the increased scale of industrial establishments is the starting-point for a more comprehensive organization of the collective work of many, for a wider development of their material motive force – in other words, for the progressive transformation of isolated processes of production, carried on by customary methods, into processes of production socially combined and scientifically arranged.
>
> MARX

In her path-breaking book, *The Theory of the Growth of the Firm* (1995), Edith Penrose analysed the limits to the growth of the firm. She identified a number of potential advantages that can be enjoyed by the large firm. Some of these are technological economies of scale at the plant level. However, the most significant are those advantages that accrue to the large multi-plant firm. She terms these advantages 'managerial economies'. These result when a larger firm can take advantage of an increased division of managerial labour and of the closely allied mechanization of certain administrative processes; make more intensive use of existing managerial resources by 'spreading' overheads; obtain economies from buying and selling on a larger scale; use reserves more economically; acquire capital on cheaper terms; and support large-scale research.

Penrose investigates in detail the ways in which a large, growing firm can use its resource advantages to generate further growth. Economies which are attributable to the size of firms may, up to a point, be responsible not only for lower costs of production and distribution of the existing products of larger firms. They may also provide crucial competitive advantages enabling already large firms to grow still further. Crucial to this process are the firm's research activities, enabling the development of new products, and the ability to generate the resources to introduce them. Far from management being a fixed factor of production, with diminishing returns, large firms can adapt their management structures to growth. Managerial resources become a key part of the large firm's ability to expand further: 'Once a substantial increment of growth is completed, the managerial services devoted to it become available for further expansion.

Furthermore, the growing experience of management, its knowledge of the other resources of the firm and of the potential for using them in different ways, creates incentives for further expansion as the firm searches for ways of using its own resources more profitably.' Penrose concludes that there are no theoretical limits to the size of the firm: 'We have found nothing to prevent the indefinite expansion of firms as time passes, and clearly if some of the economies of size are economies of expansion, there is no reason to assume that a firm would ever reach a size in which it has taken full advantage of all these economies'.

## Large firms and technical progress

Angus Maddison identifies technical progress as the most essential characteristic of economic growth: 'If there had been no technical progress, the whole process of accumulation would have been much more modest'. The research of Alfred Chandler has demonstrated the central role of the large, oligopolistic firm in technical progress. This was, in its turn, central to the growth of modern capitalism. In the late nineteenth century, especially in the United States, the first-mover large firms established themselves as dominant oligopolistic players and became 'the fertile learning ground for technological, managerial, and organizational knowledge for an entire economy'. These were primarily in the manufacturing sector that constituted the Second Industrial Revolution, including especially such capital-intensive activities as primary metals, petroleum refining, chemicals, electrical products and transport equipment. In these oligopolistic industries, there took place a switch from price to non-price competition:

> Oligopolistic firms competed even more effectively through functional and particularly strategic effectiveness: that is, by carrying out processes of production and distribution more capably; by improving both product and process through systematic research and development; by identifying more suitable sources of supply; by providing more effective marketing services; by product differentiation (in branded packaged products primarily through the advertising); and by moving more quickly into expanding markets and out of declining ones.

In this climate of oligopolistic competition, 'market share and profits changed constantly, which kept oligopolies from becoming stagnant and monopolistic'.

Technological advances achieved by large firms in these industries had powerful beneficial effects on the rest of the economy. They contributed to improved productivity in a wide range of other industries, including transport, communication and financial services: 'These enterprises became a rich spring of managerial and organizational information as well as technological knowledge, all of which spilled over into the wider spheres of domestic and international economies by means of networks, spin-offs and even ordinary market transactions'.

Chandler has shown the way in which the 'Third Industrial Revolution' during and after the Second World War was also 'dominated by large enterprises'. This revolution involved new technologies in chemicals, pharmaceuticals, aerospace, and electronics. With the exception of electronic data-processing technologies, 'the new technologies were commercialized by large, well-established enterprises rather than start-ups'. The modern industrial enterprise 'played a central role in creating the most technologically advanced, fastest growing industries of their day'. These industries, in turn, were 'the pace-setters of the industrial sector of their economies'. They provided an underlying dynamic in the development of modern industrial capitalism.

## The state and large firms in the 'catch-up' process: (i) the West

Far from arising spontaneously through the free play of market forces, even in the West, the rise of big business in the West was strongly influenced by the state. The British Industrial Revolution took place under a Mercantilist philosophy of high protection and export promotion, not to speak of massive territorial conquest largely in pursuit of economic benefit. Britain's 'infant industries' were heavily protected, denying the massive textile industries of China and India access to the British market. These restrictions gave Britain's infant textile industries the chance to mature and modernize through reinvested profits from heavily protected markets. By the mid-nineteenth century Britain's 'big business' (compared to the rest of the world) was able to prosper with free trade. It is questionable whether Britain rather than China would have been the 'First Industrial Nation' without extensive state intervention.

In the nineteenth century, the US industrialized behind high protectionist barriers, 'free riding on free trade'. As early as 1791, Alexander Hamilton argued for US industrialization behind tariff barriers. From 1820 through to the 1930s, US tariffs on imported manufactures were never below 25 per cent and mostly were far higher. Despite extensive public discussion and academic analysis of big business, anti-trust law in the US did little to hinder the rise of large US firms. The US merger mania of the 1890s provided the underpinnings for the business structure of the US economy for decades thereafter: 'The conversion of 71 important oligopolistic or near-competitive industries into monopolies by merger between 1890 and 1914 left an imprint on the structure of the American economy that 50 years has not yet erased'. Sixty-three of the 100 largest US firms in 1955 had experienced their main spurt of growth as a result of merger activity, including 20 in the 1895–1904 merger wave.

Having established powerful firms behind protectionist barriers, both Britain and the US became converts to free trade and the 'global level playing field', allowing their powerful businesses free access to the markets of less developed economies with weaker business structures.

Capitalism's innate tendency to concentration of economic power became manifest almost as soon as the First Industrial Revolution got under way. The earliest forms of the modern industrial enterprise were found in the railways of the United States and Europe in the mid-nineteenth century. These quickly developed into the world's largest business institutions, often with tens of thousands of employees. The railways mobilized vast sums of investment funds from an increasingly widespread body of shareholders. They developed the first significant body of salaried professional managers. These characteristic features of the modern industrial enterprise quickly spread to other parts of the economy in which large businesses emerged. These were industries characterized by greater economies of scale, greater potential gains from vertical integration, greater speed and coordination of production flows, as well as greater gains from high-volume marketing. These were notably the food, chemicals, primary metals and transportation equipment sectors. By the 1930s, the one hundred largest firms accounted for around one-quarter of total manufacturing output in Britain and the United States.

There is intense and unresolved debate as to whether the degree of dominance of large corporations increased over time within each of the advanced economies. What is beyond dispute is that in the late twentieth century, these corporations occupied immensely powerful positions within each of the advanced economies, quite at odds with the views expressed by most neoclassical economists. In 1947, the 200 largest firms in the US accounted for 30 per cent of total value-added in manufacturing. By 1987, the share had risen to over 43 per cent. In 1960, just four firms accounted for 22 per cent of total US industrial R&D expenditure. Three hundred and eighty-four firms each employing more than 5000 workers accounted for 85 per cent of the total expenditure.

## The state and large firms in the 'catch-up' process: (ii) Japan

In Japan the catch-up process after the Second World War was facilitated by the Japanese government, through a wide array of trade and industrial policies that went counter to mainstream economic theory. MITI, Japan's key planning body, did the opposite of what the American economists told them to do: 'We violated all the normal concepts'. It was in this environment of close indirect support from the state that the giant Japanese firms, that today lie at the heart of the Japanese economy, developed.

In the early postwar period, the US occupying forces imposed American anti-trust laws upon Japan. Initially these were strictly applied. They led to the dismantling of the leading pre-war *zaibatsu*, the large industrial groups which had dominated the interwar Japanese economy. However, the government soon encouraged the reconstruction of the *zaibatsu* albeit in a somewhat looser form, known as *keiretsu*. The goal of the Japanese government was explicitly to create oligopolistic competition. MITI actively encouraged mergers between leading firms in key industries. It allowed large indigenous firms to develop through draconian import controls. However, the government was acutely aware of the need to avoid monopoly and encourage oligopolistic rivalry. It closely monitored market shares and prevented any single investment from being so large as to destabilize the market. International competitiveness was encouraged through the

use of exports and international market share as the performance goals with
which to evaluate the extent of government support for big businesses.

In post-1945 Japan, the system of cross-ownership provided a powerful
mechanism through which the large Japanese corporation was able to grow at
high speed and catch up with the world leaders. Most large companies were
members of a small number of industrial groups, the *keiretsu*. A *keiretsu* usually
owned less than 2 per cent of any other member firm, but it typically had a stake
of that size in every firm in the group, so that between 30 per cent and 90 per cent
of a firm was owned by other group members. Japanese corporations have about
70 per cent of their shares held by other corporations. Through the cross-holding
process, Japanese managers effectively hired friendly owners. The system was a
kind of 'collective defence to maintain the control by management over
ownership'. The removal of ownership control meant that the unconstrained
Japanese managers could afford to ill-treat owners with impunity. In 1990, the
total dividend payout of all public corporations in Japan was 30 per cent of profits
compared with 50 per cent in Germany, 54 per cent in the US, and 66 per cent in
the UK. Japan managers spent more on corporate entertaining than they paid out
in dividends. Japanese managers could ignore short-term profitability as a
measure of their performance and concentrate instead on 'Schumpeterian'
competition, such as foreign market penetration, quality control, and long-term
product development. 'Share price increase' was their least important target, and
'market domination' their most important one.

Under this system there was only a low level of merger and acquisition. From
the managers' point of view, to be taken over by others was to surrender to their
enemies. Externally hired managers were rare, reflecting the fact that in Japan
competition was viewed as a war with no prisoners taken, with a good chance that
managers in the firm that was taken over would lose jobs after the take-over. This
life-and-death battle forced Japanese managers to build an alliance with their
employees, building long-term programmes such as housing, training, lifetime
employment, and the seniority system. Managers and workers 'agree[d] to trade
wage increases for job security or better opportunities for promotion made
possible by the growth of the firm'. Hence, the level of strikes in Japan was low.
Instead, Japanese labour unions and their members were very interested in having
a voice in management. Workers in large Japanese firms often endured hardship
in order to enable their firm to survive and grow.

Alongside rapid growth of national output, Japan's large firms grew at high
speed. In 1962 Japan had just 31 of the *Fortune 500* companies, less than either
Germany or the UK, and only marginally more than France. By 1993 the number of
Japanese firms in the *Fortune 500* had risen to 135. Not only had the number of
large Japanese firms risen at high speed, but their contribution to technical progress
in the Japanese economy had also dramatically risen. By 1993 Japan had 49 out of
the world's top 200 companies by R&D spending. By 1995 Japan had 18 of the
world's top 100 TNCs (ranked by foreign assets) and in 1996 it had 110 of the
world's top 500 companies, ranked by market capitalization. Despite the numerous

difficulties of the 1990s, the core of Japan's large business structure remains immensely strong. A large group of Japanese firms are still world leaders in terms of R&D expenditure and technological capability, as well as in terms of global brand and distribution systems. In the year 2000, Japan still had 107 firms in the *Fortune 500* (ranked by sales revenue) and 77 firms in the *FT 500* (ranked by market capitalization) and 83 of the world's top 300 firms ranked by R&D spending.

## The state and large firms in the 'catch-up' process: (iii) the Four Little Tigers

The role of the state and large firms in the Four Little Tigers was much greater than the neoclassical position allows. With the exception of Hong Kong, the Asian NICs were characterized by far-reaching, pervasive state intervention and control in almost all segments of the economy. In Taiwan, Korea and Singapore the state in each case had an extremely active industrial policy. The Taiwanese and South Korean states each went far beyond influencing the environment within which big business operated. In both cases the state played an important role in the construction of large-scale business through the direct operation of upstream, heavy industry which the private sector was unable or unwilling to undertake. Despite a quite limited role in direct ownership, both Hong Kong and Singapore had a central role for the state in developing human capital and maintaining social stability through high levels of expenditure on education, health and housing. In the populist neoclassical view of the Four Little Tigers, their rapid catch-up was reliant on small firms and perfect competition. In fact, large firms played a key role in the economic development of each of the Four Little Tigers.

Both Hong Kong and Singapore throughout their catch-up practised basically free trade regimes. As tiny city states they had little option. However, for both Taiwan and Korea, trade policy was central to their catch-up strategy. Both of them massively protected their economy through high tariff barriers in the early period of development. In Taiwan, after tariffs began to fall in the 1970s, there remained for many years a wide array of non-tariff barriers. Taiwan used a variety of measures to actively promote exports. Korea remained heavily protected right up until the late 1990s, using both tariff and non-tariff barriers.

### Taiwan
One of the most eloquent statements on the importance of the state in promoting economic development in the Far East is that of Chiang Kaishek, the leader of the Kuomintang. In 1947, in the midst of his party's struggle with the Chinese Communist Party, he wrote:

> China cannot compete with the advanced industrial nations. She must therefore adopt a protectionist policy with regard to foreign trade, and a policy of economic planning with respect to her industrial development. *Private capital alone will not be sufficient to operate on a large scale, or to compete with the trusts and government operated*

*enterprises of foreign nations.* This is the great weakness of laissez-faire economic theory and makes it unsuitable for China (emphasis added).

In the 1950s and 1960s, the state's industrial policy focused on import substitution and export promotion in labour-intensive light industry. However, in the 1970s, government policies called for a gradual shift to basic and heavy industries and as part of a backward integration process, intermediate goods industries were established. This included extensive state ownership of the 'commanding heights' of heavy industry, including steel, shipbuilding, oil refining, chemicals, and electricity generation. Even in sectors where public enterprises did not dominate, such as plastics and textiles, the state 'aggressively led private producers in the early years'. Through its extensive ownership and operation of vital upstream industries, as well as numerous other measures, such as import controls, tariffs, entry requirements, domestic content requirements, and concessional credit, the Taiwanese state strongly influenced the operation of the private sector, constantly pushing it and assisting it to upgrade technologically.

By the early 1980s, three-quarters of Taiwan's exports consisted of high and mid-tech products and 51 per cent consisted of technology-intensive products. Subsequently, policy shifted to indirect support, and eventually widespread privatization. However, there was still a strong objective of consciously transforming the economic structure towards higher value-added activities more rapidly than the free market would have produced them. For example, the government established the immensely influential Hsinchu Science Park, provided tax benefits for investment in high technology industries, and in the mid-1980s it accounted for 60 per cent of total R&D expenditure in Taiwan. By the late 1990s, over 80 per cent of Taiwan's exports were of technology-intensive products.

The stylized picture of Taiwan provided by neoclassical economists is of an economy dominated by small firms. Taiwan does have a vibrant small-scale sector. However, it also has a very strong and dynamic large-scale sector. Taiwan's large firms benefit from economies of scale and scope enabling them to compete on world markets and provide intermediate inputs in an efficient way for Taiwan's other exporters. The Taiwanese government itself describes its industrial structure as a mutually interactive relationship between large and small firms: 'The close relationship and division of labour between SMEs (small and medium-sized enterprises) and large-scale enterprises make for a very solid 'pyramid' or 'cluster' economy in terms of industrial structure, which allows the realization of operational efficiencies'.

In the early 1970s, Taiwan's large firms, with more than 500 employees, accounted for 58 per cent of manufacturing value-added, compared with 53 per cent in Korea and 49 per cent in the US. In 1979, the top 100 firms accounted for 44 per cent of total private manufacturing assets. In the 1990s, Taiwan's rapid growth of high-technology exports was spearheaded by large firms such as Acer Computer (1999 revenue $5.6bn), Taiwan Semi-Conductor (revenue $1.7bn) and Quanta Company (revenue $1.7bn). Large heavy industrial enterprises, often former state-owned firms, such as China Steel (1999 revenue $3.3bn), Formosa Chemicals (revenue $1.3bn), Formosa Plastics (revenue $1.4bn) and Nanya Plastics (revenue $4.1bn), still form the backbone of the economy. Taiwan has 26 of the top 100 firms in the non-Japan Asia-Pacific region, ranked by market capitalization.

### South Korea

The South Korean government believed strongly in the central role of big business in the catch-up process. President Park Chung Hee wrote as follows:

> One of the essential characteristics of a modern economy is its strong tendency towards centralization. Mammoth enterprise – considered indispensable, at the moment, to our country – plays not only a decisive role in the economic development and elevation of living standards, but further brings about changes in the structure of society and economy … . Therefore the key economic problems facing a free economic policy are co-ordination and supervisory guidance, by the state, of mammoth economic strength.

The government actively encouraged the growth of powerful, large-scale private businesses, the *chaebols*, by providing them with a protected domestic market, and supplying them with tightly controlled, but low interest, credit from the state-owned banking system. The South Korean state used pre-existing powerful business families as the foundation for the *chaebol* structure. Korea's large firms remained predominantly family-owned throughout its catch-up process. Like the Japanese state, South Korea was acutely aware of the importance of maintaining competition among its large oligopolistic firms. It went out of its way to ensure that big business did not collude, by allocating subsidies only in exchange for strict performance standards. Industrial policy focused initially on import substitution, with massive protection from import competition for a long period while its big businesses were nurtured, absorbing advanced technologies from abroad, and benefiting from economies of scale and scope. The state was prepared to provide long-term support until the businesses became internationally competitive, enabling firms to have long time-horizons for their investment plans. Once they were established, a key condition for continued state support was success in export markets.

The South Korean 'entrepreneurial state' instigated every major industrial diversification of the decades of the 1960s and 1970s. Alice Amsden notes:

> The state masterminded the early import-substituting projects … The transformation from light to heavy industry came at the state's behest … The government played the part of visionary in the case of Korea's first colossal shipyard … and it was responsible for the Big Push into heavy machinery and chemicals in the late 1970s. It also laid the groundwork for the new wave of import substitution that followed heavy industrialization and that carried the electronics and automobile industry beyond the simple stage of assembly. The government enacted the automobile protection law as far back as 1962, as part of its five-year economic development plan. In conjunction with this decision, it promoted the oil-refining industry.

Korea's *chaebols* were the core of the country's economic development. By the mid-1980s, the top ten *chaebols* accounted for over two-thirds of national product. The large-scale heavy industry sectors, dominated by the *chaebols* were at the heart of Korea's dynamic export performance in the 1970s and 1980s. By 1985, South Korea had 35 of the top 200 largest industrial enterprises in developing countries, including 11 of the 29 top 'high-tech' companies and 13 of the top 'mid-tech' companies within this group. By 1995 it had three of the top ten TNCs based in developing countries. Uniquely among developing countries, by 1993, South Korea had no less than four companies in the *Fortune 100* list of the world's largest companies. Even in the wake of the East Asian crisis, it still had 11 of the top 100 Asia-Pacific companies ranked by market capitalization and 12 firms in the *Fortune 500*.

### Singapore

Singapore's state had little confidence in the capability of indigenous entrepreneurs to create globally powerful firms. Instead it actively induced multinationals to establish production facilities in Singapore in selected industries. Ezra Vogel comments: 'Singapore's leaders took great care in selecting the foreign companies whose investment they approved. They sought out stable corporations that had advanced technology and were prepared to invest for the long-term'. It is no surprise that Singapore's industrial structure is dominated by multinational firms. However, alongside these firms, it has also developed a strong group of large indigenous firms. Singapore's bureaucrats over time developed a group of state-run enterprises in telecommunications, banking and transport, that began to establish a serious internationally competitive capability, including Singapore Telecoms, Development Bank of Singapore, and Singapore Airlines. However, Singapore is also the home to several powerful private sector regional banking, infrastructure and property development companies. By 1999/2000, Singapore, a tiny city-state, had three firms among the 100 largest multinationals based in developing countries, the same number as did Mexico, and ten firms among the 100 largest in East Asia (by market capitalization), more than India and Indonesia combined.

### Hong Kong

In the neoclassical view Hong Kong is the prime example of development through free markets and small competitive firms. Hong Kong has an outstanding location. It has a strong entrepreneurial tradition, particularly due to the migration of a group of powerful entrepreneurs from Shanghai after 1949. It obtained enormous benefits from trade with, and investment in, the mainland. The combination of these factors stimulated the growth of numerous powerful firms that were among the largest in non-Japan East Asia. In 2000, there were seven Hong Kong-based firms among the top 15 firms, and 20 firms among the top 100 firms in non-Japan Asia, ranked by market capitalization. Despite the rise of IT-based Indian firms, such as Wipro and Infosys, India still has only seven firms among the largest in the non-Japan Asia-Pacific region, far fewer than the tiny city-state of Hong Kong. In 1995, nine of the 50 largest firms based in developing countries were from Hong Kong. Hong Kong was the base for a larger number of firms than any other country among the 50 largest TNCs from developing countries. The sales revenues of the top five Hong Kong companies are equivalent to over 10 per cent of Hong Kong's GDP. Hong Kong's relatively large companies account for a major share of the total market capitalization of the Hong Kong stock market. The political life of Hong Kong is strongly influenced by a handful of large firms.

### *Overall*
The total population of the Four Little Tigers is just 77 million, the same size as a medium-sized Chinese province. The Four Little Tigers grew rapidly, due to a variety of state actions, both direct and indirect, the advantage of good location, and outward-oriented policies at a time when other countries, such as India and China, were inward looking. By the late 1990s they had between them 20 of the 50 largest TNCs in developing countries, and 67 of the 100 largest firms in the non-Japan Asia Pacific region. Large firms played an important role in the development of each of these economies, including even Hong Kong. The facts of the relationship between the state and industrial development, and the role of large firms during the take-off phase in these countries, are far removed from the populist neoclassical view.

## Conclusion

China's policymakers after the 1970s were deeply influenced by the industrial policy experience of the advanced capitalist countries in Europe and in the US during their 'catch-up' phase of development. Even more influential was the more recent experience of its East Asian neighbours. Among these, by far the most impressive for them was the way in which the Japanese state was able to mastermind the high-speed growth of large corporations. These were entities that came to challenge the global giants of Europe and the US within their own markets. They developed high levels of business capability, built global brands from nothing and constructed massive R&D capabilities. During the first decade or so of China's post-Mao industrial policy, Japan's large firms were viewed in the West as providing a massive challenge to the existing large corporations. By far the most influential trend in business philosophy in the West was to learn from Japanese large corporations. The key philosophy of the Chinese leadership's policies towards large-scale industry throughout this period was the attempt to emulate the East Asian late-comer countries, and by means of state support to gradually build globally powerful large corporations. This policy was in the sharpest contrast with that pursued by the former USSR.

## 1.2   **Building the national team**[1]

### Unorthodox policies and rapid growth

From the late 1980s to the late 1990s, China followed a path of experimental economic system reform alongside an over-riding commitment to maintain system stability through tight political control. This path contrasted strongly with the reform path of the former USSR. While the Russian political system and economy disintegrated, China's non-orthodox approach produced outstanding results in terms both of output growth, with an average annual growth rate of GDP of over 10 per cent from 1980 to 1990. Moreover, indicators of human welfare, such as life expectancy, child mortality and absolute poverty, improved greatly over the course of the two decades of reform.

It is widely argued that China's rapid economic development was primarily as a result of the explosive growth of small enterprises, often under *de facto* private ownership. By the end of 1996 around 70 per cent of small state-owned enterprises (SOEs) had been privatized in pioneering provinces and about 50 per cent in many other provinces. This was referred to as a 'quiet revolution from below'. The World Bank considers China's small enterprises to be 'the foundation for recent growth'. In fact large enterprises played a key role in China's economic growth in this period. The Chinese state consciously nurtured a group of large enterprises that it hoped would be able to challenge the world's leading industrial enterprises on the 'global level playing field'.

### Grasping the large

By the early 1990s, a key economic policy slogan had become 'grasp the large, let go of the small'. The determination to build such a group of globally competitive large, multi-plant corporations stemmed from deep study of the development experience of successful late-coming industrializing countries and from close observation of the industrial structure of advanced capitalism. National pride was a further powerful motive. For almost one thousand years, China had been by far the most advanced part of the global economy. As late as the mid-eighteenth century, China accounted for around one-third of total global industrial output. However, from the mid-nineteenth to the mid-twentieth century, China's political system disintegrated and China's economy advanced at a painfully slow rate. Progress was confined to a few pockets of Treaty Ports along the coast. In 1949, when the Communist Party came to power, China was extremely poor. Its share of global industrial output had shrunk to under 3 per cent. China's national aspirations to recover its former place in the world

---

[1] This section is based on the research of Dylan Sutherland, Judge Institute of Management Studies, University of Cambridge.

economy were powerfully expressed by Chairman Mao in his speech on the founding of the People's Republic of China: 'The Chinese have always been a great courageous and industrious nation; it is only in modern times that they have fallen behind. And that was entirely due to oppression and exploitation by foreign imperialism and domestic reactionary governments...Ours will no longer be a nation subject to insult and humiliation. We have stood up.' When Mao died in 1976, China had achieved considerable economic progress, but was still far behind the advanced capitalist countries. Its near neighbours, Japan and East Asian newly industrializing countries, had vastly outstripped China. Building large indigenous firms was a crucial part of China's effort to rebuild national pride.

The call for a 'national team' to compete with the large firms of the rich countries was explicit. For example, in 1997, in his speech to the 15th Party Conference President Jiang Zemin said:

> The leading role of the state-owned sectors should manifest itself mainly in its control power. We should make a strategic readjustment of the state-owned sector of the economy. The state-owned sector must be in a dominant position in major industries and key areas that concern the life-blood of the national economy ... we shall effectuate a strategic reorganization of state-owned enterprises by managing well large enterprises while adopting a flexible policy toward small ones. By using capital as the bonds and relying on market forces, China will establish highly competitive large enterprise groups with trans-regional, inter-trade, cross-ownership and trans-national operations.

In 1998, Vice-Minister Wu Banguo said:

> In reality, international economic confrontations show that if a country has several large companies or groups it will be assured of maintaining a certain market share and a position in the international economic order. America, for example, relies on General Motors, Boeing, Du Pont and a batch of other multinational companies. Japan relies on six large enterprise groups and Korea relies on ten large commercial groupings. In the same way now and in the next century our nation's position in the international economic order will be to a large extent determined by the position of our nation's large enterprises and groups.

As China's entry to the WTO grew nearer, China's leaders became even stronger in their call for the construction of a group of globally powerful indigenous corporations. In January 2000, Vice-Minister Jian Qiangui considered it 'imperative to develop a number of large enterprise groups to make up the backbone of the national economy and the country's main force to participate in international competition'.

## Policies to develop the 'national team'

Like all of China's reforms, the growth of support for large enterprises emerged from a process of experimentation, combining central directives with initiatives from below. Under the planned economy, each enterprise had operated as a relatively independent unit, with direct links to the relevant ministry. As China's enterprises began to acquire increased independence in the early phase of China's economic reform, so there quickly developed economic links between different enterprises. In July 1980 the first policy document recognizing the existence of growing inter-enterprise production agreements was published ('The State Council on pushing forward rules relating to economic links between enterprises'). By April of 1981, Erqi (Dongfeng), a large automotive producer, and arguably the leading pioneer in the trials with enterprise groups, had become one of the first large state enterprises to expand from predominantly plant-based operations to a regionally and operationally diversified group of enterprises, organized by a core plant. With the proliferation of economic linkages between enterprises in the early and mid-1980s it was not long before policy advisers started to realize the potential of further promoting some pioneering groups. By 1986 influential Chinese economists and policymakers, including Ma Hong, head of the influential State Council Development Research Centre (SCDRC), began to look at policies specifically aimed at the promotion of large business groups based around former state plants. By December 1987 the publication of 'Some opinions on arranging and developing business groups' marked the first policy document setting out the aims and means of developing enterprise groups.

In the 1990s a 'national team' of 120 large enterprise groups was selected by the State Council in two batches, in 1991 and 1997 respectively. These enterprises were predominantly in those sectors considered to be of 'strategic importance', including electricity generation (8), coal mining (3), automobiles (6), electronics (10), iron and steel (8), machinery (14), chemicals (7), construction materials (5), transport (5), aerospace (6) and pharmaceuticals (5). These sectors are those that have historically tended to be characterized by strong economies of scale and scope. They correspond closely to those sectors which Chandler identified as 'most crucial to the strength, continued growth and defence of a modern, urban, industrial and technologically advanced society'.

A number of policies were used to support the growth of the national team. Most fundamentally, they benefited from high levels of protection. China's tariff level fell substantially during the 1990s, but by 1999, the average level of tariffs still stood at almost 25 per cent. Tariffs in certain sectors were much above this. For example, they stood at 80–100 per cent on vehicle imports, and 31 per cent on farm products. In oil and petrochemicals, the average tariff had fallen to 15 per cent, and to 13 per cent for IT products, and 10 per cent for steel and pharmaceuticals. In addition, there was a battery of non-tariff barriers. These included requirements to make technology transfers for certain categories of imported goods. Chinese bureaucrats frequently selected component suppliers for multinational investors. Firms that exported to China were frequently required to source from Chinese components suppliers. Foreign firms were routinely excluded from access to domestic distribution channels. Foreign investors in many sectors were required to establish joint ventures with domestic partners, the latter often being chosen by Chinese bureaucrats.

Members of the national team typically were given enhanced rights at a relatively early stage in the economic reforms to manage the key aspects of their business, including such fundamental issues as profits retention, investment decisions and rights to engage in international trade. They were permitted to establish their own internal finance companies. They were given the right to manage other state-owned firms within the enterprise group. Many state-run R&D centres were simply transferred to members of the national team, in order to enhance their ability to sustain technical progress. Members of the national team were in the forefront of the attempt to establish a modern enterprise system, which formally separated the enterprise from the bureaucracy. The property rights of the enterprise as an independent legal entity were formally established under the 1994 Company Law. The national team was in the lead in the move to list Chinese enterprises on stock markets. By the late 1990s, almost every one of the national team was listed on the domestic stock market. Around fifty had been listed overseas. The process of overseas listing was especially tightly controlled by the Chinese government. This was an important mechanism for raising capital for China's aspiring global champions.

As well as a variety of special rights, the national team received large-scale state financial support. The four large state banks, Industrial and Commercial Bank of China (ICBC), Agricultural Bank of China (ABC), Bank of China (BOC) and the China Construction Bank (CCB) all gave special support to the emerging large enterprise groups: the '[state] banks concentrate limited funds on key state businesses, which can help the country to implement its industrial policies'. According to the ICBC vice-president, 'supporting large state enterprises is not only our duty but also a key strategy for our expansion'. The CCB claimed that 'by focusing on large conglomerates and giving up small firms with poor performances, our banks achieved good returns'. It supported the process of industrial concentration. In the late 1990s it developed a simplified loan procedure for the targeted large enterprise groups. It claimed that 95 per cent of loans were collected on time and problem loans from the large enterprises accounted for less than 1 per cent of the total. The CCB has 500 professional branches based in the large enterprises giving advice as well as providing easier access to capital markets for the groups. Encouraged by the State Council, the CBC's stated policy was to support almost 300 'prime clients', in order to 'fuel the fostering of international industrial giants', making it one of the leading supporters of the national team. The BOC has also been active in making loans to large-scale industry. For example, in 1997 it agreed to supply Konka, a leading electronics firm, with one of the largest ever loans to a manufacturing company (totalling half a billion dollars). The Export-Import Bank of China has also given export credit guarantees to large firms in sectors such as electronics, shipbuilding and high-tech machinery sectors. In 1996 alone, it financed $4.3bn-worth of electronics and machinery exports.

## Size and influence of the national team

The 120 trial enterprise groups chosen by the State Council were invariably leaders in their industries. The six trial groups in electricity generation and supply, for example, produced over half of China's electricity. The eight metallurgy groups produced 40 per cent of the nation's iron and steel and the six approved vehicle makers manufactured 57 per cent of China's vehicle output. The three civilian airlines controlled over 55 per cent of the domestic market. The groups were based upon large-scale enterprises which were the 'core members of the group' with the 'capability to act as investment centres'. In 1995 the 120 trial groups combined workforce stood at approximately 7 million, averaging about 60 000 employees per group, amounting to approximately one quarter of total employment in large-scale enterprises. In 1997 they accounted for one third of the total output value of the whole large and medium scale enterprise sector. In the same year, within the whole state-owned sector, they accounted for over 50 per cent of total profits, paid 25 per cent of taxes and made over 25 per cent of all sales. Of the 120 groups less than ten were loss-makers at the end of 1995.

# 1.3   **Case studies**

Between 1994 and 1999 Dr. Wang Xiaoqiang and I undertook a series of in-depth case studies of China's emerging 'national team'. These studies showed the intense ambition that exists in China at the level of the enterprise to build powerful modern, internationally competitive firms. We found that great progress was made in building a modern business system. By the late 1990s, China's large firms were significantly transformed compared to the former state-owned enterprises. However, the progress was not uniform and many unexpected difficulties emerged during the course of this period.

## Aerospace: AVIC

### What is AVIC?

From the early 1950s through to the 1990s, the Ministry of Aviation Industry ran China's entire aviation industry. In 1993, Aviation Industries of China (AVIC) was established, assuming responsibility for the management of all the aviation industry assets formerly under the Ministry. It was formally turned into an experimental state holding company in 1996. AVIC had around 245 enterprises under its control. These included 18 enterprises manufacturing military and civilian aircraft and helicopters, 11 enterprises manufacturing aero-engines, and 77 enterprises manufacturing airborne equipment. In addition, it had 34 research institutes. Its structure was quite different from the world's leading aerospace companies, with a core design and airframe assembly company, which buys engines and other components from a huge number of supplier firms. AVIC embraced within a single company all the elements needed to build an aircraft. The goal of the holding company was to transform the nationwide collection of enterprises into an internationally competitive aircraft company:

> AVIC is promoting itself to become a gigantic enterprise group with world-wide fame and influence ... The aviation industry has itself become one of the key high-tech industries with intensive technology and vast infrastructure. AVIC will become an ultra-large industrial group, which combines military and civil aviation, is transnational in operation, high technology and export oriented.

AVIC's enterprises were widely scattered across China. Each of the main plants together with the associated engine and components supply network, is capable of independently manufacturing complete aircraft. The vast bulk of production capabilities was intended to manufacture military aircraft.

## Military aircraft

AVIC's principal aerospace products were military planes. By the time of Mao Zedong's death in 1976, Western experts had concluded that China's military technology was 'at least two or three decades behind that of advanced industrial countries'. The military industrial base was 'incapable of producing modern arms' and the armed forces, including China's large military aircraft fleet, were equipped with 'obsolete equipment copied from Soviet models'.

China's whole military strategy was drastically overhauled at the end of the Maoist period. In his key speech in 1977, Deng Xiaoping told the PLA leaders that priority must be given to economic modernization: 'But we must take note of one condition, namely that we must proceed from actual possibilities. The state budget is limited, and moreover, the amount of our military expenditure has to be decided with a view to the overall balance. Our national defence can be modernized only on the basis of the industrial and agricultural development of the country as a whole'. Deng Xiaoping recognized that China's task of catching up in the military sphere was extremely difficult: 'Even if we gain 10 or 20 years [of peace] in which to modernize our army's equipment, it will still be inferior to the enemy's. For the enemy won't be sleeping while we are advancing. Therefore, if and when war breaks out, we will still have to triumph over superior forces with our inferior equipment'.

After the late 1970s, there was a serious fall in the government's outlays on domestically manufactured military aircraft, which had large consequences for the development path of the entire aerospace industry. Within the national budget, 'expenditure on national defense' (in real terms) fell by around 2 per cent in total from 1980 to 1995. Its share of the total budget fell from 19.1 per cent in 1971–75 to under 10 per cent in 1986–95. The output of Chinese combat aircraft production by the mid-1990s had fallen by more than one-half from the levels of the early 1980s.

In the early 1990s, the former USSR collapsed economically and politically. Russia's outlays on military aircraft procurement declined dramatically, and the defence industry contracted drastically. However, the technical level of the former USSR's military aircraft industry is far ahead of China's, with world class design capability. The Soviet defence industry was very keen indeed to earn hard currency by selling to China.

On the Chinese side, the Gulf War had a big impact on Chinese military thinking. China's military leaders realized that the country lagged badly in its defence capability, and that urgent measures were needed to deal with its backwardness. The West would not sell advanced military aircraft to China, and the Russians were able to sell advanced equipment at relatively low prices. In 1992, China placed an order for 50 Su-27s, which were delivered in 1993. This was a very symbolic move, since there had been no arms sales from Russia to China since the 1950s. In 1997, they placed a further order for 150 Su-27s, to be built under licence in China. These are truly advanced fighters, far beyond the level that China itself can produce. It was reported in 1999 that China was ordering more Su-30 fighter aircraft, technically more advanced than the Su-27s. By the late 1990s, the Su-27s had become the core of China's fighter aircraft fleet. One Western expert commented: 'Of the 5000 fixed-wing combat aircraft, more than 90 per cent are obsolete. Only the Su-27s are truly modern'. Another commented: 'The decision to import Russian fighters suggests an acceptance that indigenous designs are inadequate as front-line aircraft. China's decision to import a second batch of Su-27s in quantity implies a judgment that the process of copying the first batch – avionics, engines and missiles – would not be practicable even if manufacturing skills are improving'.

Since the 1970s, military technology outside China has advanced at high speed. A key aspect of the Gulf War was 'command and control' systems. Western experts consider that China 'has lagged badly in this area'. By the mid-1990s, Western expert opinion noted: 'China's arms industries have no experience in [designing and building] modern aircraft, nor have they experience in building and operating advanced avionics suites … China's total lack of experience in constructing modern power plants constitutes yet another hurdle to jump'. The strategy that China has adopted since the late 1970s leaves it highly reliant on imported equipment and technology for its national defence.

## Civilian aircraft

### *Market prospects*

The Chinese civilian aircraft market is one of the largest and fastest-growing in the world. It is forecast that China will acquire over 1300 aircraft between 1996 and 2014, worth a total of $100bn. This would account for 35 per cent of predicted sales for the entire Asia-Pacific region. Up until 1997, Boeing had comprehensively dominated the Chinese commercial aircraft market, selling over 240 aircraft to China compared with just 35 from Airbus. The Chinese market is important for Boeing, accounting for around 10 per cent of its total global sales in 1990–96. After 1996 Airbus sharply increased its market share in China at the expense of Boeing. In both 1997 and 1998 China ordered 19 aircraft from Airbus, amounting to around 10 per cent of Airbus' annual output in those years.

The Chinese aviation industry is still subject to a high degree of regulation by the Civil Aviation Administration of China (CAAC), which is directly responsible to the State Council. All civil aircraft purchases must be conducted through CAAC's subsidiary, CASC (the Civil Aviation Supply Company). This provides a potentially powerful instrument for industrial policy should the government choose to use it. It also provides a potentially powerful lever for influencing international relations. Under China's economic reforms CAAC has been reluctant to buy any planes other than from the leading European and US companies.

### *Yun-10 (Y-10)*

In 1970, the central government decided that China should build its own domestic large jet airliner, the Y-10, at almost the same time that France, Germany and the UK decided to attempt to break the dominance of Boeing with Airbus. The decision to start the Y-10 programme appears to have been initiated by Premier Zhou Enlai. He apparently recommended the plan to Chairman Mao, who gave it his support, and then the scheme got under way. In December 1981, Deng Xaoping issued the following instruction: 'Henceforth, China's domestic airlines should use only domestically-produced airplanes'.

Shanghai Aircraft Manufacturing Company (SAMC) was chosen as the central location from which the project was co-ordinated and at which the plane was to be assembled. Prior to the Y-10 project it was China's largest military aircraft repair plant. The Ministry of Aviation dispatched several hundred technicians from all over China to Shanghai to work on the project. The atmosphere during the project was highly patriotic. The design of the aircraft was completed in 1978 and the first test flight took place in 1980. Between 1980 and 1985 it made 130 test flights, totalling 170 hours of flying time. It demonstrated an ability to fly in any type of weather condition, and to make landings at a variety of different altitudes.

The Y-10 was modelled on the Boeing 707, with a variety of modifications. The engines were based on the Pratt and Whitney JT3D. The entire airframe was manufactured within China. 'Most' of the avionics were manufactured in China, but 'around twenty' important pieces of avionics equipment were imported. The vast bulk of domestically manufactured components were produced in different enterprises in Shanghai, with a total of 263 different work units involved. Altogether two Y-10s were assembled and the components for a third aircraft were ready for assembly, but the assembly was not undertaken due to termination of the programme. One aircraft was 'tested to destruction' in ground tests. The other was used for the test flights, and still stands parked on the airfield at the SAMC.

The Y-10 programme was halted in 1985. It is unclear why this happened. One common explanation is that it was halted for 'political reasons' after 1978, because it was associated with the Gang of Four. Others observe that the Y-10's safety record was unproven and that it would have required a great deal more investment to ensure that it met the CAAC's safety requirements, let alone those of the FAA. In the face of an uncertain market, with proven international aircraft available on attractive terms, the purely commercial justification for the Y-10 did not exist. It would have required substantial government protection in the form of a guaranteed domestic market in order to provide the initial sales needed to launch the programme commercially. Apparently, the CAAC was unwilling to make such a commitment.

For the Chinese aircraft industry the Y-10 provides an important symbol of China's capability to build a large civil airliner independently. Its successful development is seen by many people within the industry as having closed the technological gap between China and the West, as it enabled China to develop valuable skills in building a complete airliner. Design and assembly of the Y-10 in Shanghai helped rapidly push the SAMC from being a purely aircraft repair into a major assembly company. This in turn helped decide that the assembly of McDonnell Douglas aircraft would take place at the site.

### Building a modern jet airliner

After the conclusion of the Y-10 programme, China's aerospace industry re-organized its strategy. China had huge resources within the aerospace industry, despite its technical backwardness. There was a strong feeling within the industry that in such a huge country as China, employing almost three-quarters of a million people within the aircraft industry, 'the goal should be to build a large commercial airliner'. The Ministry of Aviation devised a 'three-step take-off plan', with the goal of building a 180-seater plane by 2010. This was highly ambitious, but China was stimulated by the way in which Airbus Industrie had grown from nothing to challenge Boeing's global dominance. The plan was to start with the assembly of the McDonnell Douglas 80/90 series of planes, which would provide China with an understanding of the skills needed to assemble a large modern aircraft. The second phase involved the intention to co-operate with a leading manufacturer, in order to jointly design and manufacture a state-of-the-art 100 seater plane, to go into service around 2005. The final phase involved self-design and manufacture of 180-seater aircraft. One by one each of these objectives fell by the wayside. By the autumn of 1998, the whole strategy needed to be rethought.

### MD-80 assembly

Co-operation with McDonnell Douglas (MD) began as early as 1975, when MD first put forward the proposition that MD planes might be assembled in China. For MD the move was clearly intended to facilitate its sales to the fast-growing China market. It was acutely aware of its weakness relative to Boeing, and intended to use the China market as a major weapon in its struggle with Boeing. Consequently, MD was willing to allow China to assemble the MD-82/83, whereas it appears that Boeing was unwilling to allow assembly of its aircraft to take place in China. Boeing was at that stage only willing to discuss sub-contracting arrangements with China.

From 1986 to 1993 SAMC assembled 34 MD 82/83 aircraft. In 1992, SAMC made the first of five deliveries of the aircraft to the US and the planes obtained their FAA certificate of airworthiness. Twenty-nine of the aircraft produced went into service with Chinese domestic airlines. The number of MD 82/83 aircraft in service in China rose from five in 1985 to 39 in 1996.

Although there was no large-scale transfer of technology, there were substantial gains for SAMC from the assembly contract. The income from the contract enabled SAMC to invest in large-scale purchase of advanced machine tools, and there was a large-scale transfer of knowledge from MD to the Chinese side. SAMC gained important understanding about the complex process of organizing the assembly and testing of a large modern aircraft. SAMC's quality standards were forced upwards in order to obtain FAA approval for the MD 80 series assembly line and the subcontracted components production. MD assisted the Shanghai Aviation Research Institute to advance its design skills as part of the programme. SAMC made significant gains in understanding the complex process of assembling a modern aircraft. It was positioning itself to become the core plant in any restructuring of the Chinese aviation industry, since it is the aircraft assemblers that sit at the centre of the process of aircraft production in the West.

### *MD-90 joint production*

In the early 1990s MD phased out the MD-80 series and replaced it with the MD-90. Although derived from the MD-80 series, it was a substantially different plane, requiring large-scale retooling for the assembler. The plane was longer than the MD-80 series. It was significantly wider, used a new engine, which was markedly quieter and had greater thrust. Its avionics were more advanced. The aircraft was more reliable and had lower operating costs.

Despite a broadly successful outcome of the MD-80 series assembly programme, MD was still losing out heavily to Boeing in the race for the Chinese aircraft market. By 1996 there were still only 39 MD-82s aircraft in service in China. The number of Boeing 737s and 757s rose from fifteen in 1985 to 175 in 1996. Moreover, Airbus had now appeared on the scene as a potentially formidable competitor. In order to try to capture market share from its rivals, MD agreed to build MD-90 aircraft in China, with a substantial proportion of domestically-manufactured components, mainly undertaken at three AVIC subsidiaries (Xian, Shenyang and Chengdu). Final assembly would be carried out at SAMC. Domestically produced components would account for around 80 per cent of the value of the airframe. The engines, most of the avionics, auxiliary engine, and landing gear were to be imported, so that considerably below 80 per cent of the total value of the aircraft would be domestically produced.

Nevertheless, the agreement in principle was a major breakthrough for the Chinese aviation industry. It marked a potentially significant step on the road towards designing and building a modern airliner within China.

In the initial discussion in 1992, it was suggested that MD would build 150 MD-90s in China, with the Shanghai assembly line forming one of only two that MD would have across the world, the other being Long Beach, California. When the contract was finally signed in 1993, MD's situation had changed significantly. The final agreement was signed against a background of a deteriorating situation for MD in its competition with Boeing, and it was feeling the growing force of competition with Airbus. More importantly, AVIC was unable to guarantee MD the sales to domestic aircraft companies that MD had hoped for. Indeed, Boeing's sales to China increased rapidly at the very time when MD was negotiating the agreement to produce MD-90s within China. MD's main goal was not to export from China, but to sell into the country. As a result, the final contract in 1993 stipulated that a drastically reduced number of aircraft would be manufactured within China. Instead of 150, the contract stipulated only 40. Moreover, the contract was further revised in July 1995, when it was agreed that only 20 would be manufactured in China and the remaining 20 to be sold within China would be manufactured at Long Beach. The Chinese aircraft industry was bitterly disappointed that CAAC was unable to place a larger order for a plane that would be made within China, and could form the springboard for the industry's long-term development.

Production was scheduled to begin in April 1998. The main participating Chinese factories invested heavily in setting up manufacturing facilities and sub-assembly and final assembly lines. While they were setting up the production lines the situation at MD continued to deteriorate, culminating in the merger of Boeing with MD, put into effect in 1997. Only a few months after the merger, in November 1997, Boeing announced that it was going to discontinue production of the MD-90 in 1999 and close the MD-90 assembly line at SAMC. In the end CAAC committed itself to buying just two of the MD-90s produced in China. It was said to be unwilling to invest in a plane the production of which was shortly to cease. CAAC's decision not to buy more than two MD-90s was critical for the programme. Indeed, had China bought significant quantities then export markets might even have developed. AVIC even applied to start its own airline which would have used domestically produced MD-90s, but this proposal was vetoed by CAAC.

Instead of producing 20 domestically manufactured MD-90s, the final number was reduced to three in July 1998. In August, even that number was revised down to just two. The termination of the programme involved large losses for the Chinese aircraft makers. Their investments in plant, equipment and stocks were all made on the assumption that at least 20 aircraft would be built. SAMC was the most seriously affected of the Chinese aircraft manufacturers, since it is almost entirely dependent on assembly of civil aircraft. It does not make military aircraft and has limited subcontracting compared to the other major companies in the sector. By 1998 it was reduced to negotiating with the Shanghai Automobile Company to become a partner in a bus manufacturing joint venture and abandoning any serious pretence to become an aircraft maker. The Y-10 stands as a forlorn symbol of the aspirations it once held to compete with the global giants.

### Jointly designed and built jet aircraft

In the early and mid-1990s, the Chinese civilian aircraft industry was confident of its strategy and prospects for becoming a major aircraft manufacturer. The successful programme to assemble MD-80 series planes had been completed, the next step, to produce a large number of MD-90s, with the major share of the manufacturing work being undertaken within China, was apparently well advanced. The next stage on the 'flight plan' was to co-design and build a substantial part of a small jet airliner, and thereafter to proceed to independently design and build a large airliner, albeit initially using imports of key components, such as engines and part, at least, of the avionics.

There is a fast-growing world market for jet aircraft of around 100 seats. Boeing estimates that there will be a market of 2500 in the 80–100 seater jet aircraft category over the next twenty years. Asia is the main focus for sales of regional jet aircraft. Some estimates suggest that as many as 2000 regional jets could be sold in the region over the next twenty years. China is thought likely to constitute a large share of this market.

However, this is an extremely competitive segment of the world aircraft market. Two important makers of 100-seater jets have either drastically reduced their production or left the business altogether. In the late 1970s British Aerospace gave up producing the BAC 1-11 which seated between 65–119 people. Around 230 of the aircraft were produced. In the 1980s, BAe started to produce the four-engined BAe-146 (renamed the Avro RJ), seating 75–110 passengers. It only made a profit for the first time in 1997/98. BAe only produces around 20–22 of the aircraft per year. Fokker is the world's oldest aircraft maker. By the mid-1990s it had made over 200 F-28s (70–90 seats) and over 250 F-100s (100–110 seats). However, the firm went bankrupt in 1996. Bombardier (Canada) plans to produce a 90-seat regional jet aircraft, expanding on its existing smaller aircraft. Embraer (Brazil) has also built itself into a fully-fledged regional jet aircraft maker, with the first of its 70–108 seater planes planned for delivery in 2002. Boeing and Airbus already produce highly competitive planes, the smallest versions of the B-737 and A-319 both seating just over 100 passengers. Boeing has developed at high speed a 100-seater aircraft, the B-717, based on the MD-95. This flew for the first time in September 1998, and entered service in the summer of 1999. Airbus also plans to build a 100-seater aircraft. In other words, Bombardier, Embraer, Boeing and Airbus will collide in this sector of the market.

In the early 1990s, AVIC entered intense negotiations with McDonnell Douglas, Boeing and Airbus to establish a venture to jointly design and produce a 100-seater aircraft. The stated intention was to produce in China a total of 1000 planes to be sold to both the domestic and the international market, principally regional Asian carriers. The MD proposal quickly fell by the wayside. A protracted period of negotiation took place with Airbus and Boeing over several years, with many different proposals under discussion. In the end AVIC decided to proceed with the Europeans rather than Boeing as their partners in the development of a 100-seater aircraft.

The planned aircraft was called the Air Express 100 (AE-100). The initial agreement to proceed with the scheme was signed in April 1996. The co-operative venture was hailed as a prelude to even wider co-operation, with AVIC joining Airbus as a future partner in the A3XX, Airbus's planned 'super jumbo' aircraft. Enterprises within AVIC were planned to take 51 per cent of the total work involved in the AE-100, including production of the wings, fuselage and final assembly. The agreement was hailed as 'a significant step towards the development of an indigenous Chinese aircraft industry'. It was a major boost for the Chinese aviation industry, which felt that it was now firmly on the road to developing an indigenous modern aircraft industry.

The intention of the agreement was that the AE-100 would be ready to go into service in 2005. The length of time required to design and produce a new aircraft from scratch presented genuine commercial difficulties. The B-717 was ready to go into service in the summer of 1999, and Airbus itself could rapidly develop its own 100-seater aircraft using an existing larger aircraft as the basis. Thus, the main competitors would have been well established in the market before the AE-100 had even been test-flown. A key problem for the development of the AE-100 was that CAAC refused to place any advance orders for the plane, causing intense disappointment in the Chinese aviation industry.

In September 1998, it was formally announced that the proposed joint venture had been scrapped. The announcement was coupled with the statement that Airbus intended to develop its own 100-seater aircraft, the A-318, which would be an adaptation of the existing A-320 family. It was announced that it could be developed for 'less than $500 million', and be put into service by 2002. The plane could be flown by the same pilots and maintained by the same engineers as the A-320 family of planes.

By April 1999, Airbus announced that it had attracted 109 firm orders for the plane. Most interestingly, it was announced that Airbus was 'close to an agreement with Lufthansa and Air China'. In other words, Air China was unwilling to buy the AE-100, which would have enabled the domestic industry to take off, but was willing to buy the comparable Airbus plane.

The double blows of the termination of the MD-90 programme and the AE-100 programme were perceived outside China to 'deal a severe blow to China's nascent aviation industry' and 'throw into doubt its plans to become a substantial aircraft manufacturer'. Large investments had been made in the MD-90 programme. A great deal of energy had been put into the AE-100 project. Both programmes had substantially raised the industry's hopes. The double blow of the end of both the programmes left the industry reeling. Its development strategy of 'three stage take-off' was in tatters. The coincidence of the double blow was remarkable. Many people in the Chinese aircraft industry felt that it had been let down not only by Boeing and Airbus, but also by CAAC, which had refused to order either the MD-90 or the planned AE-100. In late summer 1998, it was difficult to discuss the issues with people in the industry, since the experience was so painful for them. Great hopes had been pinned by the industry on these programmes, and deep rethinking was now necessary.

## Non-aviation production

In the early 1980s, the Ministry of Aviation Industry had under its control well over 100 production enterprises and numerous design and research institutes, as well as support units in health, education and other social functions, employing around 700 000 people. Most of these were located in remote areas away from the relatively prosperous east coast. As well as the workers themselves, there were at least one million other family members dependent on the aircraft industry for their survival. Therefore, the sharp decline in government procurement for military aircraft had major implications for the maintenance of large communities scattered across China.

Not only did AVIC face the problem of a serious decline in military aircraft orders, but it also encountered great difficulties in trying to develop its civilian aircraft industry. It met with major problems in attempting to become a manufacturer of large civilian airliners, leading to failure to generate revenue and employment from aerospace in anything like the hoped-for amounts. From the late 1970s to the late 1990s the total real value of Chinese aircraft production fell by at least 15 per cent.

In response to the emerging crisis for China's aircraft industry, the central government instituted the policy of conversion of military into civilian. In the late 1980s and early 1990s, as the market economy developed, aircraft enterprises began to produce non-aviation products such as autos, motorcycles, textile machinery, refrigerators and air conditioners. In the 1990s the scale of non-aviation production accelerated. In 1979, the share of non-aerospace sales stood at less than 10 per cent of the total sales of the Ministry of Aviation Industry. By 1997, their share had risen to more than 80 per cent. Automobiles, auto components and motorcycles together accounted for 62 per cent of AVIC's total revenue. AVIC had become a hugely diversified conglomerate, manufacturing more than 5000 types of non-aviation products.

### *Institutional change*

The rapid expansion of AVIC's non-aviation business in the 1990s created a company which consists of a relatively small aircraft firm, by all measures other than size of workforce, within the shell of a vast diversified conglomerate. No-one within the industry believed this was a viable structure upon which to build either a successful aviation business or to construct a successful non-aviation business. From almost the time it was formed, intense discussion went on within

AVIC over how to restructure it in the light of its own internal problems and the explosive changes going on in the world industry outside. This culminated in a proposal to the State Council made in the spring of 1999 to reshape AVIC fundamentally. The re-shaping of AVIC caused, unsurprisingly, intense debate within the industry. By a curious piece of timing, China's debate over the institutional structure of its aircraft industry took place alongside the similarly intense debate within the European aerospace industry. In Europe, a large fraction of the European aerospace industry was merged into a single giant company, the European Aircraft Defence and Space Corporation (EADS).

Instead of breaking the civilian away from the military aircraft, separating aero engines or airframes into separate entities, or any other of the more radical proposals that were considered, the Chinese government decided to simply split AVIC into two relatively equal integrated parts, AVIC 1 and AVIC 2. Each group contains the full range of production and sale of military and civilian aircraft, airborne equipment as well as non-aeronautical products.

The stated goal of the reform is the 'break up of monopoly and the fostering of fair market economy mechanism'. Zhu Yuli, AVIC president, said: 'The two groups will both compete and co-operate'. While the world's leading aerospace corporations are in the midst of an unprecedented epoch of merger and acquisition, the Chinese aircraft industry is being divided into smaller components. Compared to the global giants, each of China's 'competing aircraft companies' is now even more of a minnow than before the restructuring, each with aerospace revenues of no more than $400m, and each surrounded by a sea of unrelated businesses.

Not only did the State Council decided to split AVIC into two, it simultaneously decided to split into two the other main branches of national defence industries, under the State Defence Industries Commission (COSTIND). Thus, the China National Nuclear Industries General Company, the China National Aerospace Industries General Company, the China National Shipbuilding General Company, and the China National Armaments General Company, were each split into two segments in order to 'foster competition'. Instead of five aerospace and defence industry companies, China's 'restructuring' has established ten much smaller companies. China's 'restructuring' of its defence industries is moving in the opposite direction from the global trends. In the interests of increased domestic competition, China's national defence industries appear to have become much weaker in relation to the global giants.

## Postscript

The collapse of the three-stage plan for take-off of the Chinese aerospace industry caused intense debate within the industry itself as well as at the highest levels of state policymaking. In the year 2000, it appeared that the Chinese government was about to relaunch the attempt to produce an indigenously-manufactured jet airliner: 'If we are unable to build our own airliner, how can we look our parents and old people in the face?' The plan had the strong backing of the Shanghai municipal government as well as support from the central government. It was hoped that the project would be included as a key item in the Tenth Five Year Plan. Shanghai regarded this as a way of pushing forward the city's technological basis.

The goal was initially to manufacture a 100-seat aircraft, later building to a 150-seater. The objective was to sell to the international as well as the domestic market. Shanghai municipality was willing to shoulder the financial risk, and use SAMC as the core designer and assembler for the endeavour. A consortium of risk-sharing partners, including several key Shanghai companies, would be responsible for raising the launch costs, estimated to be around $700m. It was hoped that the project would be able to attract back to Shanghai a group of highly skilled Chinese technicians in the aerospace and related industries then working abroad. A crucial part of the development plan was the agreement of Shanghai Airlines, with the approval of CAAC, to be a launch customer and buy twenty of the newly-produced planes. It was acknowledged that the Chinese industry still had a great deal of ground to catch up in modern aerospace technology. However, the case of Brazil's Embraer had demonstrated that it was technically possible for a large developing country to build a successful modern airliner. Moreover, the plan had the support and partnership of the Shanghai Satellite Company, which contained advanced aerospace technological capability, and of the leading universities in the city.

## Pharmaceuticals: The Sanjiu Pharmaceutical Company

Sanjiu only began life in the mid-1980s. Less than a decade later, in terms of sales revenue it had become the country's largest pharmaceutical company and one of the top 100 firms in China. It had been selected as a member of the team of 120 'national champions' supported by central government industrial policies. It had the ambition of becoming one of the world's top ten pharmaceutical firms.

### Relationship with the PLA

The Nanfang Pharmaceuticals Plant was established in Shenzhen Special Economic Zone 1986 by the Guangzhou Army Hospital. This was the People's Liberation Army's (PLA) No. 1 Medical University, responsible to the PLA's General Logistics Department (GLD) in Beijing. The Army Hospital had its own laboratories that made traditional Chinese medicines. The leadership, in consultation with the headquarters in Beijing, decided to establish a factory of its own which made use of its own experience in making pharmaceuticals to enter this fast-growing market. The Guangzhou Army Hospital reached an agreement with Prof. Zhao Xinxian, a leading researcher in the Hospital. Under the agreement, Zhao selected a small group of co-workers from the Hospital (five in all, apart from Zhao himself), to form the management team of the plant under his command. The group were all 'military intellectuals'. They were to organize the building of the plant, for which the Hospital loaned them 5m yuan. Revenues grew rapidly, reaching the equivalent of over $100m by 1991. From 1987 to 1991 inclusive, Nanfang handed over the equivalent of around $10m to the Guangzhou Army Hospital, amounting to around one-third of its post-tax profits. Moreover, the relationship was becoming 'more and more tense', with the Army Hospital asking for greater handovers from Nanfang as the plant prospered.

The arrangements for hand-overs to the Army Hospital were *ad hoc* and informal. The removal of such a high share of profits was a source of increasing dissatisfaction to Nanfang's leadership. In the early 1990s, Zhao Xinxian found a way to increase the plant's autonomy and to retain a higher share of profits. By 1992 the GLD had set up around 35 enterprises in Shenzhen, many of which were loss-making. A deal was struck with the Nanfang leadership. Nanfang was to cease to answer directly to the Army Hospital in Guangzhou. Instead it was to be placed directly under the supervision of the General Logistics Department. Nanfang would henceforth make its handover of post-tax profits to the General Logistics Department, which was the formal owner of the firm. The General Logistics Department made a separate agreement with the Army Hospital in Guangzhou to allocate a proportion of the profits to them. The General Manager of Nanfang was now formally appointed by the Logistics Department, and could be replaced by them if they found his performance unsatisfactory. Zhao Xinxian was reaffirmed in this position.

Nanfang was permitted to put into practice a new wage system, with much enhanced differentials among regular members of the workforce (the 1:18 system). Under the deal there was an agreement that the share of profits handed over would be reduced, and would become more predictable. Moreover, Sanjiu felt that it was now able to bargain more effectively about the share of profits to be handed over to its superior authorities than before the 'deal'. The handovers to the GLD after the 'deal' was agreed were a fairly stable fixed amount, totalling around 70–80m yuan per annum. Consequently, the proportion of post-tax profits handed over fell from over 20 per cent in the early 1990s, to around 12 per cent in the late 1990s alongside powerful growth in Sanjiu's total profits. Under the deal Sanjiu was allowed operational autonomy, subject only to requiring the approval of the GLD. Zhao Xinxian, the 'legal person' who had responsibility for the firm, had complete autonomy from the GLD General Logistics Department in the appointment of his management team. Sanjiu was been praised for the clarity with which the line of responsibility was drawn between the enterprise and its superior administrative organ, the GLD.

The second part of the deal was that Nanfang would take over the General Logistics Department's mainly loss-making enterprises in Shenzhen. Nanfang would become the 'core' enterprise in a newly formed 'Sanjiu' (Three Nines) Group. During the years 1992–94 Sanjiu injected around 200m yuan into these enterprises. Their takeover was to have great significance for the future path of development of Nanfang, helping to push it towards 'conglomerate' form much more rapidly than might (if ever) have happened without the move.

Under China's economic reforms, the PLA became heavily involved in commercial activity. It is estimated that in the late 1990s the PLA controlled around 15 000–20 000 enterprises, employed around three million workers and produced about 10 per cent of China's gross industrial output value. There was extensive discussion within the Chinese leadership about the possible conflict between the PLA's commercial activities and its military functions. In recognition of the growing problems being caused by the PLA's involvement in business, the Central Military Commission set up an audit commission to restrain the PLA's business activities in 1992. In 1993 the central government banned any local PLA units from running enterprises. In some military regions, the PLA was required to hand over ownership of their enterprises to local governments. Despite the ban and the fact that almost one-third of its business ventures may have closed down or passed out of army ownership, the PLA was still heavily engaged in commercial activities. The continuing problems were highlighted by the high-profile disclosure of a $120m fraud investigation into J&A Securities, based in Shenzhen and partly funded by the Guangzhou military region.

On 22 July 1998 President Jiang Zemin (also chairman of the Central Military Commission) gave the order: 'The army and armed police forces must earnestly carry out checks on all kinds of commercial companies set up by subsidiary units, and without exception from today must not engage in their operation'. The largest PLA-owned business groups controlled at the military-command level and above were given a three-year grace period to transfer their ownership to the civilian sector.

Sanjiu's response to the central government's policy announcement of July 1998 concerning PLA-run businesses, was that this would benefit the Company's long-term development. Sanjiu believes that as one of the largest and most effective PLA-owned business, with a powerful management team, it will be able to take over weaker and smaller competitors in the period ahead. It anticipates that there will be a regrouping of the PLA's businesses, and it is likely that it will be in a strong position to take over many of the PLA's companies in the near future. As one of the best run of the PLA's businesses, Sanjiu may be allocated an expanded role in managing PLA-owned businesses, though the precise form this may take is not yet clear. Sanjiu may become a major beneficiary of the reforms, allowing it to greatly increase its strength within the Chinese pharmaceutical industry.

## Growth of the core business: Chinese medicines

### *Competition within pharmaceuticals*
The capital costs of becoming a major independent player in generic drugs are relatively high. Also, there were several large-scale established state-owned enterprises in this sector, which stood a good chance of becoming more effective

players as their management improved. This sector offered no chance to develop a high margin business. Even in the advanced economies, running a low-margin generics operation successfully has eluded many mainstream drugs companies.

The second possibility for Sanjiui was to attempt to establish itself as an independent producer of patented Western medicines. The possibility of becoming a successful independent producer of Western patented medicines was regarded as negligible. The resources required to develop a new patented drug were enormous and rising steadily in the 1980s and 1990s. In the period when Sanjiu was considering its strategy, China was liberalizing internationally, with a fast growth of Western pharmaceutical companies in China. Increasingly, Sanjiu would find itself competing with the global giants through their joint ventures in China. The Sino-foreign pharmaceutical joint ventures were backed by the vast resources of the international partner, including especially their huge R&D investment and consequent patented drugs portfolio, as well as their management and marketing expertise.

A third possibility was to establish itself through becoming a joint venture partner producing patented medicines with a multinational. This path was rejected also. Sanjiu's leadership felt that this would prevent them ever becoming a truly independent company. Moreover, it was felt that the intense competition among Chinese enterprises to attract multinational partners meant that their bargaining position was weak, and the terms obtained were unlikely to be favourable to the domestic partner. After it had become established as China's leading pharmaceutical company, Sanjiu held long discussions with Merck about a possible joint venture. Merck required that it owned 75 per cent of the joint venture, that it should choose the General Manager, select the Chairman of the Board of Directors and the Financial Manager, and that only Merck medicines with a Merck trademark should be made in the plant. Sanjiu was very reluctant to produce medicines without its trademark, and the project did not come to fruition. Sanjiu also had 'very lengthy' negotiations with Bayer about a possible joint venture, but nothing emerged.

The fourth possibility was to attempt to become a successful producer of traditional Chinese medicines. Here, Sanjiu could escape direct competition with the multinationals. The competitors were almost entirely other domestic firms. The sector was highly fragmented, with a large number of new entrants, typically poorly-run, with a large number of loss-makers struggling to survive. Conversely, as we have seen, if the firm was well-run, there were possibilities for high returns in traditional Chinese pharmaceuticals. The sector looked very much like the soft drinks market in its early stage of development in the advanced capitalist economies.

### 'Getting close to the market'
When Zhao Xinxian and his colleagues set up Nanfang none of them had any experience of business. However, they knew instinctively that to be successful they needed to 'get close to the market'.

The Chinese pattern of food consumption leads to widespread stomach acidity due to an excess of glucose arising from high grain consumption. For many years the Guangzhou Army Hospital had produced a stomach medicine, *Sanjiu Weitai* ('Three Nines Stomach Healthy'), designed to cure this condition. Zhao had accumulated over 100 000 patient histories involving treatment with this drug. This was the product on which Sanjiu built its success. In 1995 *Sanjiu Weitai* was still Nanfang's best-selling drug, accounting for 60–70 per cent of Sanjiu's total revenue from pharmaceuticals. Sanjiu accounted for around 37 per cent of the total national market for stomach medicines.

Nanfang's location adjacent to Hong Kong had a big impact on the way it used advertising. It quickly became one of the most innovative firms in China in the way in which it used the mass media. Nanfang ran its own advertising campaign and its style has had a substantial impact on the methods of advertising across China. Zhao Xinxian frankly acknowledged: 'like Coca-Cola, Nanfang's products are simple, and our competitors' products are not fundamentally different from ours'. It is relatively easy to identify the chemical composition and the herbs used in making the product although it is almost impossible to identify the sequence in which they are mixed. Nor is the production process especially complex. Consequently, advertising is a centrally important aspect of the growth of the firm.

Nanfang built its own advertising firm, and hired staff from Chinese film studios to make their advertisements. It is illegal in China to use doctors in advertisements to endorse the safety and effectiveness of pharmaceutical products. Nanfang had to search for more subtle ways to convince consumers of the quality and reliability of their brand. They used famous film stars to promote their products. For example, they hired Hou Dejian, a Taiwanese filmstar, with a huge following in Hong Kong and Taiwan, famous for his 'touching' and sentimental film roles. Their advertising campaign was especially important after the conclusion of the national court case in which Nanfang felt they had been wrongly treated by the Chinese legal system. They were allowed to register *'Sanjiu'* as their trademark, but not allowed to register the whole name *'Sanjiu weitai'* for their main product. They hired Li Moran, an actor who was famous for his portrayal of roles in traditional Chinese films in which he was associated with 'justice'. The combination of the publicity given in the press and the effectiveness of their advertising campaign, had a 'huge impact' on Nanfang's sales.

In 1995 *Sanjiu Weitai* was ranked the most valuable indigenous brand name in China, worth an estimated 3.4bn yuan. In 1997 the *'Sanjiu'* *('999')* trademark was ranked the sixth most valuable in China, valued at 4.5bn yuan.

Until the late 1980s, all pharmaceutical products, whether imported or domestically manufactured, were sold in China through state-owned wholesale and retail channels. From the late 1980s, it became possible for pharmaceutical producers and importers to establish their own distribution network, and sell directly to local distributors or even to hospitals and retailers. The change is still far from complete. Official state policy is still to restrict selling outside the state supply system. However, the changes made so far are large ones. They provide opportunities for larger firms to benefit from the economies of scope involved in constructing effective selling networks. Nanfang moved quickly to set up its own sales network. By 1995 in Sanjiu there were 62 senior business representatives in charge of the regional markets, and 229 permanent representatives in charge of regional promotion. There were a further 1017 'market information collectors' working on commission for their supervisors. There were branches of the sales network in over 100 cities across the whole of China. This was the largest sales network of any Chinese pharmaceutical company. All those employed in the marketing system are university graduates, 90 per cent of whom are either specialists in pharmacy or doctors. Sanjiu sets strict standards for the appearance of its sales staff. It has an advanced computerized system for information collection and processing, and for assisting decision-making. Sanjiu regards the creation of 'an immense sales system' as 'the guarantee of the healthy development of Sanjiu Pharmaceuticals'.

Sanjiu has set up sales offices in a number of foreign countries, including America, Germany, Russia, and South Africa and the Middle East. It has a sales network over most of Southeast Asia, where sales are strong among overseas Chinese who constitute a large potential market for traditional Chinese medicines. It has processing factories in Malaysia and Hong Kong. Sanjiu has serious ambitions to develop international sales of its medicines. Not only is there a large potential market for traditional Chinese medicines among overseas Chinese, who total around 50m, but also among Western consumers who wish to use Chinese medicines as a complement to, or even as a substitute for, Western medicines. In 1994, the Federal Drugs Administration gave Sanjiu permission to sell its main product, *Sanjiu Weitai*, in the USA.

### Modernization

In order to meet the internationally-set 'Good Manufacturing Procedures' (GMP) for the world's pharmaceutical industry, Nanfang needed to have a comprehensively modernized production process. It set about reaching these standards with a two year comprehensive modernization after 1991. Nanfang was the first firm in China to produce Chinese medicines in a Western fashion. The GMP standards that China follows are those of the US FDA and the equivalent body in Japan, which are the strictest world-wide. The GMP requirements apply to all aspects of the production process, including such matters as quality of raw materials, dust levels and quality of floor and wall tiles. Meeting the GMP standards also necessitated high worker skill levels. Production workers were each given half a year's training in GMP standards, and if they failed to meet the strict standards set by GMP they were dismissed from the firm. Its core staff of around 500 cadres mostly have university science degrees. They all have been required by company policy to attend training in order to become computer literate, with special training courses to bring the skills of older entrants up to date. Moreover, the cadres were all required to develop fluency in at least one foreign language by 1998.

## Management

In the early phase of the construction of Nanfang, Zhao Xinxian brought five army colleagues with him. They took a gamble, accepting much lower salaries than they would have received had they stayed in Guangzhou Army Hospital. They lived in rough conditions during the years of the plant's construction. Much of their time was spent physically involved in the construction of the plant. Their slogans were: 'production first, life later' and 'hard and arduous struggle'. Zhao considers their army background helped them greatly to sustain their spirit and discipline during this tough and highly uncertain phase of building their business. During these years a close bond built up among this group, who still remained at the centre of the firm's leading cadres in the late 1990s. These were all young people, recently graduated from university, led by Zhao, who was in early middle age when the endeavour began. Up until 1989, all the management level personnel were members of the People's Liberation Army. Zhao Xinxian is a powerful motivator, who was able to weld together a strong management team and provide a vision and sense of purpose to the firm. His entrepreneurial and leadership abilities (demonstrated dramatically by the subsequent growth of the firm) had been repressed under the command economy and were now given the chance to flourish.

The cadres were remunerated according to the 1:18 wage scale for cadres. The greatly enhanced differentials were a key part of the 'deal' won by Zhao Xinxian for Nanfang. In addition to their regular wage income, under the deal with the General Logistics Department, Sanjiu is allowed to allocate as bonuses 15 per cent of the post-tax profits retained by the firm. These are allocated on a much more egalitarian basis than the 1:18 wage scale. The ratio between the top and the bottom bonus is around 1:3. A significant share of Nanfang's retained profits has been ploughed into building high quality housing in the plant's quiet semi-suburban location. All the regular workers at the main Nanfang plant live in company apartments. Rents are nominal, a 'few tens' of yuan per month. Open market rents for equivalent apartments in Shenzhen are around 3–4000 yuan per month. This amounts to a large addition to the real value of workers' incomes, and constitutes a major incentive to remain in employment at Nanfang.

Most of the leading cadres have been been offered lucrative positions with other pharmaceutical firms, but they have all chosen to stay with Nanfang. This is partially a financial decision. Their income at Nanfang is high by the standards of Chinese state industry and there are plenty of fringe benefits such as good quality, highly subsidized housing and extensive foreign travel. However, the income available to such highly skilled people in a pharmaceutical joint venture is considerably above even that available at Nanfang. When questioned closely about their reason for staying with the firm, they answered that it is to a considerable degree because of their sense of involvement with an exciting endeavour which they have helped create under Zhao's leadership. His personal influence on the firm is transparent. He is a powerful personality, talking with great clarity about the firm's strategy. All leading cadres speak of him with great respect, recognizing the key role he played in the firm's successful growth and modernization.

## Pressures to diversify

### *Limits to growth within pharmaceuticals*

Sanjiu expanded within the pharmaceuticals industry both through organic growth and merger and acquisition. It took over a dozen smaller pharmaceutical firms across the country. It turned around the management systems of the newly acquired plants, re-specialized their production to make Sanjiu products, and sold their products through their own marketing system using the *Sanjiu* trademark. During its early phase of rapid expansion, Sanjiu was highly dependent on a single, non-patented product, *Sanjiu Weitai*. Although its overall share of traditional Chinese pharmaceuticals was low, it quickly established a high market share within the specialized market of traditional Chinese stomach acidity medicines, with around two-fifths of the national market. It produced a wide range of other traditional Chinese medicines, but in the absence of patented drugs, it was unable to establish such a strong market for position these products, despite the strength of its brand.

Some serious competitive threats for Sanjiu were on the horizon in the traditional Chinese medicine sector. As we have seen, other institutions, such as local governments, are capable of giving support to the growth of their own local 'champion' which might develop a powerful business system such as Sanjiu's. Multinational investors are starting to develop an interest in the sector.

In the international market, the main possibilities were among overseas Chinese. However, this market is smaller than most Chinese provinces in terms of the total population, and by the mid-1990s, the market was close to saturation. Despite having been approved by the FDA, the prospects for growth in sales of traditional Chinese medicines in the advanced economies among non-Chinese people were still weak. Their consumption remained limited to a small minority of the population. There was still no sign of a major breakthrough in the use of traditional Chinese medicines.

During its high-speed growth within traditional Chinese medicines after the late 1980s, Sanjiu developed many transferable resources that could be used within the Western patented medicine sector. These included its large R&D capabilities by Chinese standards, including both physical and human skills. It had a large and capable sales force. It had high standards of production quality. It was knowledgeable about the global marketplace. It had a small but powerful biotechnology company. However, even after it had become China's leading pharmaceutical firm, it was still far from being able to compete directly with the multinationals within patented Western medicine.

When the opportunity to diversify out of pharmaceuticals presented itself to the management of Sanjiu, it grasped the opportunity firmly. Zhao Xinxian put the situation bluntly: 'We must diversify, because we simply cannot match the multinationals in proprietary technology'. The leadership decided to diversify through venture capital in different activities, in Zhao Xinxian's phrase, 'floating boats on the water' and seeing which of them floated. This repeated the pattern under which Nanfang itself was originally set up.

### Growth of non-core business

As we have seen, a key aspect of the 1992 'deal' was that Nanfang would merge with the Logistics Department's 35 plants in Shenzhen, many of which were loss-makers. These included firms in construction, clothing, trade, printing and packaging, taxi renting, tourism and a hotel. At a stroke Nanfang, now renamed Sanjiu Group, had become a highly diversified conglomerate. The output value of the newly absorbed businesses was 37 per cent of that of the whole Sanjiu Group. These businesses were substantially less profitable than Nanfang. Indeed, many were loss-makers. In 1992 their combined pre-tax profits contributed only 18 per cent of those of the whole Sanjiu Group.

Sanjiu acquired numerous further non-core businesses and some of the newly merged businesses grew rapidly. By the mid-1990s Sanjiu received 'innumerable' requests from the administrative authorities of loss-making firms to take them over and use their investment capital, management skills, brand name and marketing network to turn the businesses around. The GLD also asked Sanjiu to take over more of its businesses in addition to those involved in the 1992 'deal'.

By 1998, Sanjiu had evolved into a very different company from that of the late 1980s and early 1990s. Like most successful East Asian diversified conglomerates, a single chief executive officer has played a central role in the Company's development. Zhao Xinxian was still the most powerful and authoritative person in Sanjiu. He devises and puts into practice all major strategies and decisions. After 1996, Sanjiu's second pillar business was the food and beverage sector. The other six major industries of Sanjiu were wine manufacturing (Western and Chinese wines, including beers), agriculture (including the manufacturing of agricultural machinery, chemical fertilizers and cultivation), tourism (including hotels), real estate (including the development of real estate, construction of infrastructure and provision of construction materials), trading (including imports and exports, franchised dealers and shops) and even automobiles (including the manufacturing of automobiles and spare parts).

Instead of a firm of around 1200 employees, mostly employed at a single site, it had grown into a vastly more complex organization. The Group now owned a second tier of around one hundred enterprises with a total of around 3000 employees in the first and second tier firms who were mostly directly paid their wages by the core firm and had their 'file' lodged at Nanfang. However, it had also a third, and much larger, tier of employees, who were not paid their wages by the core firm and whose 'file' was not deposited at the firm's headquarters. However, they were working directly for the Sanjiu Group. These included over 1000 pharmaceutical salespeople working on commission, around 3000 employees in the Sanjiu hotel chain, several thousand employees in merged businesses, and 'several tens of thousands' of workers in the Sanjiu construction company. By 1998 the total number of employees working for the Group may have been well over 50 000.

## Rethinking the business structure for the new millennium: return to the 'core business'

Even before the East Asian crisis, Sanjiu was re-evaluating the strategy of diversification, influenced by difficulties encountered with its increasingly diversified business portfolio. The East Asian crisis has explicitly stimulated an even sharper re-evaluation of the company's strategic direction. It determined to refocus on its core businesses in pharmaceuticals and closely related businesses. It decided to focus its expansion on the most profitable enterprises within the Group: in 1997 fifteen out of the total of over seventy enterprises within the Group generated profits of more than 10m yuan and accounted for more than 85 per cent of total Group profits.

The definition of 'core business' is still problematic. The view of the Sanjiu leadership is that the 'core' should include not only pharmaceuticals, but also closely related products such as food and beverages (Sanjiu's second 'pillar industry'). Sanjiu still feels that traditional Chinese medicines have a lot in common with the production and marketing of these products: they share some common elements of R&D, require high quality control over ingredients, close attention to packaging quality, need an effective sales network, and depend heavily on brand imagery. Marketing is at the centre of product success.

By 1997, it is possible that the share of non-pharmaceutical businesses in the Group's total assets and sales value may have been as high as 40 per cent, and its share of Group employment even higher. However, pharmaceuticals generated around three-quarters of the Group's total pre-tax profits. In other words, since the take-over 'deal' with the GLD in 1992, Sanjiu had rapidly built up a portfolio of poorly-performing companies in a wide variety of often unrelated businesses. Since 1991, Sanjiu had acquired seventy or more enterprises in twenty provinces, of which around one-half were outside the pharmaceutical sector. These sapped management efforts, diverted Group capital for low returns, diluted the Company's brand and added little to the Group's profit stream.

In 1997 Sanjiu Group Headquarters devised strict new guidelines to govern the Group's mergers and acquisitions. M&A targets were all to be compatible with the renewed focus on pharmaceuticals and closely related businesses. Under the new policies, Sanjiu abandoned the attempt to make automobiles a 'second pillar industry' and suspended investment in the sector. It closed down or sold off sixteen poorly-managed third-tier companies. It integrated and reshuffled the assets of those companies which had recorded losses for two consecutive years or large losses in a single year (12 out of the total of 71 enterprises in the Sanjiu Group were loss-making in 1997).

The intention in the recent reforms is to take Sanjiu firmly back to the path of being a focused modern pharmaceutical company, with some related business in the food and drinks sector. As we have noted already, the State Pharmaceutical Administration's goal is to build a small number of domestically-based giant pharmaceutical firms to compete with the multinationals. Sanjiu was selected by the SPA as one of China's five 'national champions' in the pharmaceutical sector.

# Complex equipment: Harbin Power Equipment Company

## China's power equipment needs

China's role in the future of this industry at a global level is likely to be very large. China is the world's biggest single market for power generating equipment. China's electricity output is forecast to rise from 1008bn kWh in 1995 to around 2500bn kWh in 2010. It is anticipated that China will account for about one-half of Asia's expected demand for power generating plant in the next ten years, and about one-quarter of the world's total. A central issue for the world's power equipment manufacturers and for China's power equipment manufacturers, is: who will benefit from China's huge increase in demand for power equipment?

For the foreseeable future, over 80 per cent of China's electricity will be generated by thermal power stations (coal, oil and/or gas). Coal is China's main primary energy for generating electricity. China has vast coal reserves, but relatively small proven reserves of oil and gas. The share of coal in China's total energy production rose from over 69 per cent in 1980 to 75 per cent in 1995. The huge growth in future demand for coal-fired thermal power stations provides China's large indigenous producers with a big opportunity to grow and develop their technology in this area. Many other developing country markets as well as developed countries are also likely to need coal-fired power station technology. There are strong environmental pressures to raise the share of oil and, especially, gas in the total structure. The global giants are far in the lead in the technologies of gas turbines. At the end of the 1990s, the top three global power equipment makers (GE, Siemens, and Alstom) accounted for 87 per cent of the total world market for gas turbines. Moreover, the global giants have a considerable technical lead in advanced coal-fired technology that reduces or eliminates particulate and 'greenhouse gas' emissions. The greater the emphasis that the Chinese government places on environmental controls, the stronger the competitive position of the global giants will be in the Chinese power equipment market. Despite the enormous Three Gorges Project, it is predicted that hydro power will still generate only around 16 per cent of China's electricity in the year 2010.

## State industrial policies

Up until the early 1990s, power generation and transmission was controlled by the Ministry of Machine Building Industries (MMI). In 1993 the Chinese government set up the Ministry of Electric Power (MOEP) as a separate entity from the MMI. In line with its policy of separating regulatory from commercial functions, in 1997 it set up a new body, the State Power Corporation (SPC). This formally assumed ownership of all the power generation assets over around 100mW (around 80 per cent of China's total power supply) that were owned by the Chinese state. It quickly became obvious that in the transition to the market economy, the interests of these two bodies were in conflict. The MMI wanted to build a powerful Chinese power equipment industry. The MOEP (later SPC) wanted to expand rapidly China's ability to provide cheap electricity for Chinese industry and consumers.

Up until the early 1990s, as had been the case in most Western countries until the late 1980s, power plant construction was entirely funded by the government. The share of government revenue in China's national product fell from 34.4 per cent of GNP in 1978 to just 14.1 per cent in 1993. In the early 1990s, the government recognized that the long-term solution to its power plant needs necessitated a radical rethink of its approach. It was forced to consider a number of paths towards resolving its desperate need for funds for the energy sector, using diverse sources of domestic capital, and actively pursuing international investment. By the late 1990s, less than 5 per cent of funding for power sector investment came from the central government via direct grants. Instead, it is estimated that around one-half came from 'soft loans' from state banks, 20 per cent from provincial and local governments and 17 per cent from foreign institutions and companies. Increasingly, power station operators were using commercial criteria in selecting their choice of equipment.

Up until the 1990s, the MMI was able to affect directly the choice of equipment adopted by domestic power generators. However, as power generation became more commercialized, the government turned increasingly to indirect means to stimulate the growth and modernization of the power equipment industry. In the early 1990s the Chinese power equipment industry still enjoyed substantial protection. Tariffs were lower than for most products, but were still significant. In 1994, tariffs on imported power generating equipment stood in the range 6–35 per cent for boilers and turbines, and 15–45 per cent for generators. By 1997, China's tariffs on imported power equipment had fallen substantially, and were now close to WTO levels. Foreign investment in the sector could only be undertaken with a Chinese manufacturer as a joint venture partner. When tendering for a power project took place, if the foreign and the domestic manufacturer had the same terms and conditions, preference must be given to the domestic manufacturer. In the mid-1990s imports of units of 300MW and below were prohibited, and in 1998 it was announced that thermal power plants of 600MW or less could no longer be imported. If a foreign power equipment manufacturer contracted for a foreign-financed power project, then a minimum of 30 per cent of the value of the project must be subcontracted to a domestic manufacturer. When importing large power units (600MW and above) that could be supplied from domestic sources, the amount of domestic subcontracting and technology transfer needed to be clearly specified.

In the first phase of the Three Gorges project, all fourteen of the giant 700 MW units were imported, as they were beyond the technical capabilities of the indigenous firms. The second tranche of twelve units was to be 'earmarked for indigenous manufacturers'. It remains to be seen if this definition includes multinationals producing in plants within China. A condition of the award of the contract for the first phase of the Three Gorges Project was that the successful bidders subcontracted substantial amounts of work to the leading indigenous manufacturers, and assisted them to upgrade their technical level hydro technology. Power plants constructed with foreign capital, either jointly or wholly foreign operated, were 'encouraged to adopt domestically-manufactured equipment'.

## Harbin Power Equipment Company

### Institutional change

Harbin Power Equipment Company (HPEC) is located in the city of Harbin in Heilongjiang Province in the extreme northeast of China, close to the Soviet border. Harbin is known as the 'City of Power Generating Equipment'. In the 1950s several large plants and many small ones were set up in or close to Harbin to produce different components of power plant equipment. The main factories were the Harbin Boiler Works (HBW), the Harbin Steam Turbine Plant (HTC), and the Harbin Electrical Generator Plant (HEC). Between them they produced the main parts of thermal power station units. From the 1950s to the 1980s, these plants operated under the control of the Ministry of Machine-Building Industries (MMI).

Institutional reform accelerated in the late 1980s, as the market economy developed. The State Planning Commission, and the State Committee for Restructuring the Economic System, set out the policy of organizing enterprise groups (*qiye jituan*) in order to change China's individual plants into large, multi-plant businesses that could compete in the market economy by taking advantage of economies of scale and scope. In 1987 the governments of Heilongjiang Province and Harbin City responded to the new policy by attempting to construct a 'super company' in Northeast China for power plant equipment manufacture. This would have been a highly integrated company combining a large part of the production of both the main engines and the ancillary equipment within the same 'firm'. The Liaoning Provincial Government and five of the plants in Liaoning agreed, but the proposal foundered due to opposition from Zhou Zouming, the Head of the Shenyang Transformer Plant (SYT). Zhou's plant was central to the production of the ancillary equipment. His ambition was to organize his own enterprise group, with SYT at the core of the six Liaoning plants. Zhou was successful in his goal, subsequently forming the Northeast China Electrical Equipment Company, which was floated on the Hong Kong stock market.

Instead of a super-large integrated company, a large new company was formed, which was around one-half the size of that originally proposed. It consisted wholly of firms based in or near to Harbin. The main forces within this were HBW, HEC and HTC. They were combined to form an enterprise group, known as Harbin Power Engineering Group Company (HPEGC). The formation of HPEGC involved no change in ownership. The main constituent plants remained separate independent legal entities and accounting units. The participating plants were 'linked by products, not by assets'. The new entity was designed principally to unify the operations of the three constituent entities in order to bid successfully for power equipment projects.

In 1992, the first group of nine Chinese companies was listed on overseas markets. In 1994, HPEGC was selected to be part of the second batch of 22 companies to be listed overseas. The company was further restructured for this purpose. Under the restructuring a newly formed company, Harbin Power Equipment Company Limited (HPEC), took over the entire power plant equipment manufacturing and engineering services previously carried on by HPEGC. HPEC was a holding company, the 'mother'. The 'children' were the constituent plants which remained independent legal entities owned by HPEC. The production-related businesses of the former HBW, HEC and HTC were then taken over by the newly-established Harbin Boiler Works, Harbin Turbine Company, and Harbin Electrical Machinery Company. HPEGC retained its non-production related business, such as the provision of education, housing, medical facilities, catering services and other investments not directly related to the core business of the Group.

During the restructuring, employment in HPEC fell from over 40 000 to around 27 000, with the stated intention to reduce the number to around 16–18 000 by the year 2000. HPEC's leadership believe that downsizing is crucial to the company's competitive capability. A major reason for the felt need to downsize is in order to change the mentality of employees, rather than simply to reduce the wage bill. The stated goal is to produce a firm with higher average incomes and a hard-working ethos among the workforce.

By the early 1990s, the three main production entities in HPEGC had almost 40 years of operation as separate units, albeit under state control. In the 1980s they each increased their operational independence due to the state's policies to expand enterprise autonomy through retention of increasing amounts of profits. The increasing impact of market forces led to a steady widening of the range of activities in respect of which the enterprise needed to take autonomous decisions, such as the purchase of inputs, the organization of suppliers, finding markets for their product, and responding to customers' needs for after-sales service. Each of the plants had its own social service facilities. Each had engaged in their own programme of technical transfer from international firms. Each had undertaken a substantial programme of expansion, involving both the selection and purchase of new equipment as well as the selection, purchase and up-grading of substantial amounts of second-hand equipment on the world market. Each had negotiated their separate joint venture relationship with international companies.

In the wake of the restructuring, the newly established holding company, the 'mother', recognized that with forty years of history, it would be impossible to fully control the three main individual plants, HBW, HTC, and HEC. Following the restructuring there were intense internal arguments over the allocation of the funds raised from the flotation, over the handover of profits to the 'mother' company by the 'children', and over the allocation of investment funds between the 'children'. Each of the children wished to use their revenues to expand their own business in both power equipment and subsidiary activities. In theory, the manager of each of the subsidiary companies was to be appointed by HPEC headquarters. In practice, the leadership of the subsidiaries altered little after the restructuring. The separate subsidiaries were still 'small and complete'. Each subordinate company still had its own divisions for R&D, its own design office, personnel management, accounting, product development, sales and service, quality control, and materials procurement. As well as specialized production departments, each had its own rail and truck transport departments, equipment control department, and even its own casting and forging workshops. This was a costly duplication. The subordinate companies are within a stone's throw of each other in the centre of Harbin City.

From the outside, HPEC had become a modern enterprise, floated on the international stock market, with intense ambitions to become a globally competitive firm. HPEC's impressive new headquarters are very 'lean', with only around one hundred employees. The firm downsized and upgraded its human resources. The managers of HPEC developed a detailed knowledge of the personnel and the business structure of the main multinational competitors. These acted as benchmarks for the company in its drive to modernize. Despite these significant advances, there still existed a complex, disunited and dysfunctional internal structure.

### *Growth and modernization*
From the late 1950s until the mid-1980s, Harbin was China's leading power equipment base, accounting for around one-quarter of China's total national output of power equipment. Its production capacity grew steadily, roughly doubling over these years. In the reform period its capacity expanded at high speed. Output more than doubled in physical terms from the early 1980s to the early 1990s, and rose by two-thirds from 1991 to 1994 alone. In the late 1990s, the rate of growth of demand for power equipment within China slowed down, and competition intensified, with a serious decline in HPEC's market share. From 1995 to 1998, Harbin's revenue hardly increased.

Like other large state-owned enterprises, Harbin's power equipment plants became responsible for funding their own investment out of retained profits and bank loans. They were responsible for finding their own markets rather than passively receiving orders from the MMI. In order to compete successfully, it urgently needed investment funds. Immediately before flotation, HPEC's pre-tax profit rate was reasonably high, at around 10 per cent of revenue. However, pre-tax profits amounted to only around $25m. These slumped to just $12m in 1998. HPEC's international flotation raised around $160m.

Soviet technology and equipment were central to HPEC's growth from the 1950s to the 1980s. From 1960 to the 1980s, it was almost completely cut off from international progress in the industry. It was technically far behind the world's advanced power equipment producers.

From the early 1980s onwards HPEC made considerable technical progress. In part this was achieved through self-investment. However, an important part of its technical modernization took place through policies implemented by the central government. From 1981 to 1996, the government implemented a Fifteen Year

(1981–96) Programme for Technical Transfer to the Chinese power equipment industry. It was the largest programme of technical transfer to China during this period. The main beneficiaries were HPEC and the Shanghai Electrical Company (SEC). In the late 1980s the unit capability for thermal power generation was just 125MW at Shanghai and 200MW at HPEC. The technical transfer programme raised the thermal unit production capability at Shanghai to 300MW and at HPEC to 600MW. At HPEC the technical transfer programme involved co-operation with Combustion Engineering (US) (later merged with ABB) to raise the boiler-making capability, and with Westinghouse to raise the steam turbine and electric generator capability. The programme allowed Chinese firms to purchase licences 'very cheaply'. It allowed Chinese technicians to be trained in the foreign firm. Chinese technicians participated in co-design of the (for them) new generation of equipment, and were involved in on-site management of the supply of the new equipment.

The second major state-orchestrated programme of technical transfer was that associated with the Three Gorges Project. HPEC was a major beneficiary of the technology transfer requirement placed upon foreign firms winning the first tranche of contracts to supply the Three Gorges project. The objective was to enable HPEC to supply complete 700MW hydro-power units.

In addition to co-operation with foreign manufacturers, HPEC has undertaken its own research and development. In the mid-1990s HPEC employed over 1500 staff in research and development, of which 24 were high-level experts with national recognition, and 1320 were senior engineers. HPEC contains the Harbin Research Institute of Large Electrical Machinery, established in 1958. It employs over 600 staff. It is designated by the PRC government as the authority responsible for the research and development on hydro turbines and large electrical machinery for the whole country. It is the centre responsible for evaluating the technical performance and quality of China's power generating equipment. It has independently designed and started production of 600MW and 1000MW nuclear steam turbines, 800mW supercritical steam turbines and 25MW gas turbines for ships.

From the late 1970s onwards, HPEC rapidly updated its equipment. By the late 1990s, around two-thirds of the total value of HPEC's equipment was imported, including many leading-edge machine tools from international leaders in the field. As well as extensive purchase of new imported equipment, HPEC imported a large amount of second-hand equipment. For example, HTC's main engine workshops in the 1980s purchased eight large US-made numerically-controlled machine tools from a bankrupt factory, and in the 1990s bought a number of large, advanced numerically-controlled machine tools from bankrupt factories in Russia and Rumania. Despite these significant efforts to upgrade its equipment, in the mid-1990s, the total value of HPEC's plant and equipment was less than $100m, pathetically small compared to the global giants.

A key part of competitive capability in the power equipment industry is the ability to organize a large 'external firm' of components suppliers. For the leading global firms, the supply chain is global, closely integrated by modern information technology.

Around 40–50 per cent of the value of a complete power plant unit produced by HPEC is composed of ancillary equipment from external suppliers. For equipment sold on the domestic market, the ancillary equipment is supplied from a network of around 200 suppliers, most of which are not specialized in the power industry. Several of these have joint ventures with international companies, which has enabled them to raise their technical level since the 1970s. However, the business and technical capability of the domestic components supply network that HPEC must rely on, is drastically inferior to that of the global giants in the industry.

As domestic and international competition in this sector intensified within China in the 1990s, the Chinese reaffirmed the special position of HPEC as China's 'national champion'. In an effort to meet the intensifying competition in the domestic market HPEC negotiated with several multinational companies to set up a series of joint ventures. In 1994 it signed memoranda with each of the companies concerned. Under the agreement, each of HPEC's subordinate plants was to have set up a joint venture with either GE or ABB, each of which was to have been 70 per cent owned by the Chinese side and 30 per cent by the foreign partner. The package was approved by the Harbin City government, and by the Ministry of Machinery. However it was turned down by the State Council because they considered that HPEC was 'one of the largest industrial groups in China and should, accordingly, remain in Chinese hands, owned by the state'.

This decision had some benefits for HPEC. It meant that a disproportionate share of government assistance would be channelled towards HPEC, instead of towards the Sino-foreign joint ventures that were being established simultaneously in other firms in the sector. In July 1996, HPEC was formally identified as one of China's keypoint large enterprises. In August 1997, the State Development Bank agreed to provide two large loans for expanding the Company's capacity to manufacture large-scale hydro power equipment and technological improvements to enable HPEC to compete in supplying hydro equipment for the Three Gorges Project. The loans totalled $84m. A further advantage for HPEC in remaining independent of the multinational suppliers was that any given multinational company would be unlikely to subcontract to another multinational competitor's joint venture within China, thereby making HPEC a relatively attractive firm with which to subcontract.

*Competition*

Despite rapid advance in almost all aspect of its business, at the end of the 1990s HPEC still lacked the capability to compete seriously in international markets. Its exports increased substantially in the 1990s, and HPEC was much the largest Chinese exporter in this sector, accounting for around 80 per cent of China's total exports of large-scale power plant equipment. However, the bulk of its exports were through political channels to friendly developing countries, especially Pakistan. Their average annual value remained tiny compared to that of the global giants, at less than $US50m in the mid-1990s. Moreover, a large fraction of its exports consisted of subcontracts for the global giants, who took the role of lead contractor, sourcing the supply of components from HPEC.

In the 1980s China's three principal manufacturers, Harbin, Shanghai and Dongfang, accounted for over two-thirds of national output. In the post-reform economy, HPEC began to accustom itself to competition with the other major domestic producers. Like HPEC, Shanghai and Dongfeng became increasingly autonomous and increased their competitive capability. The intensity of inter-enterprise competition was enhanced by the fact that in 1983, property rights for the three plants were transferred to the respective provincial/municipal governments.

In the reform years HPEC managed to sustained itself in its leading position in the domestic market, still accounting for around 30 per cent of domestic output in the early 1990s. So long as the Chinese government remained the sole supplier of funds for the construction of power stations, and as long as multinational power plants were not permitted to invest in the Chinese power equipment industry, then the main competitive struggle would have been between HPEC and its domestic rivals. This position was very like that in which the major Western power equipment companies grew to maturity. However, the nature of competition altered sharply in the 1990s.

In the 1990s, the market became truly global. There was intense interest among Western power equipment producers in the possibility of gaining a share of the potentially vast Chinese market. Increasingly competition came from imports and from the domestic joint ventures of the multinational giants. The scale of the Chinese market 'encouraged every big manufacturer to bid for business, driving down prices'. Chinese bidding contests were fiercely contested, because 'all the large integrated groups have seen the country as their top market and have been willing to sacrifice margins for establishing their presence'. HPEC was now forced to operate in this brutally competitive environment even within the domestic economy.

Westinghouse was extremely keen to enter the Chinese market. In order to gain entry it was willing to engage in a large-scale technology transfer programme with Shanghai Electrical (Group) Corporation (SEC). This programme, begun in 1981, enabled SEC to develop manufacturing capability for 300MW and 600MW units. The co-operation was expanded greatly in 1995, with the conclusion of a full-scale joint venture, sub-divided into four separate agreements with each of SEC's subordinate units. Westinghouse was a minority partner in each of them, with an ownership share of between 30–40 per cent. Westinghouse committed itself to investing $100m in modernizing the plants in Shanghai. A key part of the joint venture was Westinghouse's commitment to transfer further technologies to the Chinese side. After absorption of the new technologies, the joint ventures would have the capacity to design and manufacture 1000MW thermal power sets with sub-critical and super-critical parameters. Soon after the establishment of the joint venture, Siemens purchased Westinghouse's non-nuclear business, in the process taking over Westinghouse's share of the joint venture with SEC. This provided Siemens with a way into the China market through one of the major domestic players. SEC's output advanced much more rapidly than that of HPEC during the mid/late 1990s, at least in part due to the contribution of Westinghouse to its technological progress and through substantial investment in the joint venture. With Siemens as its joint venture partner, SEC constituted an even more formidable competitor for HPEC than it had under Westinghouse.

In 1994 the Dongfang Power Equipment Company (Sichuan) floated its turbine generator plant on the Hong Kong stock market. 'H-share' holders accounted for around 38 per cent of the share ownership after the flotation. Subsequently, it set up a joint venture between its hydro generator plant and GE (Canada), owned 70 per cent by Dongfeng and 30 per cent by GE (Canada). Dongfang's Jiaxiang (Zhejiang Province) boiler plant set up a separate joint venture with Hitachi. The equity was split 50/50 between Dongfang and Hitachi. A condition of the joint venture was that Hitachi transfer technology for the manufacture of sub-critical steam turbines.

The combination of devolution of asset ownership rights to the local authorities, international flotation and international joint ventures with different sub-parts of the business meant that a merger of one or more of China's leading players in this sector became more difficult.

By the late 1990s, both of HPEC's main competitors had established joint ventures with the global giants of the sector. HPEC considered this to be 'very dangerous'. Under a combination of increased imports and intensified competition from the domestic joint venture partners of the multinational giants, HPEC's share of the national market for power equipment declined significantly, falling from a peak of almost one-third in 1992, to less than one-fifth in 1996.

## Oil and petrochemicals: CNPC and Sinopec

### Increased enterprise autonomy: formation of the holding companies

Under the post-Mao economic reforms China's oil and petrochemical industry was mainly organized into two separate entities, upstream and downstream respectively. On the upstream side, prior to the 1980s, the country's entire oil and gas exploration and production had been controlled by the Ministry of Petroleum Industry (MPI). In 1988, the Ministry was reorganized into the China National Petroleum Corporation (CNPC), vested with control over the assets formerly under the MPI. CNPC was transformed from a Ministry into a holding company, with formalized ownership rights over the constituent production enterprises. The key entity on the downstream side was Sinopec, established in 1983 as a state holding company. Sinopec spanned the full range of petrochemical industry production including crude oil refining, oil products, the manufacture of petrochemicals, chemical fertilizers, synthetic resins, fibres and rubbers, and the marketing of these products. Almost the entire national oil and petrochemical industry was included in these two giant holding companies.

Under the Chinese enterprise reform, individual production enterprises within CNPC and Sinopec were granted the status of incorporated legal persons, able to sign contracts, responsible for their own profits and losses, and able to retain profits. Many of them established large-scale joint ventures with multinational companies, and floated on international stock markets. In the case of the key large-scale enterprises within both Sinopec and CNPC, the enhanced autonomy of the reform period built upon already strong traditions of enterprise identity. It was far from clear where the 'enterprise' that constituted the heart of China's 'enterprise' reform would finally be located in the oil and gas sector. Individual large enterprises under Sinopec and CNPC had reason to believe that they might indeed end up as autonomous firms, which would form the key entities around which China's industrial strategy for this sector would be organized. Many of the key enterprises began to develop a real sense of 'corporate identity', striving to increase their autonomy from the holding company.

The establishment of CNPC and Sinopec as state holding companies signalled an important transition from the purely administrative control functions of the Ministry towards a market-oriented method of functioning. However, it was still unclear where the 'firm' would be located. Would CNPC and Sinopec become truly independent companies, owning and managing the subordinate production units under its control, or would they simply act as quasi-Ministries with declining ownership and management rights over the subordinate entities? The period from the early 1980s until 1998 was one of experimentation, groping towards the correct business structure for the industry. Not until the 1998 restructuring was it finally decided by the central policymakers that CNPC and Sinopec would each indeed become a truly integrated company, casting off its old 'ministerial' functions.

The tensions caused by the policy of increasing enterprise autonomy can be seen from the examples of the giant Daqing oilfield within CNPC and Shanghai Petrochemical Corporation within Sinopec.

### Daqing: oilfield or company?
Over a long period, Daqing Petroleum Administration was much the most important single production unit in the Chinese oil industry. It was the largest single enterprise in the entire Chinese economy, with revenues the equivalent of over $US5bn in 1996. In that year, it accounted for two-fifths of the physical output of CNPC, and almost two-thirds of CNPC's pre-tax profits. Daqing employed around 250 000 people. Around 800 000 people were directly dependent on a member of their family working in Daqing. The total population

of Daqing is around two million, the livelihoods of almost all of whom are closely linked to the prosperity of Daqing.

Daqing's ambitions were fuelled strongly by the enterprise reforms after the mid-1980s, which allowed enterprises to retain a significant proportion of their profits. They were given even stronger impetus by the intense discussions and policy experiments to create large enterprise groups in the 1990s. In 1996, under the 'visionary' leadership of Ding Guiming, Daqing developed its own reform plan. The reform plan charted a course for Daqing to develop autonomously into a global giant corporation. Daqing planned to use its abundant accumulated financial reserves to acquire international oil assets, particularly in the former USSR. This is extremely important since it is predicted that, at the most, Daqing will have another ten years or so of life left in the Daqing oilfield. If permitted, Daqing would have taken over other domestic oilfields. A crucial part of the enterprise's strategy was to become a fully integrated oil company with extensive refining and petrochemical operations. Daqing planned a series of large-scale mergers with other strong Chinese companies. It strongly wished to avoid merging with weak companies. Daqing planned to merge with refineries in the north-east of China so that a close integration could be developed with its oil supply. Even more ambitiously, the plan included a merger with Shanghai Petrochemical Company (SPC) in Shanghai. Exploratory talks were even held with SPC. Daqing already supplied around one-third of SPC's crude oil supply. In addition, SPC's location would have provided Daqing with a base in the fast-growing coastal area of China, surrounded by a huge and highly dynamic market and low transport costs to other highly developed parts of China. Daqing held talks also with Yanshan Petrochemical Corporation (Beijing) with a view to merger and developing its vertically integrated operations.

Daqing recognized the key importance of developing downstream operations, and planned also to develop a network of petrol stations along high-speed motorways in the coastal areas. It planned to take over or merge with chain stores that would co-operate in the development of high margin retail stores to sell food and other products at petrol stations. It explored the possibility of developing its own tanker fleet. It held talks with Dalian port, through which Daqing's oil is exported, with a view to merger. It held talks with China's largest automobile companies, Yiqi and Erqi, with the objective of establishing joint ventures to co-operate in the development of high quality lubricants. Daqing even contemplated merging with Sinochem, the giant China National Chemicals Import and Export Corporation, in order to provide Daqing with a direct link to international markets.

In sum, by the mid-1990s, Daqing had developed intense ambitions for domestic and international expansion. The goal of the leadership was to make Daqing the core of a new giant integrated oil and petrochemical company, that would lead the Chinese industry in its competition with the global giants of the industry. A key part of the strategy was to focus on the core business of oil, oil products and petrochemicals, integrating upstream and downstream. The emphasis would be on growing by merging with or taking over other strong companies 'through the market', in order to conjoin the business interests of the two enterprises.

Daqing's ambitious plans were resolutely opposed by the headquarters of CNPC. If Daqing had succeeded in achieving its goals for 'restructuring through the market', it would have meant the death of CNPC. In the words of one industry expert, CNPC would have had to face the question: 'If you are a giant, who am I?' After fierce discussion, the central government supported CNPC headquarters and rejected the Daqing plan. Instead, the central government decided to support the path of reconstruction to build global giant companies through administrative means. The basis for these new companies was to be the old ministries and their quasi-ministerial successors, CNPC and Sinopec. This firmly turned the government's back on the possibility of allowing and encouraging competitive giant firms to emerge 'from below' as the basis for industrial reform to build competitive giant companies. This was a highly significant decision in the history of China's industrial reform. It decisively set the industrial reform path in a new and different direction in the oil and petrochemical sector, and has profound implications for the whole of China's reform of large-scale industry. Following the defeat of Daqing's plans, its ambitious leaders were transferred to other parts of CNPC.

### Shanghai Petrochemical Corporation (SPC)

SPC was the most important subordinate enterprise within Sinopec, contributing a greater volume of pre-tax profits than any other production unit. It was one of the ten largest enterprises of any kind in China in the mid-1990s. By the early 1990s, SPC had become a formal legal person, with operational and financial autonomy. Although Sinopec was the majority owner of the enterprise, SPC had strong ambitions of its own. SPC has the strong support of the Shanghai municipal government, which is keen to see SPC develop into a world class competitive company, alongside other Shanghai 'giants', notably Baoshan Iron and Steel Corporation and Shanghai Automobile Corporation. The period after the 1970s saw the gradual development of a sense of corporate identity and ambition at SPC. SPC successfully lobbied the central government to allow SPC to be the site for a large (300 000 ton) imported ethylene unit. It borrowed heavily in order to be able to finance the purchase, much of the loan coming from international markets, repayable in hard currency.

SPC successfully lobbied the central government to allow it to become the first Chinese company listed on international markets. Through the initial listing, and subsequent share issues, the ownership share of Sinopec fell from 100 per cent in the early 1990s to 56 per cent in 1997. The President of SPC, Wu Yixin, reported that he would be quite happy to see the ownership share of Sinopec fall below 50 per cent, though he thought it unlikely that it would fall below 30 per cent. Through the flotation and subsequent share issue, SPC raised a total of nearly $380m. This was used mainly to repay loans taken out to expand capacity.

International joint ventures were a major route for SPC to realize its ambitious expansion plans. Prior to 1996, SPC had already established several joint ventures. In 1996, the level was sharply stepped up with the announcement of two major projects. The smaller of these was a $100m project to build a 100 000 ton per annum linear low density polyethylene plant, in partnership with Phillips Petroleum. The project is 60 per cent owned by SPC, and was completed in 1998. This important project was dwarfed by the announcement later in 1996 of a $2.5bn joint venture with BP. The core of the joint venture was to be a 650 000 ton ethylene plant. This project will increase SPC's ethylene capacity from 400 000 tons in 1998 to over 1m tons, making it one of the world's largest ethylene plants.

Once the central government announced that it wished to allow the development of a number of large-scale petrochemical companies through merger and acquisition, SPC began to acquire other petrochemical companies. In 1996 SPC acquired the Shanghai Jinjiang Acrylic Fibre Plant. As a result of the merger, SPC's share of China's acrylic fibre production rose from 32 per cent to over 44 per cent. Shortly after this, SPC announced that it was taking over the Zhejiang Acrylic Fibre Plant which would 'enable the Company to increase its market share for acrylic fibre products' (SPC, 1998: p.13). SPC's share of national acrylic fibre output now surpassed one-half.

The goal SPC's leaders in the mid-1990s was to develop SPC's core business of petrochemicals by investing in new technology, lowering costs of production, changing its production structure towards high value-added products and merging with other strong firms. Under an ambitious chief executive officer, a group of leaders emerged at SPC who fought strongly for the company's independence from the headquarters of Sinopec. A major strategic goal for SPC was to merge with companies with which it had real business synergies. Such expansion, it felt, was best achieved 'through the market' rather than through state administration. SPC's ambitious leadership in the mid-1990s felt strongly that the construction of a national integrated oil and petrochemical giant company would be best accomplished by allowing increasingly autonomous entities such as SPC to merge and take over other companies, including those upstream and downstream of SPC. A key part of SPC's ambitions was to merge with a crude oil supplier: 'Without an integrated crude oil supply we are not a modern oil and petrochemical company'. One obvious possibility for merger was with Daqing, from which almost one-half of SPC's crude oil was supplied. As we have seen, at one point in the mid-1990s, SPC held serious discussions with Daqing to explore this possibility.

As well as SPC, Sinopec also contains several other companies with a strong sense of corporate identity. Each of them pursued a similar route of enhanced autonomy from the central holding company. The most important of these have all issued H-shares in Hong Kong, namely Yanhua, Yizheng, and Zhenhai.

### *Restructuring and flotation: from holding companies to integrated oil and petrochemical companies*

*Restructuring (1).* The structure that was painfully established in the Chinese oil and petrochemicals sector from the early 1980s through to the late 1990s produced a great many unresolved problems. There was intense debate about how to restructure this vast industry at the heart of the Chinese economy. Moreover, the debate was given dramatically increased intensity by the sudden explosion of mergers and acquisitions in the world's oil and petrochemical industry in the late 1990s. Chinese policymakers openly acknowledged the inadequacies of the industry. The over-arching problems were the ambiguity of the relationship between the headquarters and the subordinate production units, the separation of the upstream and downstream parts of the industry and the urgent necessity to drive the industry towards a modern management system. In June 1998, after years of intense debate and experimentation, China's most senior policymakers decided to undertake a dramatic transformation of the institutional structure of the oil and petrochemical industry, which was far bolder than most industry observers had predicted.

The restructuring programme for the oil and petrochemical industry created two new giant, vertically integrated oil and petrochemical groups: [New] China National Petrochemical Corporation (Sinopec) and [New] China National Petroleum Corporation (CNPC). Together, they account for 11 per cent of China's industrial output value. The government's stated aim was to establish completely independent companies. Their only aim was to be the pursuit of profits. They were to be given complete operational independence. They were to be allowed and encouraged to compete with each other as giant oligopolistic companies. The assets of Sinopec and CNPC were reorganized along geographical lines, with those located in eastern and southern China coming under the management of Sinopec and those in northern and western China coming under CNPC. Under the reorganization scheme, Sinopec transferred 19 petrochemical enterprises to CNPC, of which 14 are engaged in production and five in marketing. CNPC transferred to Sinopec 12 enterprises, of which 11 were engaged in oil exploration and production; the twelfth enterprise was Zhongyuan Petrochemical.

The new Sinopec accounts for about 60 per cent of China's total refining capacity and about 30 per cent of the onshore crude production capacity, and well over half of total Chinese output of the main petrochemical products. The new CNPC accounts for 40 per cent of China's refining capacity and 69 per cent of onshore crude production capacity. Within China they are massively dominant. Together, they account for around 90 per cent of crude oil production in China, and are responsible for over 75 per cent of the output of natural gas. Combined oil refining capacity amounts to over 95 per cent of the total in China. The two companies also account for 90 per cent of the ethylene cracking capacity. All the provincial state-owned petroleum companies and their petrol stations were placed under CNPC and Sinopec. CNPC was allocated the companies in the north and west, and Sinopec was allocated the remainder. Each was encouraged to compete in the other's territory, and there is some evidence that this has already begun.

*Restructuring (2)*. The restructuring of 1998 created two giant, vertically integrated companies. Almost as soon as this restructuring had been completed, the Chinese government announced that the restructured companies were to issue H-shares in Hong Kong. Feverish activity took place in both companies in order to get them ready for flotation. The flotation involved a further, even more dramatic 'restructuring' process. The goal was to produce companies that looked like the global giants in their fundamental business structure.

Restructuring CNPC and Sinopec for flotation produced intense conflict between the central holding companies and the subordinate entities. After almost two decades of gradually developing their autonomy and sense of corporate identity, the large subordinate enterprises within each holding company were required to relinquish power to the central holding company. The flotation involved an intense internal political battle involving the 'relocation' of key officers in the major subordinate companies. The process involved separation of 'core' from 'non-core' business. The core businesses included all the key production assets in oil and petrochemicals. The non-core business included some specialist oilfield engineering services, but principally involved non-oil and petrochemical business, including utilities, social welfare, and 'diversified undertakings'. The floated companies included the former, and the non-floated 'mother' company included the latter. Across China, within every enterprise in CNPC and Sinopec a ferocious struggle took place to separate the business into two components. At Daqing, for example, 106 000 workers were separated into Petrochina, the new national company that was to be floated internationally, and 180 000 employees were to be left in the non-core 'continuing enterprises'. Daqing, like most large Chinese enterprises, had formerly been a single large socioeconomic unit. Now it was cut in two and its autonomy taken from it. For Daqing's employees, this was equivalent to 'killing' Daqing.

After the restructuring, the two entities to be floated, PetroChina and China Petroleum and Chemical Corporation (Sinopec) respectively, were left with the 'cream' of the oil and petrochemical assets. They drastically downsized in terms of employees. PetroChina contains 480 000 employees, compared with 1.54m in the original CNPC. The China and Petroleum and Chemical Corporation (CPCC) contains 400 000 employees, compared with 1.12m in the old Sinopec. PetroChina and CPCC both floated in the year 2000, each selling around 10 per cent of their total equity value on international markets. The remaining equity share was still owned by the respective 'mother' companies, CNPC and Sinopec. The flotations raised around $3.0bn and $3.5bn respectively. A major reason for the relative success of the flotation was the participation of the global giant companies. BP Amoco purchased $620m-worth of the PetroChina flotation. In return for their contribution to the flotations, the global giants were promised greatly increased access to the lucrative 'downstream' market, notably petrol stations. A consortium of the three giant companies, BP Amoco, Exxon Mobil and Shell, together agreed to subscribe to a large fraction of the share issue of CPCC.

By the year 2000, after a long and tortuous path of reform, China's oil and petrochemical industry had grown to outwardly resemble the middle-ranking global integrated oil and petrochemical companies, such as ENI or Repsol. Like them it was following a path of gradually reducing the state's ownership share and building a modern competitive business. The particular path of reform that China had followed produced an intense struggle to create a unified company for flotation. Large questions remained about the degree to which the floated entities would be truly independent of interference from the mother company. It remained uncertain how far the finances raised through flotation would be used for expansion of business capabilities and how far they would be used to ease the pain of separation for the huge number of employees that remained in the respective mother companies. The multinational giants not only had large investments in joint ventures with the separate subordinate entities within CNPC and Sinopec, but were now also acquiring significant ownership shares in the floated entities. The long-term relationship between the global giants and the newly created Chinese entities was far from clear.

## Autos and components: the case of Yuchai Diesel Engine Company

### Growth and concentration in the Chinese vehicle industry

China's rapid economic growth after the 1970s stimulated a matching increase in demand for motor vehicles. National output of all types of automobiles rose from 150 000 in 1978 to 1.6m in 1998. Over the same period, output of trucks rose from 96 000 to 480 000. The government designated the vehicle industry a 'pillar' sector to be strongly supported. It tightly controlled legal vehicle imports and strongly promoted domestic vehicle and component production. Right up to the late 1990s, vehicle imports were subject to strict licensing and high tariffs. The components industry grew in tandem with vehicle output growth, spurred by tough local content rules, lower transport costs and the imperative of 'just-in-time' production required by global vehicle makers. The components industry was heavily protected. For example, in the mid-1990s, the tariff on imported diesel engines still stood at 35 per cent.

After the 1970s, China's economic reforms stimulated a rapid growth of demand for vehicles. Alongside high levels of protection, this encouraged a proliferation of vehicle makers. Demand greatly exceeded supply for some years, encouraging new entrants into the industry, often producing on an extremely small scale. The number of automobile assembly plants rose from around 50 in the mid-1970s to over 120 in the early 1990s. In 1990 only two of the vehicle manufacturers had an annual output of more than 50 000 units. As early as 1987 the Chinese government announced its intention to attempt to concentrate the automobile industry into much larger units which could benefit from economies of scale. In 1994 the Chinese government reiterated its commitment to concentrating vehicle production in a small number of large firms. These firms were to be the 'national champions', that would be able to withstand the onslaught from international competition when China's protection was reduced. The government's goal was to reshuffle the top twenty or so vehicle manufacturers into just three or four enterprise groups by the turn of the century 'in order to meet foreign competition'.

The rapid growth of output from the government's targeted keypoint plants produced an explosive process of concentration of market share in saloon vehicle production. By 1996 Shanghai Automobile Corporation's joint venture with VW accounted for 47 per cent of total domestic saloon car production. and the Tianjin Charade joint venture accounted for 20 per cent. At the start of the reform process, there were already two dominant truck-making enterprises, Yiqi and Erqi (Dongfeng). These two entities were strongly supported by central government policy during the reforms, as the pillars of the Chinese truck industry.

Consolidation of the auto components industry lagged behind that in vehicle assembly. A large number of vehicle makers produced vehicles in small batches, with low quality and price, using cheap, low quality components manufactured by local firms, typically township and village enterprises, with small entry costs. By the mid-1990s it is estimated that there were almost 5000 components manufacturers across the country, most of which were tiny. In the late 1980s there were at least 200 enterprises manufacturing internal combustion engines. The government's goal in the components sectors, as in vehicle assembly, increasingly became the creation of a small group of powerful indigenous manufacturers. By the turn of the century the Chinese government aimed to have a network of just five to ten internationally competitive components manufacturers.

## Yuchai

### Growth and collapse

Prior to 1984 Yuchai was a small producer of low-power diesel engines for agricultural machinery, ranked 173rd among China's internal combustion engine producers. Experimental production of the medium-duty truck diesel engine, the 6105, began in 1981 and full production began in 1984. By 1993, Yuchai had become China's largest diesel engine manufacturer. Its share of China's medium-duty truck engine market climbed sharply from zero in the early 1980s to around 49 per cent in 1995. This was a remarkable story of growth, from nothing to almost one-half of the total market for one of China's most important, fast-growing and technically demanding products. Within only two years, however, Yuchai's position had deteriorated to the point at which it was close to bankruptcy. By August 1997, there was 'no production at all'. Employees were working in rotation, being paid for less than one day out of three. By the autumn of 1997 Yuchai was unable to pay many of its creditors. The outlook was bleak. The story of its rise and fall is closely related to its failed attempt to become one of China's key components makers supported by the central government's industrial policy.

### Wang Jianming

Wang Jianming was crucial to Yuchai's success. He arrived at Yuchai in 1970 as a Red Guard from Shanghai. He quickly rose to become Deputy Head of the Yuchai Revolutionary Committee, but he was then demoted to be head of the casting workshop. In 1983 he won the highest number of votes in a workers' poll, and was appointed deputy manager. However, Wang felt that he deserved to be made head of Yuchai. Shortly afterwards, when the then Director visited Beijing, Wang talked with the Guangxi Provincial Ministry of Machinery (Yuchai's superior body) and won them over to support him. When the director arrived back at Nanning airport, he was dismissed from his post and Wang Jianming appointed in his place.

This proved to be the turning point for Yuchai. When Wang Jianming took over the plant in the mid-1980s it was deeply indebted. From early on Wang Jianming drove Yuchai to 'look towards the market', and change its traditional pattern of behaviour. He was directly responsible for the huge change in Yuchai's institutional structure, for mapping out its course of becoming a Joint-Stock Company, a Sino-foreign joint venture and its flotation on the New York Stock Market.

Wang was directly responsible for the transformation of the firm's philosophy in marketing its products, and in trying to capture large areas of the truck engine market through raising capital to upgrade its technical level. Wang Jianming's position may be closely analogous to that of the head of a powerful Western family business, such as Michelin or Ikea. There were no serious rivals for Wang's position once the firm started its high-speed growth in the late 1980s, and few people who understood the business like Wang. Like the heads of strong family-run firms, Wang's visionary leadership was strongly growth-oriented, rather than short-term profit-oriented and risk minimizing. Even after its flotation on the New York Stock Market, there is little evidence that Wang Jianming was much concerned about Yuchai's stock market price. His main interest in the flotation had been to raise cash to finance Yuchai's ambitious expansion plans.

Yulin is a rough, backward city compared to China's coastal cities. The quality of the local labour force is poor. A major objective of Wang Jianming's management was to build a professional 'modern enterprise system' at Yuchai. In its struggle to become the number one engine maker in China, Yuchai set great store by upgrading its human resources: 'If you don't have the personnel, then everything is a waste of time'. In the 1990s, Yuchai allocated around 5 per cent of the total wage bill to training, a high proportion for a Chinese company. From the 1980s, it established its own internal training programme to upgrade existing workers' technical skills, especially in computing and internal combustion engine technology. By the mid-1990s Yuchai had built up a core of highly qualified technical personnel. In 1995 it had more than 550 engineers, over one-half of whom were devoted to research and development, product enhancement and new designs. It had a staff of approximately 1000 employees in its technology and engineering department. In the early 1990s it head-hunted key personnel from the Shanghai Internal Combustion Engine Research Institute in order to help it upgrade its engines. As the plant modernized, so the quality of workers required rose steadily. The new production lines require more skilful, computer-literate workers than previously. After 1993, as Yuchai began its accelerated drive for growth and modernization, it recruited high level technical specialists and senior engineers from all over China. Yuchai was allowed by the Guangxi government to introduce 'revolutionary' changes in the wage system. It radically increased wage differentials. In 1992 their new bonus system caused a 'sensation' in Guangxi province. An annual bonus of up to around the same amount as the basic wage was introduced, its award being dependent upon the achievement of a variety of targets.

### *Institutional change*
Faced with a booming domestic market for medium-duty trucks, and the possibility of even faster growth in heavy-duty trucks, Yuchai embarked on a colossal institutional transformation in the 1990s, led by its dynamic chief executive officer. The driving force behind this was the urgent need to obtain capital to finance the company's expansion plans. Guangxi is a poor region, and the provincial government had limited financial means with which to assist local businesses. From the early 1980s onwards, following a path common across Chinese industry, Yuchai was allowed to retain a portion of the profits it generated. By the late 1980s, Yuchai was allowed to retain a large fraction of realized profits and taxes.

The approach of the Guangxi Provincial Government towards Yuchai changed sharply in the late 1980s as Yuchai commenced its high-speed growth. In order to meet the anticipated growth in demand, Yuchai wanted to buy the production line for the 6112 heavy-duty engine from Ford in Brazil. They had heard in 1992 of its availability for purchase. Long discussions were held between Yuchai and the Guangxi government, including the Ministry of Machine Building, to investigate how to help. The provincial government was not able to offer substantial financial support, but it was able to 'support Yuchai with policies'. They quickly gave their support to Yuchai's proposal to establish a Sino-foreign joint venture as a way to raise funds to support Yuchai's expansion. They accepted that this would mean a great dilution of direct state control over the enterprise. A major reason for giving Yuchai such support was that a successful Yuchai was able to make a large financial contribution to the region's prosperity. Yuchai turned towards international capital at least in part in order to fund its ambitious expansion plans, since the Guangxi government was unable to provide the necessary funding. A further reason for Yuchai pursuing this path was in order to increase its degree of independence from the Guangxi government's administrative control. In July

1992, with the help of advice from the System Reform Commission under the Chinese State Council, the diesel engine business of Yuchai (formerly Yulin Diesel) became a formally approved joint stock company, the first SOE in Guangxi to be allowed to do so. In May 1993 Yuchai became a Sino-foreign Joint Stock Company. The Guangxi government gave its approval for a radical dilution of the state's ownership of the firm, and a massive change in its structure. Majority ownership (51.3 per cent of the then-outstanding Yuchai shares) passed into the hands of various foreign share owners, of which much the most important was Hong Leong Holdings (Singapore). The establishment of the Sino-foreign Joint Stock Company raised a capital injection of $52.3m into Yuchai, further increasing its ability to finance its ambitious expansion plans.

Hong Leong (HLA) is an overseas Chinese company. It is one of the top five groups in Singapore. It invested in Yuchai because they believed that it had the potential to become the dominant diesel engine manufacturer in China. They considered that in a developing country the heart of a truck is the engine. They were confident that a strong truck engine manufacturer had high long-term growth prospects. They pinned their hopes on the possibility that with their investment and the capital from the New York flotation (see below), Yuchai would be able to upgrade the 6105 into the 6108, maintaining Yuchai's leading position, and become a leading supplier of heavy-duty engines through the 6112 model using the second hand Ford (Brazil) line. In November 1994 the company was further restructured prior to the 16 November flotation on the New York Stock Market. The state's ownership share in Yuchai Machinery Company was further diluted, falling to 22.1 per cent at the point of flotation. The floated entity, China Yuchai International (CYI), owned 76.4 per cent of Yuchai and the share of indigenous Chinese institutions fell to 1.5 per cent. Foreign public shareholders purchased 30 per cent of the share value of CYI, raising around $64m to finance Yuchai's ambitious expansion plans.

### *Market structure*
China's high-speed growth of national product was accompanied by a fast growth of vehicle output. In the mid-1980s, trucks still accounted for over two-fifths of total vehicle output. Moreover, medium-duty trucks constitute the principle carrier of cargo by road. The use of heavy-duty trucks is limited by the narrowness and poor maintenance of roads which place a premium on manoeuvrability. In 1993 there were over 178 000 medium-duty trucks produced in China, compared to just 10 000 heavy-duty trucks.

The demand for diesel engines for medium-duty trucks rose exceptionally fast in the 1990s, not only due to the fast growth of demand for medium duty trucks, but also because diesel engines were replacing petrol ones as the choice of truck purchasers. Although diesel engines are more expensive to buy, they are preferred because of their higher power, fuel efficiency and reliability. By 1995, almost all new heavy-duty trucks, over one-half of new medium-duty and over one-third of new light-duty trucks were fitted with diesel engines. Over the long term, as road conditions improve, it is to be expected that the share of large trucks in freight haulage will rise. The nature of demand also altered in the 1990s in respect of the type of purchaser. Instead of state units, there occurred a rapid growth of individual purchasers due to the rise of private and collective transport companies, and the leasing out of transport units by state-owned enterprises. Consequently, consumers became much more discriminating, with much closer attention to the purchase price, reliability and operating costs of the engines.

### Product choice and development
Yuchai's period of explosive growth in the late 1980s/early 1990s was based on the 6105 engine (that is, a six cylinder engine with a 105mm bore). This was a more powerful engine than that produced at the time by Yuchai's chief rivals, which mattered greatly in the competitive struggle for the Chinese medium-duty engine market. However, as the 1990s progressed, other domestic producers were quickly catching up. The two diesel engine producers within the Yiqi Group, Dalian and Wuxi, could both produce by 1996 engines of 110mm bore, achieving even greater power than Yuchai's 6105 engine.

Yuchai could foresee these problems. It attempted to keep itself ahead of the competition through a variety of strategies. It attempted to upgrade the quality of the 6105 to a 108mm bore (6108), enabling the engine to generate greater power. The development of the new engine and associated production facilities cost 500–600m yuan, using the bulk of the revenue from the New York listing. Unfortunately, development of the engine encountered major technical problems, and Yuchai was unable to produce the 6108 commercially. A second plank of Wang Jianming's strategy was the purchase of a second hand production line from Ford (Brazil) to produce a six cylinder, 112mm bore engine (the 6112 model). It had a design capacity of 45000 engines, and was intended to supply the heavy-duty truck market. The plant was purchased for 'just' $16m, but the engine was a 'poor performer', and had serious emission problems even in terms of China's lax pollution controls. It basically found no market at all. In the late 1990s the plant was lying idle.

By 1997/8, Yuchai faced the situation that in the medium-duty truck market, the mainstay of Yuchai's growth, the 6105 was no longer able to command a mass market due to the development of technically superior and attractively priced competitors. The medium-duty 6108 was a technical failure. In the heavy-duty market, the 6112 failed to find a market due to its technical backwardness. Yuchai had the capacity to produce annually around 70000 of the 6105 engines, around 70000 of the 6108 engines and around 50000 of the 6112 engines. In 1997 Yuchai sold well under 30000 units, not even one-half of the production capacity of one of the three engines that it was then able to produce.

### Customers
In 1995 there were around eighty truck producers in China. However, we have seen that Yiqi and Dongfeng comprehensively dominated domestic production of

heavy- and medium-duty trucks. In 1998, Dongfeng alone accounted for over one-half of total domestic production of heavy duty trucks, while Dongfeng and Yiqi together accounted for 67 per cent of total national output. In medium duty trucks, Yiqi was the number one producer with 56 per cent of the national market, while Yiqi and Dongfeng together accounted for 91 per cent of national output. Without the market for these two leading producers, the future of an independent Chinese medium- and heavy-duty diesel engine maker would be severely constrained.

In 1995 Yuchai sold its engines to 37 factories, but a small number of these were disproportionately important. In total, over three-fifths of Yuchai's sales in the mid-1990s were to plants within the Dongfeng 'system'. From negligible production levels in the early 1980s, supplying only a small fraction of the engine needs of the Dongfeng Group, by the mid-1990s Yuchai had become much the most important supplier of diesel engines to the Group, China's leading truck manufacturer. By 1995, Yuchai was supplying close to one-half of the Group's diesel engines. Dongfeng had not anticipated the rapid growth of demand for diesel engines, and had invested mainly in building up its petrol engine capacity. It was initially pleased to be able to buy high quality products in large numbers from Yuchai, that in turn helped to sell its own vehicles more effectively.

To be so reliant on a single customer proved extremely dangerous for Yuchai. This was especially so since Yuchai's main customers turned out to be Yuchai's main competitors. Yuchai's very success became a serious problem. Yuchai realized that the shift towards high quality diesel engines was so strong that truck operators could be persuaded to swap their petrol engine for a Yuchai diesel engine. Yiqi and Dongfeng had to 'bear the ignominy of seeing new trucks having their engines ripped out and replaced by Yuchai engines almost as soon as they left the factory'. The heads of Yiqi and Dongfeng were extremely angry at what they considered to be Yuchai's predatory behaviour, which caused them much embarrassment and loss of face for their companies.

### *Marketing*

Not only did Yuchai develop a strong product. Yuchai was able to capture a fast-growing market share because it also developed an advanced system of advertising and service provision. Yuchai was in the vanguard of a revolution in Chinese advertising. For example, in a most unusual move for an engine-making company, it put great efforts into TV advertising. It used China Central TV to make advertisements that were very sophisticated by Chinese standards at that time. It targeted peak times, such as immediately after the evening news bulletin, just before the weather forecast. It developed strong brand imagery, with Yuchai championed as the 'king of engines'.

Yuchai was the first Chinese engine maker to put into practice the concept of an engine guarantee and to develop a comprehensive, nationwide service network. Yuchai carefully studied the world's leading diesel engine companies and realized the crucial importance of a service network for establishing competitive advantage in the diesel engine industry. By the end of 1996 Yuchai had established a network of around 450 franchised service stations. These had all to meet strict Yuchai standards for repair quality, personnel capability, space and equipment quality, and staff had to undergo training by Yuchai. Yuchai pioneered the concept of engine guarantees, steadily increasing the guaranteed mileage from 30 000 kms in 1993 to 150 000 kms by 1996.

### Competitors

In the West, especially in the US, there has been a large role for independent diesel engine makers. The volume of diesel engine production is much less than for petrol engines, and the level of technical sophistication of the engines is high. A central issue for Yuchai is the degree to which there is also a role in China for a large independent manufacturer in this sector at this stage in China's economic development. Wang Jianming's explicit goal was to turn Yuchai into a Chinese version of Caterpillar, Cummins Diesel or Detroit Diesel. Together they accounted for around 80 per cent of the North American market for heavy duty diesel engines in the 1990s. However, even in the West there is considerable debate about the degree to which it is desirable to buy in, as opposed to manufacture diesel engines in-house. The major European-based truck makers produce most of their diesel engines in-house. In the US, a much large share of diesel engines are bought from stand-alone firms. However, one of the most important of these, Detroit Diesel, was bought by Daimler-Chrysler in July 2000, and there were doubts about how long Cummins could remain an independent entity.

Wang Jianming believed that in trying to replicate the North American giants in the field, he was swimming with the tide of Chinese policy towards the components sector, namely to construct large firms which would benefit from economies of scale and would be the instruments through which international technology would be transferred to China via joint ventures and technology licensing agreements. Having launched Yuchai into a leading position by the mid-1990s, Wang Jianming was confident that he would be able to take advantage of his first-mover position to remain China's number one diesel engine maker.

As China's largest truck maker, Yiqi was a potentially very important market for Yuchai. It was also a potentially key competitor. Within the Yiqi 'system' were three major diesel engine producers, Chaoyang, Dalian and Wuxi. Along with several other formerly independent plants these were transferred to the 'control' of Yiqi in the late 1980s as part of the government's policy of forming large automobile 'enterprise groups'. In 1995, with the support of the central government, following its renewed commitment to create powerful large-scale automobile companies, Yiqi took full control of both Dalian and Wuxi Diesel Plants. The transformation of these two major diesel engine plants into tightly controlled subsidiaries of Yiqi was highly significant for the Chinese diesel engine industry. It took Yiqi down the 'Fordist' path of increasing the degree of vertical integration. Even though Yiqi had never been a large market for Yuchai, this significant development cast a shadow over Yuchai's long-term strategy.

After this move, *ceteris paribus*, a multinational diesel engine company would have been more inclined to invest in the tightly controlled diesel engine subsidiaries of Yiqi than in an independent supplier such as Yuchai.

Dongfeng seems from early on to have been keen to develop its own diesel engine production within the Group. In order to enhance its technical capabilities in diesel engine manufacture, in 1986 it concluded a collaboration agreement with Cummins diesel engine company (US). In the mid-1990s this was turned into a full joint venture. By 1996, Xiangfan was able to produce the 6100 series diesel engines, directly competitive with those produced by Yuchai. In 1994, Dongfeng increased its diesel engine capability when it took over the Chaoyang Diesel engine plant, which had formerly been within the Yiqi system.

By 1996/7 neither Chaoyang nor Xiangfan was able to produce engines of as high a power as those from Yuchai, let alone those of Dalian and Wuxi. Both were still confined to the relatively low-powered 4102 or 6102 diesel engine. Consequently, Dongfeng was forced to rely on Yuchai to supply a large fraction of its medium-duty diesel engine needs. However, their technology was in the process of being fast transformed by the joint venture with Cummins. Like Yiqi, Dongfeng had taken the highly significant step in the mid-1990s of increasing the diesel engine production facilities under its direct ownership and control. Both the joint venture with Cummins and the transfer of Chaoyang from Yiqi to Dongfeng's ownership were highly significant for Yuchai's long-term prospects. They signalled Dongfeng's wish to produce a large number of diesel engines within the first and second tier companies of the Dongfeng system, and to ensure that the technical level of these developed fast.

In sum, the combination of developments at Yiqi and Dongfeng in the mid-1990s were ominous for Yuchai's aspirations to become a Chinese equivalent of Caterpillar, Cummins or Detroit Diesel.

In the heavy duty truck sector, Yuchai faced even more intense competitive pressures. We have seen that the output of heavy duty trucks is even more concentrated than for medium duty trucks. Each of the main producers in China wishes to be self-sufficient in heavy-duty engines, following the pattern of Volvo and Mercedes. Almost all the engines they use are produced within the firm. The dominant multinationals quickly entered China in this field. Not only had Erqi established a joint venture with Cummins, which also produce heavy-duty diesel engines, as well as smaller-sized engines, but the China Heavy Duty Truck Corporation produces Steyer trucks and engines under licence. In 1997 it concluded a joint venture with Volvo to produce both trucks and engines. Freightliner (the US subsidiary of Mercedes-Benz) established a joint venture in Shanghai to produce heavy-duty trucks, at least initially using imported Cummins diesel engines. Yuchai's gamble with the purchase of the Brazilian heavy-duty engine plant was a complete failure. As we have seen, the plant was simply idle. The fact that the industry was so highly oligopolistic made it especially difficult to break into the heavy-duty diesel engine market against the established producers in alliance with multinational investment and technology.

In the mid-1990s Wang Jianming intensively lobbied the central government. His goal was for them to agree to support Yuchai as China's flagship diesel maker, to rival the world's leading companies, Caterpillar, Cummins, and Detroit Diesel. A major part of his strategy was to persuade the central authorities (Ministry of Machinery) to encourage and/or instruct Yiqi and Erqi (Dongfeng) to give up their self-reliant strategy in diesel engines, and allow Yuchai to take over the ownership of their associated diesel engine plants. However, the combined might of Yiqi and Erqi enabled them to persuade the Ministry of Machinery to reject Wang Jianming's proposal. During the course of the lobbying by Wang Jianming, relationships with Yiqi and Erqi became highly strained. Yiqi and Erqi were afraid of the market power that a greatly enlarged Yuchai would have. They were highly uneasy about being greatly dependent upon Yuchai for their key component for truck production, the engine.

## Steel: Shougang Iron and Steel Corporation

### The Chinese steel industry

Fast-growing developing countries typically generate fast growth of demand for steel. China's steel consumption rose from 32m tons in 1980 to 104m tons in 1997, or an annual average rate of 10.0 per cent. No country has witnessed such a massive rise in steel consumption in such a short period of time. It is forecast that China's steel consumption will reach 115–120m tons in the year 2000, rising to 140m tons in 2010. This provides a huge opportunity for China's steelmakers and the associated industries. It is also a highly significant market in which the multinational companies would wish to be involved. The domestic steel market was substantially liberalized in the 1990s. In addition, import tariffs on steel halved from 24 per cent in 1992 to 12 per cent in 1996. However, powerful new non-tariff barriers to protect the steel industry were erected in the mid-1990s. These included import 'registration', which could be withheld if there was felt to be a 'market need', and 'canalization' of steel imports through selected state importing companies.

In lower-quality products, China is substantially self-sufficient. However, China faces the prospect of a fast growth of demand for higher quality, higher value-added products in the years ahead. In the 1990s, China's demand for high value-added steel products greatly exceeded domestic supply capabilities. For example, in 1996, imports accounted for 43 per cent of China's consumption of hot rolled sheets, 50 per cent of car sheets, 56 per cent of cold rolled sheets, 53 per cent of galvanized sheet, 71 per cent of tin sheet, 73 per cent of container plate, 81 per cent of stainless sheet, and 87 per cent of domestic appliance sheet. A major policy aim in the steel industry is to increase rapidly the domestic supply of high value-added products.

In the reform years, faced with surging demand for steel, local small-scale plants made rapid progress. However, the large 'keypoint' enterprises still made up the core of China's iron and steel industry. In 1997 the top 20 steel enterprises accounted for 62 per cent of national steel output. Among these was a group of four super-large integrated steel enterprises (Angang, Shougang, Baogang and Wugang) which accounted for 28 per cent of national output. The Chinese government wishes to develop these enterprises into world-class companies, rivalling Nippon Steel and Posco for efficiency and global influence.

## Shougang Iron and Steel Corporation

### *Gaining autonomy*

In 1979, the Chinese government began to experiment with the system of enterprise profit retention. Shougang was one of the first pilot enterprises to undertake this reform. In 1981 it put into effect its famous contract. It was struck with Shougang's direct administrative superior, the Beijing city government. It was of fifteen years' duration, from 1981 to 1995. The Shougang contract was relatively simple. Profits handed over to the state were to increase by 7.2 per cent annually – the base figure was the profit submitted in 1981. Any profits over this amount were retained by the enterprise. Of the retained profit, 60 per cent was to be used as development funds, 20 per cent as collective welfare funds, and 20 per cent as bonuses for the employees: this was the 6:2:2 system. For the Beijing City government, the incentive was not just that it received a guaranteed handover of profits, but also that the financing of investment in the contracting plants was removed from the government's budgetary responsibility. When the contract was put into place, the city government was desperately short of funds with which to assist the growth of Shougang, so they 'helped Shougang with policy instead'. Shougang was granted 'complete autonomy' in the way in which it allocated its resources earmarked for investment, as long as it fulfilled its target for profits handover to the state.

For almost the entire period of the contract system, Shougang's Chairman and Party Secretary was Zhou Guanwu, a former army commander and senior figure in the Communist Party. Zhou had serious ambitions to build Shougang into China's leading steel producer, and to make it one of the leading steel companies in the world, alongside Nippon Steel and Posco. Zhou retired in February 1995, amid great controversy about the sources of growth at Shougang.

### *Shougang's high-speed growth*

In 1978, Shougang was a traditional large, integrated iron and steel producer, located at a single site in Beijing. It is still a state owned plant. After 1978, under the contract system and Zhou Guanwu's leadership, Shougang grew at high speed. Shougang's output of crude steel rose from 1.7 million tons in 1978 to 8.3 million tons in 1994, around 10 per cent per annum. In 1978, it was only China's seventh largest steel plant. By 1996, it was poised to become China's largest steel producer. It had become one of the twenty largest steel producing firms in the world.

Zhou Guanwu had planned to build a second huge steel plant at Qilu in Shandong Province. Had Qilu been completed, Shougang's crude steel production capacity would have increased by 10m tons. It would have become one of the world's top three steel firms in terms of physical output. The central authorities vetoed these plans after prolonged debate. Shortly afterwards, Zhou Guanwu retired, marking the end of an extraordinary epoch in Shougang's history. The shelving of the Qilu project had enormous implications for the whole expansion strategy that Shougang mapped out in the final phase of Zhou's period as head of the Corporation.

### Growth through administrative merger

In the 1980s and 1990s, almost all large and medium-sized enterprises were state-owned. Mergers between them were typically handled by administrative co-ordination, either by a single local government, or between different local governments. Shougang was in the vanguard of the gradually developing merger movement within China. Under Zhou Guanwu it merged with more than 100 large and medium-sized enterprises. Total employment in Shougang rose from around 110 000 in 1978 to over 260 000 in the mid-1990s.

In 1983, Shougang merged with 17 large profit-making steel works in the Beijing area, with a total of around 30 000 employees. The merged enterprises were all in the steel-processing sector and used to be consumers of Shougang's iron. In the 1980s and early 1990s, the price of iron was set far below that of steel and steel products. It was much less profitable to produce iron than to produce steel and steel products. Once enterprises such as Shougang were given autonomy, they were unwilling to continue supplying cheap iron to other enterprises for them to make high profits, adding value in the downstream parts of the industry. These plants became the main force in Shougang's expansion of its steel processing capacity. Their equipment was modernized with investment from Shougang. Their output structure was reorganized by Shougang's headquarters. Shougang gained access to the more profitable downstream segment of the iron and steel chain of production.

In 1992, Shougang administratively took over two construction companies with a total of 16 000 employees from the China National Non-ferrous Metals Corporation. The main goal of these takeovers was to assist in the construction of the Qilu plant. In 1992 Shougang took over the Beijing Heavy Machinery Factory, and incorporated it into the Shougang Heavy Machinery Corporation. It had a workforce of around 7000, and was heavily loss-making at the time of the takeover. Shougang employed its managerial skills to transform its operational mechanism. It adopted the contract responsibility system and assumed sole responsibility for its profits and losses. Shougang itself became the main customer for the plant, purchasing many large pieces of machinery in order to meet its urgent expansion needs.

In 1988, Shougang merged with 33 large enterprises. They had a total of 59 000 employees in ten provinces and six industries. They included Kaifeng Combine

Harvester Plant (one of the largest agricultural machinery makers in China), Qinhuangdao Tractor Component Plant, Jinzhou Electronic Computer Plant, and Zhenjiang Shipbuilding Plant. Also included in the 33 enterprises merged in 1988 were 13 large military plants, with 45 000 workers. They were mainly 'Third Front' factories located in remote inland areas such as Gansu province and Ningxia Autonomous Region. They were all loss-making and with old equipment. Shougang's enhanced independence compared to many other large enterprises also carried with it special responsibilities to the Chinese state. The administrative mergers with the military enterprises put a great financial burden upon Shougang. Unlike the other enterprises that Shougang had acquired, it was not allowed to return them to their previous owners, even though they were losing a great deal of money and unable to fulfil the contracts.

### Modernization of the core steel-making business

*Growth begets growth.* The high-speed growth of demand for steel provided a large opportunity for Chinese steel firms. Shougang's contract system provided it with a mechanism to fund high-speed expansion. By generating profits from meeting this high-speed demand growth, it was able to reinvest to fund further expansion to meet the surging demand. This market environment provided a high incentive to bring production capacity on-stream as fast as possible. However, Shougang faced the booming market demand after the late 1970s with such outdated facilities that foreign visitors in the early years of reform called it a 'museum of metallurgical history'. It was imperative to both grow and modernize simultaneously.

Shougang's success in rapidly increasing steel output to meet the surging demand generated a rapid growth in profits for reinvestment: retained profits after payment of all taxes and handovers to the Beijing government reportedly increased by 34 per cent per annum from 1980 to 1992. During the years of the contract system, enormous physical investment took place at Shougang. From 1980 to 1990, Shougang spent a total of 4.27bn yuan (roughly $1.56bn) for technical renovation and capital construction: 108 key projects and thousands of minor ones were completed. Shougang hugely upgraded its R&D and design capability and comprehensively automated its main production processes. After 1978, Shougang comprehensively modernized its blast-furnaces, and by the early 1990s, nearly all its steel was produced by oxygen converters. By the late 1990s, its output per worker was 50–100 per cent above that at old integrated steel plants and costs of production were significantly below these plants.

*Good luck: the industrial flea market.* Under the contract system Shougang did not have access to substantial external funding or technical assistance from a leading international steelmaker. Therefore, in order to meet its goal to introduce the most advanced equipment at the lowest cost, Shougang relied heavily on purchasing second-hand equipment. It was fortunate for Shougang that the world steel industry experienced a serious recession during this period. Under the contract system, Shougang imported hundreds of pieces of second-hand equipment. Many of these were major items. It frequently combined the imported units with indigenous technology in order to reduce the overall cost. Shougang typically purchased equipment that was in good condition but was not highly automated, and itself automated the equipment. Shougang's technically successful purchase of second-hand equipment reflected its own relatively high technical skills. The process of purchase and installation also helped to promote those skills, creating a virtuous circle of advance.

For example, in 1984, Shougang planned to build a new mill to expand steel production capacity. At that stage it was unable to produce complete steelmaking equipment itself. The Seraing Works in Belgium with a design production capacity of 2.5m tons and a technical level from the 1970s was up for sale. The second-hand cost of the mill, 40m yuan, plus the cost of moving, was one-tenth of the estimated cost for new plant and equipment. Also buying equipment already in operation reduced the construction period by two to three years. Shougang shipped them by sea to China in August 1985 and the mill was put into operation in August 1987.

In October 1992, Shougang bought the California Iron and Steel Company's Second Converter Steel Mill. When it opened in 1978, the mill was among the most formidable steelmaking facilities in the world. The two huge Voest-Alpine furnaces could produce up to 2.8m tons of high-grade carbon steel annually. It had originally cost \$287m to build. But soon after it was built the plant encountered new environmental regulations and rapidly rising union wages, making the mill uncompetitive compared to US mini-mills and overseas producers. Within just five years of its opening, the plant had been closed. Shougang paid only \$15m to purchase it, and sent a team of 290 engineers and labourers to dismantle their new possession, pack it up and ship it back to China. It was intended to incorporate it into the new Shougang plant at Qilu.

### Management method: military-style organization

*Technical renovation as a series of battles.* Limited funds and constraints of space at the main site in Beijing, meant that Shougang had to rely heavily on upgrading existing facilities. It impelled them to carry out technological transformation as quickly as possible. Under the contract system, time was money. Time spent in renovation meant income foregone from having segments of the plant shut down. It was from this income that the resources for further renovation came. In this sense the contract system imposed the hardest of budget constraints upon Shougang.

From the late 1970s through to the early 1990s, each of the major technological renovations was treated as a battle, with the Corporation organized like an army. From 1992 to 1995 alone, Shougang carried out more than ten large technological renovation projects. The renovation of the No. 2 Blast Furnace involved the investment of 130m yuan, dismantling 13 000 tons of material and installing a further 25 000 tons. Over 7000 workers were assigned to work day and night in an area of just 100 cubic metres. The original time limit for the project was 104 days, but in the end it was completed in only 55 days.

*Unified command system.* Because of the long chain of production that is at the heart of integrated steel production, different subordinate units were treated as part of a technologically unified structure. The requirement to treat each renovation task as a strictly unified planned activity was made even more imperative by the fact that Shougang itself carried out the entire technological renovation using its own construction units. Under the contract system, even the second-tier companies were managed tightly by Shougang's headquarters, closely integrated into the overall strategy for modernization and growth.

*Strict discipline.* The industry's technological characteristics combined with the renovation battles helped produce a highly disciplinarian style of management. In the same fashion as in an army, a mistake by a single individual in the renovation 'battle' can result in the loss of the whole battle. Under Zhou Guanwu, Shougang was famous for its strict discipline. The 'three one hundred per cent system' was introduced in 1980. Every employee had to obey regulations 'one hundred per cent'. Any violation of the regulations had to be recorded and reported 'one hundred per cent'. Violators were deprived of their bonus 'one hundred per cent', no matter what the financial consequence might be for the family of the person who had violated the code of discipline. The strict discipline did not just apply to workers, but to cadres also. From 1978 to 1990, 678 of Shougang's cadres at and above the level of subordinate plant and division management were either demoted (643) or dismissed entirely (35), amounting to almost 10 per cent of the total. This was, almost certainly, the highest ratio in any large enterprise in China.

*Full mobilization.* Each of Shougang's subdivisions and each member of the staff knew their responsibility for the fulfilment of the overall output, profit and other economic and technical tasks. There were numerous contracted targets for each individual in the Corporation. These targets linked each employee's responsibility and reward with Shougang's overall goal. The function of the internal contract system was to mobilize rather than to monitor. It owed much more to the mobilizatory tradition of the Chinese Communist Party and the People's Liberation Army than to study of Western management theory.

Under the contract system, training was an important mechanism, not only for advancing the technical level of the workforce, but also for further mobilizing Shougang's employees for the 'battles'. Training programmes went far beyond simply improving skills. They had the same function as those in an army, namely raising the employees' fighting spirit for the battle. Shougang used the slogans, 'The contract is the base' and 'the people are the base'. Other means of mobilization included meetings and study sessions, frequently out of regular working hours, encouraging employees to make suggestions which might reduce costs, increase quality and efficiency (there were more than 10 000 rationalization suggestions from the workshops over the period of the contract system).

*The military approach to management.* The head of Shougang under the contract system, Zhou Guanwu, was the leader of a guerrilla unit in the anti-Japanese struggle. In contrast to the traditional theory of consumer economics and profit maximization, Lester Thurow has suggested that an alternative way of approaching economic activity is 'producer economics, in which power and conquest are the basic motivation for the firm'. He has argued that in Japan during its rise to global power in the 1980s, competition was treated as warfare rather than a rational process of profit maximization. He believes that 'a content analysis of military metaphors would surely show their much more widespread usage in Japan [than in the West]'. Janelli's account of a large Korean firm speaks of a 'military style of life [that] pervaded the enterprise'. Shougang's management style under the contract system is a variant of the same East Asian tradition. Shougang under the contract system had a central goal, to become China's largest steel producer. However, its ambitions extended beyond that. Zhou Guanwu seriously intended that Shougang would become the number one steel company in the world. Construction of the Qilu plant would have taken the company a long way down this path. Such an ambition is not the unique prerogative of the leader of a 'Communist, state-owned' steel company. A similar ambition drove Andrew Carnegie when he built US Steel. It drove the leaders of Nippon Steel. Today it drives the leaders of Posco.

### Merger, diversification, transnationalization

It takes time for factor and product markets to emerge in less developed countries in general and in Communist, reforming, less developed countries in particular. A huge number of transactions between firms, which formerly were administered through the command system of material balance planning, now needed to be organized in a different way. This creates pressure for large firms to cut through the uncertainty, delay and absence of legally enforceable contracts to create their own internal supply networks, minimizing the cost of organizing these activities through the still highly imperfect market apparatus. This in turn helps push emerging large firms towards diversification via internal growth, acquisition and merger, over and above the forces that assist the emergence of large firms in many sectors in the developed economies.

The main channel for Shougang's expansion in steel production after 1995 was intended to be through the planned construction of the new ten million ton plant, Qilu Iron and Steel. Much of Shougang's diversification and transnationalization in the later phase of the contract system was related to this goal.

*Machine-building capability.* We have seen that under the contract system, Shougang took over several large-scale machine-building enterprises. After reorganization, the plants were linked up to form a single, large machinery engineering company under Shougang's control, the Shougang Heavy Machinery Corporation. This Corporation was now responsible for the design and manufacture of machinery for the metallurgical and mining industries. A major goal was to supply equipment for Shougang's own needs, including, eventually, construction of the new plant at Qilu. By 1994, Shougang was able to design, manufacture and erect large-sized machinery and equipment. It could manufacture a full set of metallurgical and mining equipment, non-standard machines plus components for the chemical and textile industries, as well as general-purpose equipment. Shougang now had more than 20 machinery plants scattered in eight provinces. It began also to export metallurgical equipment, internal combustion engines, large-sized farming machinery, automobile components, hardware and tools, as well as various ships.

*Construction capacity.* By 1985, Shougang had eight construction companies, comprising the Shougang Construction Corporation, with a total of 80 000 employees. They were engaged in the construction, installation and commissioning of blast furnaces, steel-making factories, oxygen plants, power stations, and other heavy auxiliary equipment relating to the steel industry. In 1991, the annual output of steel structures exceeded 10 000 tons, all of which was for Shougang itself. In 1992, Shougang took over a further two construction companies, mainly in order to meet the anticipated construction needs of the Qilu plant.

*Electronic control capability.* In 1984, Shougang began to computerize management control systems with a total of only eight specialists in charge of computer hardware development, software design and installation. Over the course of three years' intense effort they automated four converters. By 1994, Shougang Electronics Corporation employed 3000 technicians and professionals experienced in electronics design, programming, engineering and manufacturing. In 1990 a team of engineers carried out the design, programming and engineering of two computerized supervisory and process control systems for seven basic oxygen furnaces of USX (formerly US Steel), the leading steelmaker in the US, and for the Geneva Steel Works in Switzerland.

*Design capability.* In 1993, Shougang allocated 320m yuan to scientific development, equivalent to 2.5 per cent of total sales value and around 10 per cent of total profits in that year. In 1980 Shougang had a total of around 2500 research personnel. By 1994, Shougang had three design institutes and 72 research institutes, employing a total of around 8000 full-time research personnel. This was an enormous expansion of Shougang's research capability. It constituted a potential source of competitive advantage compared to even the most powerful multinational steel company. By the early 1990s, Shougang had developed the capability to produce every component for an integrated steel plant with hot-rolling capability for steel flats. In 1991, Shougang manufactured its first complete blast furnace in which all the parts, including the computer control system, were produced within the Corporation.

Shougang's technical capability was greatly extended by its policy on overseas acquisition. In July 1988, Shougang Corporation purchased 70 per cent of the shares of the Mesta Engineering Company in Pittsburgh for $3.4m. This famous company has designed more than 600 rolling mills world-wide. More than half of the total working rolling mills in the world have the Mesta trademark. At the time of its purchase by Shougang, Mesta was one of the technological leaders in the world's metallurgy industry. The purpose of this purchase was to combine Mesta's technology with Shougang's own machine-making capability in order to manufacture large continuous-casting and steel rolling equipment for both domestic and overseas clients. This gave Shougang a powerful design capability both to assist the growth of its own continuous-casting capability, and to be well-positioned to meet growing domestic and international demand for continuous-casting equipment.

*Mining capability.* China's iron ore is mostly of poor grade. One estimate is that by the year 2010, China will need to import around 100m tons of iron ore annually, worth $3.2bn at today's prices, which is equivalent to one-quarter of the total amount of iron ore traded world-wide today. The domestic shortage of iron ore has prompted representatives from many large Chinese iron and steel works to look for foreign sources of supply. In November 1992, Shougang purchased the Hierro iron mine in Peru for $120m. This was the biggest purchase abroad by a Chinese institution up until that point. A major objective of the purchase was to guarantee the supply of raw material for Qilu. It was also thought that it might provide a secure and relatively cheap source of iron ore supply for Shougang in Beijing, as well as supplying other Chinese steel plants.

### Summary: Shougang under Zhou Guanwu
Analyses of Shougang have focused almost exclusively on the expanded autonomy given to Shougang as the explanation of its exceptional growth under the contract system. However, many other enterprises eventually adopted the 'Shougang system', but few were as successful as Shougang. The most outstanding success story using the 'Shougang' contract system was Erqi, China's number two motor vehicle manufacturer. No one has seriously suggested that the contract system is sufficient to explain Erqi's rapid growth after the early 1980s.

A distinctive feature of Shougang's growth was the central role for industrial entrepreneurship. The government's reforms encouraged entrepreneurship in a general sense, but did not specifically target industrial entrepreneurship. Industrial entrepreneurs played an important role in the rise of big business in the West. People such as Ford and Carnegie who devoted their entire working life to building an empire in one sector of the economy are very different from the classic entrepreneur, for whom the technical characteristics of the entrepreneurial activity are irrelevant. The goal is to switch capital to whatever yields the highest return over a specific period. In a sense, the industrial entrepreneurs of early big business in the West can be thought of as economically irrational. Whereas Carnegie fought for supremacy within steel, its successor, USX, has diversified into oil as the main line of business. Yonekura had noted that the integrated diversification at New Japan Steel is quite different from the path followed at the New US Steel: 'Nippon Steel utilized accumulated technology in its diversification moves. This was in sharp contrast to the situation with its American counterparts. US Steel Corporation (now USX), for example, diversified into the oil business ... while National Steel diversified into financial services and food business ...The Americans seemed to utilize only accumulated capital, while technological continuity did not appear so important.'

In China during the period of the contract system at Shougang there were numerous outlets for investment capital, including many forms of short-term speculation. The rational choice for profit-making enterprises, state-owned and private enterprises alike, was often not to invest in long-gestating industrial projects, such as the Qilu steel plant, with all the complex of investments associated with it. Rather, it was frequently more rational to reinvest profits into speculation, such as property, or deposit funds in financial institutions. Frequently, those Chinese firms which issued shares abroad held on to their inflow of cash, using it for short-term speculative gain rather than the long-term industrial investment which they informed potential investors was their main aim in going to the stock market. Shougang's firm focus on growth within the steel industry and related businesses is all the more striking in that its period of most rapid technological up-grading was the early 1990s, which coincided with a property speculation boom in which most Chinese firms participated, whether or not they were state-owned. Shougang's ambition was for projects rather than profits, so that it might become the world's number one steel producer. Industrial entrepreneurs like those at Shougang work for growth within their industry rather than for short-term profit maximization.

For an industrial entrepreneur, such as Zhou Guanwu or Nishiyama Yataro of Japan's Kawasaki Steel, competition is about battles for growth, modernization and supremacy, with profits as the means for growth rather than the end purpose. In order to be victorious, industrial entrepreneurs may organize their firms as troops fighting a battle rather than as contractual institutions, but in the fight there is no room for democracy and negotiation, nor even a guarantee that everyone will become better off. Rather, there is a unified command system, strict discipline, full mobilization, and well-organized rear-service support. If necessary, part of the army can be sacrificed. To succeed in battle, there can be no free-riding.

From the early 1980s to the mid-1990s, Shougang's behaviour was sharply against the mainstream thinking of neoclassical economics. It raised many doubts in the public perception. There were many criticisms not only from outside, but from inside Shougang also. This was the price of building a fighting unit, rather than one whose goal was profit maximization. Shougang challenged not only the traditional theory of the firm, but also the liberal neoclassical ideology which was battling for supremacy in China.

# Coal: The Shenhua Coal Company

## The Chinese coal industry

China's rapid industrialization since the late 1970s has required a matching rapid growth in energy supply. China's capability to substitute other domestic sources of energy for coal is limited: China is an energy-scarce economy, with *per capita* energy endowments far below the world average. China's *per capita* reserves of crude oil are just 3 tons, compared to a global average of 28 tons. Its *per capita* reserves of natural gas are just 1416 cubic metres, compared to a global average of 28 400 cubic metres. Since 1993 China has been a net importer of petroleum, and became a net importer of crude oil in 1996. Faced with disappointing finds from the domestic oil and natural gas sector, in 1981 the Chinese began an explicit policy of 'substituting coal for oil', in order to ensure that the main source of fuel for power generation came from domestic sources. The share of coal-fired power stations in total electricity generation rose from 60 per cent in 1980 to 68 per cent in 1995, and they are planned to account for 80 per cent of new capacity.

In the late 1970s, the central authorities gave greatly increased autonomy to localities to encourage the development of local mines using local resources. The demand for coal from local markets exploded from the early 1980s onwards alongside the boom in output from the township and village enterprises (TVEs). By the late 1990s, there were over 60 000 TVE coal mines, and an unknown number of small-scale private coal mines. By the late 1990s, small mines with an annual output of less than 30 000 tons each accounted for 44 per cent of total Chinese coal output. Local governments were keen for local coal mines to develop, since they solved pressing local shortages of energy that emerged as rural industrialization proceeded at high speed. They provided sources of employment and income for under-employed farmers. At least two million people work in TVE mines. Not only was employment provided directly in large numbers in labour-intensive mines, but there was also a large amount of employment and income generated through the labour-intensive transport of coal, mainly in trucks. Moreover, a wide variety of service sector activities sprang up around the production and transport of coal.

Despite the rapid rise of small-scale coal mines, large state-owned coal mines are still the mainstay of the industry. Just 90 large-scale SOE coal mines account for around three-quarters of the total fixed assets in the coalmining sector and over one-half of the number of employees. China's state-owned coal mines have chronic financial difficulties. Of the hundred or so keypoint state coalmining enterprises, a mere 13 were reported to be making profits in 1998. Thirty were breaking even and the remainder were all loss-makers. There are around 20 'natural loss-making' keypoint coal mines, accounting for only around 10 per cent of the output of keypoint coal mines, but close to 40 per cent of their total losses. These mines have encountered fundamental natural problems, such as exhaustion of reserves or technically insurmountable problems with the exploitation of reserves.

In December 1998 the central government announced that it planned to close 26 000 small coal mines. It estimated that the closure would mean the loss of almost one million jobs in the coal industry. The closure of small mines was explicitly linked with an attempt to raise the profitability of the large state-owned coal mines. However, few industry experts believed that this administrative measure would lead to a genuine closure of small mines on anything like the scale that the government hoped. The pressure of market forces and the pressure from local governments to continue to allow small coal mines to operate is intense.

## Shenhua

### *Strategic importance of Shenhua*

The Shenhua Project began in 1985 and will be completed by around the year 2005. Many of China's old-established large-scale mines face increasing costs due to the exhaustion of easily-worked seams and steadily increasing depth. China's long-run energy requirements meant that China needed to find reliable low-cost sources of coal. The huge, virtually unexploited deposits beneath the Ordos Plateau, that make up the Shenfu Dongsheng coalfield, provided such an opportunity. The high quality of the coal in this coalfield provides an opportunity to supply coal that is suitable for the modern, low-emission power stations that form an increasing part of China's energy portfolio. The combination of the large size of the deposits and the high quality of the coal provide an opportunity for China to develop a competitive international supplier of steam coal. However, a major reason that the coalfield was not developed earlier is its remoteness, around 800 km from the coast. To develop the Shenfu Dongsheng coalfield required not only large outlays to develop the mines, but also large matching expenditure on rail and port facilities. The coalfield needed to be developed as a large-scale integrated project. The aggregate investment over the 20 year period will be the equivalent of over $9bn, making it one of the world's largest single projects.

The Shenhua Group Company is 100 per cent owned by the state. The company was established with stockholder rights formally exercised by the State Planning Commission. Its board of directors consists of fourteen people. Eight of these are from Shenhua itself. The others are from related state institutions that have a close interest in Shenhua. These include the provinces of Shanxi, Shaanxi, and Hebei, Inner Mongolia Autonomous Region, the Ministry of Railways and the Ministry of Transportation. The Group makes no distribution of profits, as its assets are owned entirely by the state. The company has initially been granted property rights by the Chinese state to develop a large segment of the coalfield (3500 sq. km), with the implicit right to eventually develop the entire field.

The high importance that the Chinese government attaches to the project is indicated by the fact that the chairman of Shenhua is Ye Qing. He was appointed by the State Council and took up his position as head of Shenhua in 1998. Ye Qing was formerly the deputy director of the State Planning Commission, with special responsibility for energy. Ye Qing is acutely aware of the nature of international competition in this industry. His strategy for the company is driven by the knowledge that Shenhua must compete with the global leaders in the mining industry both within China and in global markets. His goal is to turn Shenhua into a globally competitive mining company to rank with the world leaders. In order to ensure that Shenhua's costs are in line with its global competitors Ye Qing is trying to ensure that manning levels at Shenhua are comparable with those in the international giant companies. He has tried to instil a market orientation to the company. This has been reflected especially in his drive to increase Shenhua's exports. By the year 2000, Shenhua's exports had risen from negligible levels to 10m tons and Ye Qing's intention was to build Shenhua into a major player in international markets, directly challenging the international giant companies exporting to East Asia. In order to develop markets for Shenhua's coal in domestic markets, Ye Qing has begun to invest in large modern power stations. In order to raise revenue for expansion, he plans that Shenhua will gradually issue shares on international markets, taking Shenhua's best assets and piece by piece floating them. In this way, he will be able to put pressure on the company to steadily improve its management level, since successful further share issues will depend on the good financial performance of the existing flotations. Ye Qing believes that Shenhua must replicate the structure of the global mining giants, such as Rio Tinto, by developing mining businesses other than coal.

### Reserves

The Shenfu Dongsheng coalfield is one of the world's largest and richest coalfields. Shenhua itself estimates that the coalfield has proven reserves of 224bn tons. These figures compare with an official estimate of only 126bn tons for 'proven reserves' for the whole of China. The Shenfu Dongsheng coalfield is one of the world's largest major coalfields remaining undeveloped. The Shenhua Group Company has overall responsibility for developing the entire coalfield. This provides the company with secure access to one of the world's largest concentrations of high quality coal. The reserves under the control of Shenhua dwarf those of other coalmining companies in China, and of any of the current leading multinational coal companies. Not only does Shenhua have vast reserves under its control, at least as important is the fact that the average depth of the reserves is shallow, at between 30–70 metres below the surface. Much of the coal is accessible using modern open-cast techniques.

Not only is the Shenfu Dongsheng coalfield of huge size, but the fact that the coal is also of high quality is a large advantage in an epoch in which coal is increasingly being differentiated by the category and quality of the product. This provides Shenhua with firm long-run market potential in view of the intensifying pressure within and outside China to reduce emissions from power stations and other coal users. The ash content is 'low', and the sulphur content is 'very low'. These characteristics make Shenhua's coal excellent for use as steam coal, for coal gasification and for coal chemistry applications. It means that Shenhua's coal has strong long-term prospects for market growth through the sale of high quality coal to modern power stations, for use in households and industrial boilers in areas that have tight controls over pollution.

### Transport

The main reason for the lack of development at the Shenfu Dongsheng coalfield has been the considerable distance from the major centres of coal consumption in China, and to the ports from which to export. The construction of a dedicated rail link to the coast is central to the Shenhua scheme. When it is completed the rail link from Da Liu Ta in the heart of the Shenfu Dongsheng coalfield, to the port of Huanghua, will total 825 km. The construction of a dedicated railway for Shenhua provides an enormous potential advantage. Instead of having to contest for space with both large- and small-scale coal in order to get their goods on the train, Shenhua can in principle have the entire railway dedicated to the transport of its goods. This will be of great advantage in guaranteeing timely delivery of goods. The much-reduced distance over which Shenhua's coal will be transported will considerably reduce Shenhua's transport costs per ton.

A large fraction of China's coal shipments in North China has been channelled through Qinghuangdao, but the port is subject to severe congestion. A key part of the Shenhua Project has been the construction of a dedicated port alongside the Huanghua railway and coalfield development. The construction period will last from 1998 to 2004. The construction of a dedicated port facility will potentially add greatly to Shenhua's competitive advantage.

However, a major uncertainty remains in relation to the eventual property rights to the railway and the port. The main part of the rail system is being constructed by the Shenhua Railway Company, which is an equity joint venture between the Shenhua Group (45 per cent of the equity), the Ministry of Railways (44 per cent of the equity), and the related local governments of Hebei (10 per cent) and Shanxi (1 per cent) provinces. Huanghua Port is being built by the Shenhua Huanghua Port Company Limited (see below), of which Shenhua Group is the holding company. The Company has equity contributed by both the Shenhua Group (67 per cent) and Hebei Provincial Government (44 per cent). The final status of the property rights of the port and railway is uncertain. The railway and port have been built with large loans from the state. A Shenhua official commented bluntly: 'It cannot be imagined that the port and railway will ultimately belong to Shenhua'.

### Finance

The vast bulk of the funding for the project is in the form of loans to the Shenhua Group. Shenhua is intended to be a model for China's modern enterprise system, with real economic independence. Part of this process is for Shenhua to be responsible for earning profits to repay the loans necessary to build the company. The State Development Bank (SDB) is much the most important lender to Shenhua. By year-end 1998, it had lent 11.8bn yuan (the equivalent of $1.4bn), amounting to one-sixth of its total loans of 70bn yuan (over $8bn) to the entire coal industry. These are all technically 'hard' loans, with an annual interest rate that varies from a low of 8.01 per cent to a high of 15.3 per cent, with different rates for different tranches. The repayment period is 15 years. The implications for Shenhua's future cost structure and profitability of the treatment of its domestic debt are enormous. The greater the degree to which the government decides to treat the loans from the SDB as capital injections, the greater the profits Shenhua will be able to earn and the more powerful it will be relative to both domestic and international competitors. The issue of the final status of Shenhua's long-term debt to the SDB is far from resolved.

One important route for raising capital is through flotation. China's ambitious plans for flotation were sharply cut back in the wake of the East Asian crisis, the collapse of the Hong Kong stock market and the sharp decline in international investors' confidence in Chinese business institutions. However, in the year 2000, large international flotations by Chinese state-owned companies again got under way. Shenhua was known to be actively considering the possibility of floating parts of the company on international stock markets. Ye Qing favoured the piecemeal approach, in order to place pressure on the company's management to operate in an efficient fashion, so as to ensure that each successive flotation was successful, rather than using a single flotation simply as a way to obtain funds from international markets.

### *Labour productivity*

Shenhua started life from scratch in 1985. This provides it with the advantage that it begins life with much lower manning levels than most other large state-owned enterprises. Moreover, Shenhua has bought mainly advanced imported equipment. In the early 1990s, China's 90 largest state-owned mines had an average of over 39 000 employees each. By 1997, Shenhua had already become one of China's twenty largest coal companies, with an output of almost 8m tons. Early in the next century its output is planned to reach 60m tons. China's largest coalmining company today, Datong, produces 37m tons. The Shenhua Group employs around 9000 people. Not only are the numbers of employees much smaller, and the output per worker far higher than in traditional state-owned enterprises. A further large source of competitive advantage for Shenhua is the absence of traditional labour attitudes. The workforce is relatively young and flexible. Moreover, the company is able to pay significantly higher wages than other large Chinese coal mines, enabling it to attract high quality personnel.

Ye Qing plans to reduce the total number of employees at Shenhua even further. He believes that the proportion of non-production workers is too great for an internationally competitive coal company. Output per worker at Shenhua is already around 850 tons. This is far above the industry average of 230 tons for the whole of China, and greater than the level in Poland and Germany. As production grows towards full capacity, it should rise to an output per worker of over 5000 tons early in the next century, which would surpass that achieved in

Colombia, the UK and South Africa and begin to approach that of Australia and North America. In the medium-term, Shenhua's goal is to reduce employment to around 5000 and maintain this level until output reaches 50–60m tons. If this were achieved, it would mean that output per worker would be 10 000 tons or even higher, on a par with productivity in the Australian and North American coal industries.

*Markets*

In the 1990s, the Chinese electricity generation industry altered rapidly. The main changes included increasingly stringent anti-pollution regulations, development of the national grid network facilitating inter-regional transmission of electricity, growing commercialization of the production and sale of electricity, expansion of foreign investment, advances in the technical capabilities of domestic power equipment makers and growing imports of power equipment. Taken together, these forces have pushed the industry towards larger-scale, modern equipment. The net effect is that a fast-growing share of the new additions to China's power stations consists of large-scale modern units, designed to use cleaner coal for greater efficiency and in order to meet tougher environmental standards. Shenhua already has letters of intent for the supply of 50m tons of coal annually to the large power stations that will be built in the next few years.

Not only does Shenhua wish to sell coal to modern large coal-fired domestic power stations. It also intends to develop a network of power stations along the Huanghua railway. It is possible that these may be partially invested in by Shenhua, and will then provide an assured market for its coal. The target is to build power stations with a total capacity of 6–7000MW, providing demand for 10m tons of Shenhua steam coal, in addition to the 30m tons that Shenhua hopes to sell to domestic power stations in which it does not have ownership rights.

It is not only China's power stations that are shifting to cleaner coals. Direct consumption of coal by industry and households still accounts for over 60 per cent of total coal use in China. Coal is the major cause of the extremely high levels of suspended particulates in China. Further serious attempts to improve the quality of urban air would provide an important potential market for Shenhua's coal, and one in which it has strong competitive advantages. In the late 1990s, Shenhua was already supplying 2m tons of clean coal to Beijing and hoped that the city's consumption of Shenhua coal would rise to 5m tons by 2000. If Shanghai, Tianjin and other more economically and culturally advanced cities also pass more stringent regulations governing the quality of coal used, then the market for Shenhua coal will widen still further.

Shenhua has a genuine chance to become a significant international competitor. Shenhua possesses one of the world's largest high quality coal reserves in a single location. The Shenfu Dongsheng field is in its infancy. It will be several decades before Shenhua has to extract higher cost reserves at greater depths or in less easily extractable locations and structures. Once established, the rail link will serve the company for an indefinite period of time, long after the large initial capital cost has been repaid. Unlike competitor companies, Shenhua will not have to go through the costly process of undertaking surveys of new coalfields, as it possesses a single massive site. Unlike international competitors, Shenhua will not have to go through costly processes of negotiating with indigenous peoples and national governments in order to gain access to new resources. Shenhua's products are of the type that should face attractive market prospects in surrounding East Asian countries, and even further afield. Shenhua's physical closeness to the world's fastest-growing markets for steam coal, which are in East Asia, is a big advantage. This gives it an advantage in terms of sea transport costs over Australian and other more distant suppliers. It may also give Shenhua a competitive edge in terms of cultural and political links that surrounding East Asian countries may wish to build with China over the long term.

Shenhua must establish a reputation for itself as a reliable supplier of competitively-priced high quality produce. Building a reputation is crucial in order to be a competitive international supplier. This process takes time. In 1996 Shenhua gained the rights to independently export coal. This enables Shenhua to establish direct long-term relationships with foreign customers. At least as important, it can control the quality of its exports. It now has direct responsibility for ensuring that there is no foreign matter in the coal it supplies and for ensuring timely delivery. Shenhua is acutely aware that this provides it with the opportunity to develop its international reputation as a reliable supplier of high quality coal. By the year 2000, its exports had already reached around 10m tons, accounting for around one-quarter of China's total coal exports.

### Merger with the 'Five Western District Mines'

In August 1998 the nature of Shenhua and its development strategy was sharply altered. Through an administrative decision taken by the State Council, Shenhua was instructed to take over the 'Five Western District Mines' in Inner Mongolia: Wuda, Haibowan, Baotou, Wanli and Zhunge'er. Baotou, Wuda and Haibowan are three old state coal mines in the area around the Shenfu Dongsheng coalfield. These are heavily loss-making mines, each making an average of over 100m yuan in losses in 1997. They have only around twenty years of recoverable reserves left. They are each deep mines, with an average depth of 350–440 metres. The quality of the reserves is below that at Shenhua. They employ a total of over 70 000 people to produce an output of only 5–6m tons. Moreover, within this number are included around 20 000 retired personnel. In recent years, the employees have often not been paid wages for 'several months on end'.

The other two mines included in the administrative merger have very different characteristics. Zhunge'er is around 50–80 km to the east of the Shenfu Dongsheng coalfield. It is in its early stages of development. It has plentiful reserves that can be mined with low-cost open-cast methods. The coal is of excellent quality, and is suitable for modern power stations, though it does have a much higher ash and sulphur content than Shenhua's coal that necessitates washing. Zhunge'er already has letters of intent to supply 20m tons of coal per annum to nine power stations in the region. In addition, the Ministry of Electricity Industry has approved plans to build two pit-head power stations close to Zhunge'er, with a total of over 2m kW of generation capacity.

Wanli is the final mine in the group transferred to Shenhua in 1998. Wanli is under construction; so far, it only has two pits in operation. These have a devised capacity of 1.2m tons. In addition, Wanli has taken over two local coal mines, with a devised capacity totalling 3.1m tons. As a new mine, growing incrementally in the face of difficult market conditions, Wanli is the best of the 'Five Western Region Mines' in terms of its current profitability. It has a total of 1200 employees, far below the level that would be employed in a traditional SOE company of this level of output.

The merger of Shenhua with the 'Five Western District Mines' overnight transformed the company's structure. Immediately before the merger, Shenhua was a company with 9000 employees producing 8m tons of high quality coal. It would soon be producing 30m tons, and in the medium-term, it would be producing up to 60m tons with no increase in the workforce. Following the merger, Shenhua had become a company with around 80 000 employees producing 18m tons of coal. Much of the additional coal was of low quality. Three of the mines were close to exhaustion and heavily loss-making. The social problems of trying to integrate such a diverse group of mines presents great challenges to the Shenhua leadership. Instead of trying to build a modern mining company, it has to cope simultaneously with the run-down of non-viable mines employing large numbers of workers.

The administrative merger that has transformed Shenhua stands in the starkest contrast to the merger wave that has engulfed the advanced capitalist countries in the last few years. The main characteristic of the Western merger wave has been the merging of 'strong with strong' through the marketplace. Leading international metals and minerals producers have been expanding their portfolio by establishing new mines with high quality reserves and merging with or taking over companies, or parts of companies, with high quality reserves. They have pushed forward with large increases in labour productivity, necessitating fewer and fewer workers to produce a given output. Through these cost-effective expansions, the competitive position of the leading multinationals has increased. In the sharpest contrast, China's emerging big businesses have to fight with one hand behind their backs. The potentially internationally competitive Shenhua coal company has had its competitive advantage greatly weakened. It is still too early to predict the final impact that the merger will have on the shape of the company. The final nature of the relationship with Shenhua is still under discussion. However, it is hard to imagine that it will do anything other than substantially weaken its competitive capability in the foreseeable future.

# 1.4　Internal problems in building the national team

In their battle to build large, globally competitive corporations, China faced many special internal difficulties that were not encountered by other successful late-comer industrializing countries during their attempts to catch up at the level of the large firm.

## Where is the firm?

China's reform path from the early 1980s onwards centred on the attempt to expand enterprise autonomy while cautiously and incrementally changing ownership structures. The central drive of policy was to increase the autonomy of the operational unit, the plant or 'enterprise', from the central authorities charged with administrative authority over it. In other words, China's 'enterprise' reform enhanced the autonomy of entities that in the world's largest corporations were essentially business units within a multi-plant company.

In the public sector restructuring in Western countries in the 1980s and 1990s, the fundamental unit of enhanced enterprise autonomy and ultimately of privatization, has been the multi-plant company, not the individual subordinate plants. The unit that was privatized typically constituted the bulk of the state's assets within any given sector. This was the case in the steel sector (for example, Usinor, British Steel), in telecoms (for example, British Telecom, Telecom Italia, Deutsche Telecom, France Telecom, Telefonica), in aerospace (for example, Aerospatiale, Rolls-Royce, Casa and British Aerospace), in the auto sector (for example, Renault, British Motor Corporation) and in oil and petrochemicals (for example, British Petroleum, Elf Aquitaine, ENI, Repsol). Each of these entities contained numerous subordinate operating units. However, the chosen level at which to enhance enterprise autonomy and, ultimately, the vehicle for privatization, was the large-scale, multi-plant entity which would be able directly to challenge existing private sector global giants in terms of their assets, revenues, R&D, and market share. At the time of their privatization, most of the firms were already large companies with the capability to compete on the global level playing field, provided management was given genuine autonomy.

The experimental path chosen for China's reforms was to take its firms along a very different path for state enterprise restructuring than that followed in the West. It left a legacy of many related unresolved issues in China's emerging business structure.

China's reform process has thrown up a group of powerful, visionary, industrial entrepreneurs who have led large-scale transformations of the businesses under their control. Such leaders include Zhou Guanwu at Shougang, Ding Guiming at Daqing, Wu Yixin at Shanghai Petrochemical Corporation, Zhu Yuli at AVIC, Zhao Xinxian at Sanjiu, Ye Qing at Shenhua and

Wang Jianming at Yuchai. In other countries, a key aspect of the transformation of failing state-owned enterprises or the successful operation of newly-established state-owned enterprises has been the appointment of powerful chief executive officers. They have been given comprehensive autonomy to manage and undertake capital market operations, including mergers and acquisitions at home and abroad, disposal of unwanted businesses, downsizing and changes in remuneration systems. They have frequently undertaken comprehensive restructuring of the enterprises under their management. Such managers include Louis Schweitzer at Renault, Francis Mer at Usinor, Franco Bernabe at ENI, and Ian MacGregor at the British National Coal Board and then at British Steel. Comparable leaders in China's large enterprises have rarely been given consistent long-term support by the Chinese central authorities. Strong leaders at the enterprise level have frequently been dismissed by the central authorities who are fearful of the enterprise leaders' intense struggle to develop autonomous enterprises freed from central control. Often, the dismissal of strong enterprise leaders has been permitted because they have lost powerful patrons in the central government.

During the reform period, many of China's large state-owned enterprises developed a strong sense of corporate identity. The initial key to their ambition was the contract system of the 1980s which allowed the retention of a large fraction of enterprise profits. This was reinforced by the establishment of 'legal person' rights at the level of the enterprise or operating unit. Subsequently, the 'enterprise' became the main unit through which domestic and international stock market flotations were made. It was also the main entity through which joint ventures were established. Numerous benefits could flow for both employees and the local community from successful growth. Most of the enterprises which carried out research developed intense corporate ambitions. Over and over again the senior managers spoke of their ambition to make their enterprise number one in China and eventually to become a world leader in their chosen field. In pursuit of this aim a group of large state enterprises responded to the growing impact of market forces in the context of a fast-growing domestic market through the pursuit of organic growth via different paths. They reinvested heavily, improved product quality and product mix, developed their marketing skills, developed their brand, reduced costs of production, invested in R&D, and acquired technology through joint ventures.

Ambitious large state-owned enterprises encountered major difficulties in attempting to expand within their core business. Large-scale projects involving organic growth outside the home territory typically require approval by central authorities, whether in the relevant ministry, its successor department or in the State Council. It was common for key projects that enterprises wished to undertake to be refused permission by superior authorities for a variety of reasons. For example, Shougang's strategy under Zhou Guanwu was based around the intention to build a second major steel plant at Qilu in Shandong province, following a similar expansion path in this respect as South Korea's

Posco, now the world's largest steel company. After a tortuous bureaucratic wrangle, the Qilu project was eventually turned down by the central government, leaving Shougang's strategy in tatters, and rendering many of its acquisitions useless. A second example is Daqing's persistent wish to be allowed to use its vast financial reserves to expand into the former Soviet Union. However, such expansion was over-ruled by Daqing's superior authorities in the central government.

A substantial group of Chinese state-owned enterprises is now floated on international stock markets. However, there are strict limits on the enterprises which are permitted to float and on the extent of the flotations. Many ambitious large enterprises that wished to float were not permitted to do so, with superior authorities that were fearful of the independence that this would provide for these enterprises through this independent source of capital. Daqing, for example, persistently requested permission to float internationally but was not allowed to do so by its superior authorities. Those that did float were typically subject to strict controls on the extent to which they issued shares, with stringent limitations on the degree of dilution of state ownership. Even domestic flotation was under tight bureaucratic control. Bribery of officials to obtain approval for listing has been openly reported. For example, in late 1999 it was publicly reported that top managers at Daqing had been arrested for bribing officials in order to allow the domestic listing, in 1997, of Daqing Lianyi oil refineries, part of the Daqing oilfield complex.

A major path through which ambitious state-owned enterprises wished to expand was through merger and acquisition in their core business within China. A persistent theme is their stated wish to expand through merging 'through the markets' with other strong businesses in the same sector or by taking them over. It is easy to take over loss-making enterprises in the same sector, since this can take a poorly-performing business off the hands of the relevant central or local authorities. However, attempts by strong state-owned enterprises to merge with other strong state-owned enterprises were persistently thwarted by the superior authorities. Daqing tried repeatedly to merge with strong refineries. SPC tried to merge with other strong petrochemical companies and even held talks with Daqing about a merger to become a vertically integrated oil and petrochemical firm. Harbin Power Equipment Company tried to merge with a group of powerful northeastern electrical companies. Yuchai tried to merge with other strong engine companies and with strong vehicle makers. Each of these attempts to build a powerful company through large-scale merger within the relevant core business was prevented by the enterprises' superior authorities, or by resistance from other local authorities within whose jurisdiction one of the enterprises lay. Frequently, when asked about the reason for the absence of a merger with a relevant firm within China, the large state-owned enterprise replied that there was no point in even pursuing the matter, since the chance of success was so low. In striking contrast to the massive boom in mergers and acquisitions between 'strong and strong' in the West since the early 1980s, China has not had any examples of merger of a strong state-owned company with another strong company within the same sector.

The inability of large, ambitious state-owned enterprises to be allowed to merge with and acquire other large state enterprises in the same sector has had a powerful effect on the nature of industrial reform in China. The reform process stimulated a significant growth of enterprise ambition and wish for autonomy from the superior authorities, but severely restricted the extent to which that autonomy could be exercised. The powerful group of enterprises analysed in these studies were each prevented from expanding in a way comparable to that employed by large Western firms in the capitalist big business revolution of the 1990s. This pushed them into other forms of business behaviour, especially large-scale diversification.

In the late 1990s, there were signs that the central policymakers had realized the negative consequences of this path. The dramatic growth of globally powerful firms based around a core business, achieved through massive mergers, became a more and more striking object lesson for the Chinese leaders. The attempt to construct two huge vertically integrated companies in the shape of Sinopec and CNPC represented a belated attempt to support the growth of a different type of firm. Instead of allowing increased autonomy to the enterprise, this represented an attempt to construct a unified multi-plant firm that spanned many production units. However, the subordinate enterprises had gained so much autonomy and developed such intense corporate ambitions, that it proved difficult to reintegrate the different subordinate enterprises. Having been through two decades of 'enterprise' reform based around enhanced 'enterprise autonomy', it unsurprisingly proved difficult to recentralize power within a multi-plant firm embracing a large part of any given sector. Not only were there strong controls on the expansion of ambitious enterprises through mergers with strong domestic firms. There were, additionally, serious barriers to their growth caused by mergers imposed by higher-level bureaucrats on unwilling, ambitious firms. Shougang was forced to take over a group of heavily loss-making 'Third Front' military factories. Shenhua was forced to take over the loss-making 'Five Western District Mines'. The leadership of CNPC and Sinopec were each forced to take over a substantial group of small-scale loss-making refineries, formerly under the Ministry of Chemical Industries, on their restructuring in 1998. SPC came close to being forced into an unwanted merger with a massive local diversified chemicals conglomerate, producing everything from washing powder to rubber tyres.

## Special difficulties of building successful large, competitive firms based in a developing country

The environment in which large Chinese firms are attempting to construct globally competitive companies is very different from that of the global giant corporations.

### Battle with domestic small and medium-sized enterprises

A large fraction of the sales revenue of powerful multinational companies consists of high value-added goods and services sold in high income countries. In a huge, poor, developing country such as China there is still a high degree of market segmentation by product type and quality. A large fraction of demand is still for low quality, low price products. Moreover, markets tend to be much less well-integrated, separated to a greater degree than in advanced economies by the isolation of geographical distance, and poorly developed transport and information systems. An important part of the struggle for sales faced by large indigenous firms is with domestic small and medium-scale producers. Large indigenous firms typically have to pay a much higher wage than small local competitors. Also, they must shoulder the burden of welfare payments. They typically have a commitment to lifetime employment, unlike the flexible, non-unionized workforce of small enterprises. Many of the products produced by large enterprises for these markets are unbranded goods, with little benefit from R&D input.

We have seen many examples of the ferocious nature of the struggle between aspiring global giants and the myriad small and medium enterprises with which they must compete in domestic markets. For example, Shougang's main products are low value-added building steel. In this sector they face a fierce battle with township and village enterprises producing large quantities of low-quality steel for China's housing construction industry. Shenhua is engaged in ferocious competition with surrounding township and village mining enterprises. The small coalmining enterprises have virtually zero opportunity cost of labour and bear little of the costs of pollution. They are strongly supported by local governments for which they provide crucial local employment and income tax. They grew at high speed during the reform period to seriously challenge the dominance of the large state coal mines. Sanjiu faces a constant battle with the thousands of small and medium traditional Chinese pharmaceutical companies. The township and village enterprises typically have low start-up costs in this sector, require little R&D and produce goods for which there are typically no patents. Major oil and petrochemical companies, such as CNPC and Sinopec, face intense competition from small-scale enterprises in the refining and retail market. Such enterprises have low entry costs, can often evade legal control over their safety requirements and sell inferior, polluting products at a relatively low price in a market which typically is in a state of shortage.

In so far as China's aspiring large global firms are forced into diversified production, they almost always produce with low economies of scale, little focused R&D, little brand development and limited marketing capability. Each of the firms studied faces intense competition in its myriad 'diversified undertakings' with a sea of small and medium enterprises. For example, on the one hand, Xian Aircraft Corporation is vying with leading Japanese corporations as a global subcontractor for advanced aerospace components. On the other hand, it is battling with hundreds of Chinese township and village enterprises in the market for aluminium beams for building construction.

*Downsizing and restructuring is more difficult than in an advanced economy*
The restructuring of the leading state-owned firms in the advanced economies
took place in economies with sophisticated welfare systems and relatively large
savings within employees' families. Prior to restructuring, the number of
employees was well below that of present-day China's large state enterprises.
In China over 100 000 employees at a single production location is not
uncommon. Indeed, the number of employees at a Chinese firm can frequently
total many hundreds of thousands of people, or as much as a million or more
in some cases, such as CNPC and Sinopec. We have seen that using the levels
of employment per unit of output found in leading global corporations would
produce downsizing far exceeding that in the West in the 1990s. For example,
using the manning levels of the global giants, the entire aerospace division of
AVIC might employ less than 10 000 people. Much more so than in the West,
employees in China's large enterprises constituted a privileged elite amidst a
sea of underdevelopment and poverty. Downsizing substantially is an even
more complex political task than in the advanced economies of Western Europe
or in Japan, due to the dramatic change in both status and income that might
confront a large body of the workforce, especially older and less well-trained
employees.

*Weak supplier network*
The quality of the supplier network around large Chinese firms is radically
different from that which surrounds a global giant based in the advanced
economies. For example, globally competitive companies manufacturing large
complex machinery are rapidly moving towards a closely integrated network of
global suppliers. In sharp contrast, the manufacturers of complex machinery
analysed in these studies each operates with a network of predominantly local
suppliers. For example, Harbin Power Equipment Company has a large network
of suppliers in the northeast of China, mostly themselves producing on a small
scale, with limited R&D capability. The same is true for Yuchai and many of the
branches of AVIC. This means that China is able to produce relatively cheap final
products, such as Xifei's Y-7 turbo-prop passenger plane, Yuchai's medium-duty
truck engines, and Harbin's electric power plants. However, their products'
operating costs are often much above comparable global leaders' products, and
their performance in terms of key criteria such as energy efficiency, pollution,
reliability and functional capability, are often far below those of the products of
global leaders. Global corporations increasingly purchase huge volumes of inputs
through central global procurement. This gives them enormous cost advantages
over Chinese large-scale competitors which buy from small-scale local suppliers
or in much smaller quantities from global suppliers. The sophisticated
procurement system of the global giants dealing predominantly with other global
companies as suppliers enables more timely delivery of inputs, with consequent
cost-savings. Boeing or Airbus are able to achieve more timely delivery of a piece
of a tailplane subcontracted from China to Seattle or Toulouse than Xian Aircraft

Corporation is able to achieve for a subcontracted component of the Y-7 from a domestic Chinese supplier within AVIC.

### Spatial distribution of industrial assets

Many of China's large enterprises are located in areas far from China's major markets. They were established because of the need to be self-sufficient during the long period of isolation from the world economy, especially after the split with the USSR in 1960. Many of China's natural resources were developed in order to ensure the country was self-sufficient in time of war rather than to achieve maximum economic efficiency. A significant fraction of China's industrial assets was established in remote areas designed to enable China to survive a nuclear war. By the late 1970s around two-thirds of China's industrial fixed assets were located away from the coastal areas. A large fraction of China's aerospace, power equipment, coal mining, automobile, oil and petrochemical industries, is located far inland. This imposes a large transport cost burden upon China's aspiring global giants.

## The drive to diversify

A central feature of the capitalist big business revolution of the 1990s has been the remorseless drive to focus on core business. China's emerging large firms have demonstrated a very different tendency. In common with many other East Asian businesses China's large firms have demonstrated a powerful tendency to diversify into non-core businesses or 'diversified undertakings'. In the extreme case of AVIC, China's 'national champion' aircraft maker, as much as two-thirds of total revenue comes from non-core business in a vast array of different industries. Even China's largest, most focused and internationally competitive steel company, Baogang, is in the process of diversifying into a wide range of businesses. China's largest single entity in the oil and petrochemicals sector, Daqing oilfield, has a huge array of over 1000 companies engaged in 'diversified undertakings'. The world's leading pharmaceutical corporations have steadily shed non-core business to focus exclusively on their core products. Alongside its rise to become one of China's top two pharmaceutical companies, Sanjiu acquired a bewildering array of businesses, from large-scale construction and vehicles to beer, wine and hotels.

There were many reasons for this pronounced trend. First, China's large enterprises needed to provide for huge workforces. Innumerable studies have investigated the extent of 'overmanning' in China's industrial enterprises. Multinational corporations in China with only a small fraction of the number of employees have typically produced similar or greater output than comparable Chinese companies. However, Chinese state-owned enterprises are not only units of production. They are also social entities, providing cradle-to-grave care for the employees and their families. A central aspect of the reform process has been to separate the 'productive' from the 'unproductive' aspects of enterprise activity.

However, state-run welfare systems are still rudimentary and the enterprise still feels a strong commitment to assisting the 'downsized' workers to find employment. A central motivation for diversification has been an attempt to provide employment for the large surplus workforces that exist in most of the large state enterprises.

Secondly, China has imperfect markets with high transaction costs. China is still a poor country with a poorly developed transport system, including massive railway bottlenecks. Information flows are moving faster and faster, but are still far behind the sophisticated IT of most global leader firms. Furthermore, a large part of the output of China's large-scale enterprises is competing in the relatively low value-added part of the relevant markets, in which the need for, and the proportion of, high quality, cutting-edge technology components is relatively small. These pressures increase the incentive to produce in a far more vertically integrated fashion than international competitor firms. The tendency to 'large and complete' stems in part from a rational response to the environment faced by the large Chinese firm. Whereas the leading international giant company integrates the 'external firm' across the value chain, a large Chinese firm is often trying to reduce transaction costs by internalizing a high share of the components and equipment necessary for the final product. This was a major reason for the diversification at Shougang into iron ore, steel machinery, and construction. The same tendency exists to a greater or lesser degree in each of the other companies analysed in the case studies. However, on the global level playing field, such firms are at a severe disadvantage compared with their competitor firms, which purchase a large fraction of their inputs of goods and services from specialist firms that in turn benefit from economies of scale and scope.

Thirdly, there were serious barriers to mergers and acquisition within the core business. We have seen repeatedly that the efforts by increasingly autonomous firms to merge with other strong firms have been blocked. The merger of a majority state-owned firm requires the agreement of the superior authority. The central ministry or holding company has frequently opposed such mergers as the resulting powerful entities might undermine their authority: 'If two strong companies, X and Y, merge and expand their autonomy, who are we?' Merger of one large firm with another also typically requires the agreement of the local authorities within whose jurisdiction the enterprises are situated. Just as European governments have resisted the merger of national champions with other countries' national champions, so too do China's local authorities often resist such mergers. Each local authority fears that 'their' enterprise will be the one to suffer the bulk of redundancies or will be allocated the less attractive parts of any business expansion.

Even highly rational mergers which could bring large savings in costs, and which are not opposed by higher level authorities, can be resisted for mainly personal reasons. In Western companies, many large mergers do not take place because the chief executive of the weaker company fears s/he will lose their job or be demoted after the merger. However, shareholders get some chance to express their opinion by selling shares in the company. Moreover, there is always the possibility of a hostile takeover. In China, neither of these paths is possible. We have seen examples in these studies of an apparently rational merger successfully resisted by an unwilling chief executive officer. For example, the attempt to form a large northeast China power equipment company, involving the merger of Harbin Power Equipment Company with several other strong companies in related sectors, appeared to founder mainly due to the strong opposition of the chief executive officer of the most important potential company that might have joined such an entity. We have seen also that the attempt to merge Yuchai Diesel Engine Company with Erqi Motor Corporation, and, separately, to form a single large diesel engine company, merging with other entities in the sector, foundered for reasons that were at least partially personality related.

Fourthly, there were constraints on organic growth. Not only is growth through merger and acquisition limited mainly to takeovers of relatively weaker and small-scale businesses. In addition, as we have noted above, large-scale organic growth away from the main production site often faces substantial constraints. Major investments in new capacity can frequently be opposed successfully. Such opposition can be due to fears by central ministries or holding companies that the expansion will threaten their control by allowing autonomous growth of the technically subordinate entity. It can also be due to protectionism by the local authority within which the planned new venture is to be situated. A major new production facility might prove unwished-for competition for the 'local firm' in the same sector.

Fifthly, China's large enterprises face serious weakness in competing on world markets. Despite many major improvements in management and technology and substantial increases in scale, most of China's large firms are unable to compete directly on the global level playing field outside China. To be able to directly compete in global markets with firms making complex and high technology products, such as Nippon Steel, Usinor or British Steel in high quality steel, Siemens, GE or ABB Alstom in power equipment, Boeing, Airbus, BAe and Lockheed Martin in aircraft, Cummins Diesel in diesel engines, Pfizer or Merck in pharmaceuticals, or with Exxon/Mobil, Shell and BP Amoco in oil, petrol and petrochemicals, would require a massive leap in capability. It is questionable how rational it is for a large Chinese company to undertake large-scale investment in new technology which would still leave the firm far short of the technical capability of the global leader. In a comparable Western firm, the management would probably decide to exit the business rather than invest in a vain attempt to catch up with the market leader: in the often-repeated sentence: 'if you're not number one, two or three in the world, you should leave the business'. In export markets, China's aspiring global giant corporations must content themselves mainly with selling lower-end sophisticated products (for example, power stations, steel mills, fighter planes) mainly to other developing countries. China's aspiring indigenous global giant firms have mainly to confine themselves to the domestic market. They must leave export markets mainly to indigenous large firms producing relatively simple products at the lower end of the Second Industrial Revolution, such as white goods, bicycles and motorbikes and to small-scale firms, including massive domestic subcontracting for multinational giant companies.

Faced with such limitations on international core business expansion, China's aspiring global champions have to confine themselves mainly to domestic markets. Here, their growth is limited also. They are constrained by the absence of a developed capital market which would allow them to merge with and/or acquire other large domestic firms, linking 'strong with strong' in the way that is happening at high speed within the advanced economies.

Faced with these constraints on expansion of their core business in domestic and international markets, there is a strong incentive for China's large enterprises to use their investment resources to develop diversified operations alongside organic growth. The contrast with the global big business revolution could hardly be stronger. The rapid collapse of international barriers on capital flows, the virtual disappearance of the concept of a national strategic industry, and the massive opening up through privatization of huge areas of business activity to the free flow of capital, have combined to produce an epoch of unprecedented freedom of international, transnational and transcontinental merger, facilitating the dynamic advance of core businesses. China still remains deeply limited in the freedom to merge, acquire and dispose of large businesses freely. The result has been a vicious circle in a tendency to diversify.

Complex forms of property rights have developed under China's reforms. The core company can be the full owner of diversified undertakings. It may have a majority stake, a minority holding, a joint venture or even act simply as a bank to business activities being set up by employees. Typically a large enterprise will have a wide range of business investments of all different types, with little knowledge of the business it has invested in. The drive to diversify also allows a cascade of investments from the mother company through a succession of layers of 'children', 'grandchildren' and 'great-grandchildren'. Such property rights arrangements can bring large problems of evaluating the quality of investments and monitoring the investments once undertaken. These problems were dramatically revealed when international accountants undertook extensive investigations of a bankrupt red chip company in Hong Kong with large mainland interests. They revealed a catalogue of poor project evaluation and monitoring, and multi-million dollar theft.

One consequence of the trend to diversify is the illusion of scale. Within an apparently huge business, employing a vast number of people and sometimes with large revenues, there was in fact a small core business and a sea of small-scale businesses, often far below the economically efficient scale necessary for survival and prosperity on the global level playing field. After two decades of reform, apparently huge firms often contain a myriad of businesses without any significant R&D capability, without a marketing capability or a meaningful brand. In their core business, they often are relatively small scale.

## Political constraints

The special features of China's politics led to at least two important limitations on China's capability to build globally competitive firms.

Firstly, in sharp contrast with other successful examples of catch-up, China's policymakers remained committed throughout to maintaining the commanding heights of large-scale industry in state ownership. Large state enterprises were allowed gradually to expand the absorption of capital from non-state sources, including Sino-foreign joint ventures, and flotation on domestic and international stock markets. However, even after two decades of enterprise reform, the government remained committed to substantial public ownership of large enterprises, providing a continued channel for bureaucratic intervention in large firms' management, despite persistent attempts to 'separate ownership from management'. This was in sharp contrast with Japan and South Korea during their catch-up. It also ran counter to the trend in the advanced economies in which a string of global leading firms evolved out of privatized state enterprises. These included Usinor, Arbed, Corus (formerly British Steel), Posco and China Steel (Taiwan) in the steel sector, Elf Aquitaine, ENI, Repson/YPF and BP Amoco in oil and petrochemicals, Rolls-Royce, British Aerospace and Aerospatiale-Matra in aerospace, VW and Renault in autos, and British Telecom, Deutsche Telecom, France Telecom, and Telecom Italia in telecoms.

By the year 2000, not one of the world's top 300 firms by R&D spending, and only a tiny handful of the world's top 500 companies by value of sales, was in the public sector. Whereas Japan and South Korea had a relatively simple non-ideological goal of building globally competitive giant corporations, China's industrial policy remained suffused with ideology intertwined with the objective of building global giant corporations. The ideological objective provided a justification for central bureaucratic intervention to limit the expansion of ambitious and increasingly autonomous large enterprises such as Shougang, SPC and Daqing, and for the persistence of bureaucratic interference in the management of technically autonomous large enterprises.

Secondly, the bureaucratic apparatus with which China was attempting to implement industrial policy was very different from that in Japan or South Korea. The latter countries relied on relatively small professional civil services. These were powerfully imbued with a commitment to achieve economic advance in the face of massive military defeat in the one case and serious international threat in the other. China's bureaucracy was vastly greater absolutely and larger even in relative terms. It lacked the intense commitment to national development of its neighbours in northeast Asia. Despite great advances in its technical capabilities and important successes in aspects of industrial policy, it was unable to truly separate itself from the operations of the leading enterprises. Even after twenty years of reform, the Party remained deeply imbued with corruption, which seriously inhibited its efforts to implement a consistent, effective industrial policy.

## Conclusion

China's large firms made significant progress during the two decades of reform. Despite this significant progress there were a number of difficulties that they encountered due to the particular domestic environment in which they operated. Even more importantly, the global business environment was being transformed at high speed. The large corporation based in the advanced capitalist countries was going through the most revolutionary change in the history of capitalism. This change was to pose even greater challenges for China's aspiring global champions. Part 2 will examine the nature of this challenge.

# The Challenge of the Global Big Business Revolution

## 2.1   General features of the business revolution

Part 1 analysed the way in which China pursued an industrial policy which had the objective of creating large firms that could challenge the giant global corporations of the advanced economies. China faces a special challenge which did not confront other countries that successfully built globally powerful large firms through industrial policy: China is attempting to catch up at the level of the large firm in the midst of the most profound revolution in business systems that the world has ever seen. This revolution presents a fundamental challenge not only for China's industrial policy, but for industrial policy in developing countries as a whole. The global business revolution has produced an unprecedented concentration of business power in large corporations head-quartered in the high income countries. It is an interesting paradox that the influence of mainstream neoclassical ideas, which emphasize small firms and competitive markets, has increased greatly within Chinese policymaking circles in precisely the epoch of unprecedented concentration of global business power.

### Drivers of the big business revolution

Several forces interacted to drive forward the global big business revolution in the 1990s.

### Trade liberalization

Despite slow long-term liberalization under the GATT, the average tariffs on manufactures in developing countries still stood at 34 per cent in 1987, reaching as high as 81 per cent in South Asia. Tariff protection in the advanced economies fell from moderate levels in the early 1950s to low levels in the late 1980s, when they averaged only around 6 per cent. After the mid-1980s, the pace of trade liberalization accelerated. The Uruguay Round of the GATT began in 1985 and was completed in 1993. However, even before the conclusion of the Uruguay Round, many developing countries had substantially reduced their import duties. The Uruguay Round resulted in even further reductions in developed country tariffs, and large reductions in developing country tariffs. Alongside the fall in tariffs, there was also an overall reduction in many types of non-tariff barriers (NTBs), although the period did witness a substantial rise in the use of anti-dumping measures, 'diluting market access and the gains from trade liberalization'. The period saw a significant widening in  the scope of trade liberalization measures, including trade and foreign investment in services. By the late 1990s, 47 per cent of service sectors in industrialized countries and 16 per cent in developing countries had been liberalized. The membership of the GATT and, subsequently, the WTO, has widened greatly. By 1999 it included not only the 24 core members in the OECD, but also 110 members from outside it.

The progressive reduction in trade barriers stimulated the long-term growth of international trade. Over several decades the rate of growth of world trade powerfully outdistanced that of national output. However, the disparity between output growth and trade growth increased sharply in the 1990s. In the 1980s, world trade grew 60 per cent faster than world output, but in the 1990s trade grew at almost twice the pace of world output. A major part of the rapid growth in exports from developing countries has been associated with the process of 'slicing up the value chain' in different countries, locating different parts of the process in the lowest cost location. By the mid-1990s almost one-third of all world trade took place within global production networks.

## Liberalization of capital flows

Accelerated international flows of long-term capital were at the heart of the global business revolution. Foreign direct investment (FDI) rose enormously from the early 1980s to the late 1990s: average annual inflows in 1981–85 stood at just $48bn. By 1998 they had reached $644bn. Inflows of FDI into developing countries accelerated from an annual average of around $22bn in 1984–89 to $166bn in 1998. The share going to developing countries sharply increased, from under 20 per cent in 1984–89, to 40 per cent in 1994, falling back somewhat to 26 per cent in 1998. The inflows were concentrated heavily in a relatively small number of countries. The three largest, Brazil, Mexico and China, together accounted for 30 per cent of FDI inflows into developing countries in 1987–92 and 51 per cent in 1998.

Despite the large rise in capital flows to developing countries, the vast bulk of FDI flows were between the advanced economies. The developed countries have consistently accounted for over 90 per cent of outflows of world FDI (93 per cent in 1987–92, and 92 per cent in 1998) and their share of inflows is typically around three quarters of the world total. The US has been much the largest recipient of FDI inflows, accounting for 30 per cent of the world total in 1998.

Over the long run, the postwar world boom was 'export driven', in the sense that the growth of trade was much faster than the growth of output. However, in the 1990s, the growth of FDI was faster even than that of trade. From 1988 to 1998, FDI grew by 15 per cent per annum, compared to 8 per cent per annum for annual growth of world merchandise exports. By the 1990s, a large and rising share of total manufacturing production of firms based in advanced capitalist economies was located abroad. The output of foreign operations of US-owned corporations in the early 1990s amounted to more than one trillion dollars, roughly four times the value of US exports of goods manufactured in the US.

Since the 1980s there has been a progressive liberalization of international short-term capital flows. Across both the developed and the developing world, it has become progressively easier to move short-term capital from one location to another. In the advanced economies, financial markets have 'melded into a global financial system'. Rapid improvements in the technologies for collecting, analysing and disseminating information have stimulated financial innovation, and created a multi-billion dollar pool of internationally mobile capital. The growth of international trade, and especially the acceleration of international capital flows, has created a massive rise in foreign exchange transactions: in 1998, the *daily* total stood at around $1.5 trillion, an amount equal to one-sixth of the *annual* output of the US economy. A major driver of the growth of international short-term capital flows has been the rise of institutional investors in the advanced economies, with a large fraction of the funds allocated to equity investments. In 1995, these investors controlled $20 trillion, around one-fifth of it invested abroad.

## Privatization

Only a decade or so ago, a vast swathe of economic activity was directly owned and controlled by the state. The extent of privatization has been enormous, opening up huge areas of the economy to private capital. It has included large parts of Europe, the former Communist countries and developing countries. Privatization has included telecoms, airlines, postal services, power generation, transmission and sale, aerospace, defence equipment, motor vehicles, coal, steel, public transport, oil and petrochemicals. Privatization of formerly state-owned services such as airlines, telecoms, power generation and transmission, has had a cascading effect on sectors that supply these sectors with complex equipment, forcing intense competition upon them.

## Collapse of Communism

More than two-fifths of the world's population in the late 1970s lived in countries ruled by Communist parties. Global capital was drastically limited in its access to these potentially vast markets. By the early 1990s, almost the whole of this area was opened up to global capital. The opening-up process radically enhanced the growth prospects of capitalist firms. Large areas of the world had become potential purchasers of OECD countries' products, recipients of OECD countries' capital, and potential locations for extending their global production base. This provided an important stimulus to the 'animal spirits' of OECD countries' investors and production enterprises.

## Information technology

I shall discuss later the dramatic changes in information technology since the 1980s. At this juncture it is necessary to emphasize how central this phenomenon has been to many key aspects of institutional change in the epoch of the big business revolution. For example, it has facilitated the revolution in global capital markets, in the management of a global supply chain, in the development of global brand names, and in the design and maintenance of complex equipment.

## Migration

Mass migration constituted a major exception to the general pattern of liberalization. In the late nineteenth and early twentieth centuries, migration played a substantial role in the international economy. Around 60 million people left Europe for the Americas, Oceania, and South and East Africa. In the interwar period, international migration drastically declined. Although numbers increased subsequently, with increased flows from poor to rich countries, the level of migration has never recaptured that of pre-1914. In the 1990s, each year around 2-3 million people migrate internationally. The total number of migrants living outside their home country is thus only around 2–3 per cent of the world's population. There are significant opportunities for women to migrate as temporary domestic workers, and there is a relatively large international criminal traffic in women for prostitution. However, apart from these special categories, long-term migration of unskilled people from poor to rich countries is very limited. Hirst and Thompson note: 'A world market for labour just does not exist in the same way as it does for goods and services. Most labour markets continue to be nationally regulated and accessible only marginally to outsiders, whether legal or illegal migrants or professional manpower. Moving goods and services is infinitely easier than moving labour.'

However, international migration of highly skilled people became a central part of the global business revolution. A key feature of the global business revolution is the great excess demand within the advanced economies for highly skilled labour, especially in the industries of the Third Technological Revolution. A significant proportion of the most highly-skilled workers in developing countries has migrated to work in the knowledge-intensive industries of the high income countries. In the advanced countries, the ageing of population and waning interest in studying science and technology among young people is likely to accentuate the drive to absorb high quality human resources from developing countries.

## Competitive advantage

### Core business

After the 1970s, the extent of the market was dramatically widened by the liberalization of wide swathes of the world that had formerly been closed to international capitalism. This created a strong incentive for large firms to narrow their scope of business activity but still become fast-growing corporations within that narrowed range of business activity. The global business revolution witnessed a widespread narrowing of the range of business activity undertaken by the individual large firm. There took place a massive restructuring of assets, with firms extensively selling off 'non-core businesses' in order to develop their 'core businesses'. The goal for most large capitalist firms became the maintenance or establishment of their position as one of the top two or three companies in the global market-place. This position was to be achieved through sharply focusing R&D and marketing resources upon a narrower range of products in order to develop and enhance competitive advantage in the chosen areas of core competence. This period saw significant increases in R&D and marketing spending by leading corporations, but the range of activities upon which this expenditure was concentrated became much narrower for any given firm. The mantra for globally successful business became: 'If you're not number one, two or three in the world, you shouldn't stay in the business'.

## Brand

The epoch of the global big business revolution has seen for the first time the emergence of truly global brands. Their penetration of consumers' consciousness across the world has been facilitated not only by the spread of production centres across the world, but also by the explosion of global culture through the globalized mass media. Successful brands spend billions of dollars on marketing. This includes not only the obvious forms of brand-building, notably advertising, but also less obvious forms, such as building a global network of marketing machinery, such as freezers, coolers and dispensing machines, to distribute branded goods in close proximity to customers. It includes constant promotion of new forms of packaging. The first-movers in the great race for the global market-place of branded consumer goods are able to shape the consumption habits of the world's population for a long period to come. They possess powerful, sustainable competitive advantage.

## R&D

Spending on R&D by the world's leading firms rose at high speed alongside the acceleration in mergers and acquisitions. From a plateau of around $160–170bn in the early 1990s, R&D spending by the world's top 300 firms accelerated to over $240bn in 1998. The technical capability of the world's leading firms advanced rapidly in this epoch: 'Large MNCs are the chief repositories of the world's stock of economically useful knowledge and skills. All the screaming in the world will not change this.' (Martin Wolf, *Financial Times*.) In the USA in 1994 just five firms accounted for 21 per cent of total US industrial R&D expenditure. Twenty firms accounted for 41 per cent and 123 firms accounted for 68 per cent of total US industrial R&D expenditure. The key to the technical progress and economic advance of the US economy in the private sector lies in the hands of a small number of giant oligopolistic firms. As far as the overall technical progress of the US economy is concerned, the role of the state is also crucially important. Thirty-six per cent of total US expenditure on R&D is funded by the Federal Government. A large fraction of this funding for R&D is channelled to the giant corporations that dominate private R&D spending.

## IT expenditure

The period of the big business revolution saw a massive increase in expenditure by the world's leading firms on IT hardware, software and services. Data transmission within and between firms grew at an explosive rate, facilitated by the technological revolution. Despite a dramatic advance in the functional capability that can be purchased for a given investment, a major source of competitive advantage for globally successful firms is their ability to undertake larger investment in IT systems. Such investment facilitates numerous competitive advantages. These include deeper and more effective interactions with suppliers and consumers, centralized global procurement, downsizing of the number of employees, more effective interactions between remaining employees, deeper research using data that can be analysed by new IT systems, better and more effective R&D programmes, and better monitoring of performance of complex equipment installed by customers.

## Financial resources

The big business revolution coincided with the largest and most prolonged boom ever seen in Western stockmarkets. This process was fed by, and in turn fed, the explosion in mergers and acquisitions. Investors, especially the fast-rising institutional investors, increasingly shifted their portfolios to the world's leading companies, with high global market share, global brands, high R&D, and core business focus that enable the businesses to be transparently analysed. The lift in share values facilitated further mergers through offering shares in the dominant partner's company. By the time the stockmarket began to cool in the US and Europe in the year 2000, massive institutional change had already been wrought.

## Industrial concentration

It is possible that the epoch of greatest concentration of market power in the hands of large corporations was immediately after the Second World War. By the 1930s, most analysts agree that the US was highly concentrated. The effect of the Second World War was to destroy vast swathes of production within the former USSR and in Eastern Europe, in large parts of Western Europe and in Japan. This allowed a unique period of dominance of the global economy by giant US corporations. In the ensuing forty years or so, output grew rapidly in Japan and Europe as well as within the former Soviet bloc. Within both Europe and Japan, large indigenous corporations emerged to challenge the dominance of US large firms, often with powerful direct and indirect state support. It is plausible that the degree of concentration at a global level declined between the late 1940s and the mid-1980s, though this is hard to pin down empirically.

By the late 1990s, there was a high degree of firm-level concentration on a global scale in a wide range of sectors. It is likely that the extent of firm-level concentration increased significantly after the mid-1980s. The process of concentration was most visible at the level of the global system integrators. A powerful trend increase in the extent of firm-level concentration of global market share could be observed in industries as diverse as aerospace and defence, pharmaceuticals, automobiles, trucks, power equipment, farm equipment, oil and petrochemicals, mining, pulp and paper, brewing, banking, insurance, advertising, and mass media (see Section 2.2 for evidence from several sectors).

It quickly became apparent that a powerful associated process of firm-level concentration was at work at a lower level of the business structure. Associated with the fast-growing concentration of market share among global systems integrators there was taking place a process of intensified pressure on the surrounding network of suppliers. In sector after sector, leading firms, with powerful technologies and marketing capabilities, were actively selecting the most capable among their numerous suppliers, in a form of 'industrial planning' to select 'aligned suppliers' who could work with them across the world. Only those suppliers that were able to undertake the requisite R&D and investment in information technology were able to qualify as long-term business partners for the global giants. Across a wide range of activities a 'cascade effect' began to work in which intense pressures developed for first-tier suppliers of goods and services to the global giants to themselves merge and acquire, and develop leading global positions. These, in their turn, passed on intense pressure upon their own supplier networks. The result was a fast-developing process of concentration at a global level in numerous industries supplying goods and services to the systems integrators. The process was most visible in the vehicle components industry, but was taking place in numerous sectors that supplied the systems integrators, including such diverse activities as metal cans, high value-added steel, aerospace components, and print machinery.

Across a wide range of business activity, instead of competition between anonymous firms, competition had become oligopolistic at a global level, not only among the systems integrators, but, increasingly, among the first-tier suppliers. Leading firms at a global level increasingly competed with the clearly identified firms that occupied the commanding heights in a wide range of business activities.

## Merger frenzy

Merger activity typically intensifies in the final phase of a bull market on the stock exchange, as firms use their increased stock market 'wealth' to finance takeovers. The speed of transnational merger and acquisition in the 1990s has increased at an extraordinary rate. From 'just' $156bn in transactions in 1992, the global total soared to $1100bn in 1997, doubled to over $2000bn in 1998, and in 1999, reached over $3300bn. In the year 2000, the merger frenzy finally began to subside. The merger and acquisition explosion of the 1990s will shape the fundamental features of the global business system well into the twenty-first century. US big business is at the heart of this structure.

## Market share

In sector after sector, the 1990s saw a sharp increase in the global market share of leading companies. The process was inexorable, permeating almost every sector. Middle-sized firms were squeezed out remorselessly. Hardly a sector did not see this process. The 1990s witnessed a massive process of asset reorganization within large capitalist firms. Following the extensive diversification of the 1980s, the 1990s saw a dramatic change in big business philosophy and practice. Firm after firm shed non-core business in order to focus on the areas in which the firm could compete globally. This sharp focus enabled firms to develop vast global businesses within a much narrower range of competence than previously. Moreover, the sharpening of focus meant that large businesses could now devote much greater resources to their chosen activities. In sector after sector a small number of firms accounts for over one-half of global sales (Table 2.1).

**Table 2.1** *Global oligopoly in the business revolution (1998–2000)*

| Company name | Sector | Global market share (%) |
| --- | --- | --- |
| **Aerospace** | | |
| Boeing | Commercial aircraft orders over 100 seats | 70 |
| Airbus | Commercial aircraft orders over 100 seats | 30 |
| Rolls-Royce | Aero-engine orders | 34 |
| GE | Aero-engine orders | 53 |
| Pratt & Whitney | Aero-engine orders | 13 |
| **IT** | | |
| Lucent | Internet and telecoms equipment | 17 |
| Intel | Micro-processors | 85 |
| Microsoft | PC operating systems | 85 |
| Microsoft | Business desktop computer applications | 90 |
| Cisco | Computer routers | 66 |
| | : high end routers | 80 |
| Corning | Optical fibres | 50 |
| Hyundai Electronics | DRAMS | 21 |
| Samsung Electronics | DRAMS | 20 |
| Sony | Electronic games | 67 |
| Nintendo | Electronic games | 29 |
| Ericsson | Mobile phones | 15 |
| Nokia | Mobile phones | 23 |
| Motorola | Mobile phones | 20 |

| Company name | Sector | Global market share (%) |
|---|---|---|
| **Pharmaceuticals** | | |
| Glaxo Wellcome/SKB | Prescription drugs | 7 |
| | : central nervous system | 12 |
| | : anti-infection | 17 |
| | : respiratory | 17 |
| | : anti-asthma | 31 |
| | : anti-herpes | 49 |
| Merck | Prescription drugs | 5 |
| | : statin anti-cholesterol | 40 |
| | : angiotension converting enzyme inhibitors | 30 |
| Medtronic | Implantable/interventional therapy technologies* | 45 |
| | : pacemakers | 50+ |
| **Vehicles** | | |
| Ford/Mazda/Volvo | Automobiles | 16 |
| GM | Automobiles | 15 |
| Daimler-Chrysler | Automobiles | 10 |
| VW | Automobiles | 9 |
| Toyota | Automobiles | 9 |
| Renault/Nissan | Automobiles | 9 |
| **Vehicle Components** | | |
| Pilkington | Auto glass | 25 |
| GKN | Constant velocity joints | 40 |
| Tenneco | Shock absorbers/car exhaust systems | 25 |
| Lucas | Brake systems | 25 |
| Bosch | Brake systems | 31 |
| Bridgestone | Tyres | 19 |
| Michelin | Tyres | 18 |
| Goodyear | Tyres | 14 |
| **Petrochemicals** | | |
| BP Amoco | PTA | 37 |
| | Acetic acid (technology licences) | 70 |
| | Acrylonite(technology licences) | 90 |
| **Complex Equipment** | | |
| Invensys | Control/automation equipment | 11 |
| Siemens | Control/automation equipment | 10 |
| ABB | Control/automation equipment | 9 |
| Emerson | Control/automation equipment | 8 |
| Fanuc | Machine tool controls | 45 |
| Schindler | Lifts | 25 |
| Otis | Lifts | 18 |
| Mitsubishi | Lifts | 13 |
| Kone | Lifts | 9 |

| Company name | Sector | Global market share (%) |
|---|---|---|
| **Fast Moving Consumer Goods** | | |
| Coca-Cola | Carbonated soft drinks | 51 |
| Procter and Gamble | Tampons | 48 |
| Gillette | Razors | 70 |
| Fuji Film | Camera films | 35 |
| Chupa Chups | Lollipops | 34 |
| Nike | Sneakers | 36 |
| **Packaging** | | |
| Toray | Polyester film | 60 |
| Sidel | PET plastic packaging machines | 55 |
| Alcoa/Reynolds | Aluminium | 24 |
| **Power Equipment** | | |
| GE | Gas turbines (1993–98) | 34 |
| Siemens/Westinghouse | Gas turbines (1993–98) | 32 |
| ABB/Alstom | Gas turbines (1993–98) | 21 |

*Notes:* * Including pacemakers, implantable defibrillators, leads, programmers for treatment of patients with irregular heart-beats.

## 2.2   Consolidation in selected sectors during the big business revolution

Part 1 examined case studies from several different sectors of the Chinese economy. During the years that China pursued its industrial policy of attempting to build national champions, dramatic changes took place in the industrial structure of each of these industries. These changes posed huge challenges for China's ambitions to catch up with the leading businesses from the high-income countries.

### Aerospace

The aerospace sector is characterized by large economies of scale and scope, lending itself to a highly concentrated structure. In the 1990s the pressures pushing towards concentration intensified greatly. The industry requires huge development costs for new models, has very high requirements for R&D expenditures, needs complex systems integration skills and high expenditures to integrate the supplier network, and requires the construction of the highest degree of trust in the brand.

The prize for the 'winners' in the global aerospace battle is the vast market that exists today and which will grow much larger in the years ahead. Over the next two decades, the world's civilian airlines are predicted to buy around 14 000 new and replacement aircraft over that period with a total value of $1200bn. The period since the Cold War has seen a drastic reduction in defence spending in both the US and Europe. However, the market for defence equipment is still enormous, with military aircraft the most important single item. In 1999 total defence expenditure stood at $253bn in the US and $135bn in Europe (NATO). International arms sales in 1998 stood at $56bn. The fastest-growing markets were in the Far East, where arms sales rose from under $10bn in 1987 to over $13bn in 1998.

The 1990s witnessed a period of unprecedented consolidation in the world's aerospace industry. In the US the initiative for military aerospace mergers came from the Pentagon. In 1993, the US Defence Secretary invited the chief executives of the biggest American defence and aerospace companies to dinner, the so-called 'Last Supper'. With the green light from the government, a colossal game of 'musical chairs' followed in the mid-1990s, with over $62bn-worth of mergers and acquisitions occurring between 1994 and 1998. At the conclusion of this process, just two front-line aircraft manufacturers were left, namely Boeing and Lockheed Martin. The most significant event in this process was the merger of Boeing with McDonnell Douglas. By any conventional criteria used in competition policy, permitting this degree of industrial concentration was unthinkable. Far from being opposed to the merger, the move received 'strong support from the US administration'. As soon as it was announced in December 1996, European aerospace executives assumed it would be allowed to proceed 'because the White House and the Pentagon wanted it to'. After the Boeing-McDonnell Douglas merger, Boeing and Lockheed Martin between them accounted for close to one-half of US defence department contracts, and completely dominated military aircraft sales to the US government.

In the civilian sector, in the early 1960s there were still three large US jet aircraft makers apart from the dominant Boeing Corporation, namely McDonnell, Douglas, and Lockheed. Douglas and McDonnell merged in 1967. Neither Lockheed nor McDonnell Douglas was able to catch up with Boeing in the ensuing race. The first-mover advantage was crucial in enabling Boeing to maintain its lead. Boeing was able to watch while first Lockheed left the field of commercial airliners, then a steadily weakening McDonnell Douglas finally gave up and agreed to merge with Boeing. By 1997, the remarkable situation had been reached that in the country with the world's largest airline market by far, there was only one producer, Boeing. After the merger with McDonnell Douglas, Boeing accounted for no less than 84 per cent of the world's total aircraft in service. The merger left Boeing with a complete monopoly on large civil aircraft: Boeing is the only company in the world that produces aircraft able to carry more than 400 passengers. Moreover, unlike Lockheed Martin, Boeing was now a colossus that spanned both the military and civilian spheres of aerospace production.

By the late 1990s, the European military aerospace industry was acutely aware of its dangerous state of fragmentation compared to the US industry: 'The writing on the wall could hardly be larger: the European aerospace and defence industry must consolidate to achieve economies of scale in a shrinking market. If it does not, European defence procurement agencies will inevitably find themselves forced for budgetary reasons to order American equipment.' The European military aerospace industry realized that it must unify or perish before the US challenge. In 1998, the 'national champions' of the UK, France and Germany, BAe, Aerospatiale and Dasa, declared their intention to unify into a single company, with a single management structure, quoted on the stock market, the European Aerospace and Defence Company (EADC). It was intended to incorporate all sectors of the European aerospace industry, including combat aircraft, military transport, guided weapons, large civil aircraft (including a restructured Airbus), helicopters, space and defence electronics.

In late 1998 BAe stood on the brink of a merger with Daimler-Chrysler of Germany. It was thought that the new company would form the core of the EADC, to be joined eventually by Aerospatiale after its privatization. However, the merger talks were protracted. The negotiations were called to an abrupt halt with the announcement of the merger of BAe with GEC-Marconi in January 1999. This move created the world's third largest aerospace company by total turnover and the world's second largest in terms purely of defence revenue. The move was a serious setback for the cause of European aerospace integration. In October 1999, Dasa and Aerospatiale-Matra announced that they would be merging into a new giant company called the European Aircraft, Defence and Space Company or EADS. However, it was far from certain that the formation of EADS would be followed by the formation of EADC, including BAe Systems.

In the 1970s, the diverse civilian aircraft manufacturing capabilities in the UK and Continental Europe were still far too small to compete effectively with the might of Boeing. Europe had failed to produce a super-large airliner to compete with the B-747, or even the smaller Lockheed Tristar and McDonnell Douglas DC-10. The US aircraft companies, and especially Boeing, established overwhelming dominance in the epoch of rapidly expanding jet travel. Airbus was born in 1970, of a wish to compete head-on with the US manufacturers before it was too late. It began life as a Franco-German joint venture, later joined by Spain and Britain. The corporate structure adopted by Airbus reflected the desire to combine economies of scale and scope with the maintenance of national sovereignty and 'national champions' in the aerospace industry within each of the partner countries. Airbus is not a company in the usual sense. It is an 'Association for developing commercial interests' (*Groupement d'intérêt économique*), which publishes no detailed accounts and makes no profits and losses in its own right. All the profits go directly to the four partners in proportion to their shareholdings. Aerospatiale and Dasa each owns 37.9 per cent, BAe has 20 per cent and Casa 4.2 per cent. The partners carry out most of the Airbus manufacturing according to the principle of *juste retour*, under which they receive work in proportion to their shareholdings. The first Airbus aircraft was delivered in 1974. In 1994, Airbus won marginally more orders than Boeing, the first time that Boeing had been toppled from the number one slot since the advent of the jet age. Although Boeing quickly regained the lead in terms of new orders, in 1999 Airbus once more overtook Boeing, with orders for around 490 aircraft compared with 390 for Boeing. Moreover, in the year 2000 Airbus announced that it intended to proceed with plans to build the super-large A3XX aircraft to directly challenge Boeing in the most lucrative segment of the market. In 1996 Airbus began the prolonged attempt to transform itself from a '*Groupement d'intérêt économique*' into a limited company floated on the stock market. Following the merger of Dasa and Aerospatiale-Matra, EADS will hold 80 per cent of Airbus, compared with just 20 per cent for BAe Systems. This should make it much easier to turn Airbus into a single company. However, the final shape of the European aerospace industry is far from certain.

Following years of merger and acquisition, by the late 1990s there were just three companies that controlled the entire world market for large aircraft engines, Pratt and Whitney (United Technologies), GE's engine division and Rolls-Royce. Moreover, there were strong rumours that one of these would shortly merge with another of the group.

The component supply industry has also been undergoing rapid change. In order to meet the demands of the global systems integrators, the major components suppliers have needed to invest heavily in R&D and to grow rapidly in order to benefit from cost reduction through economies of scale. A powerful merger movement is taking place among the first-tier suppliers to the systems integrators. By 1997, two of the world's top five aerospace companies (by value of sales), namely United Technologies and Allied Signal, were principally aerospace components suppliers to the major systems integrators. In 1999, Allied Signal strengthened its already powerful position still further when it announced that it was to merge with Honeywell. The merger created a new Honeywell, 'a global technology powerhouse' with revenues of $25bn and a staff of 120 000 in 95 countries'. The combined R&D expenditure of the two companies is almost $800m. The new company's largest single business is aerospace, with about $10.5bn in annual revenues, 'bringing together Honeywell's focus on sophisticated avionics with Allied Signal's in-flight safety products and systems'. Only a year later, in October 2000, GE announced that it was to buy Honeywell for around $42bn, to combine with its own huge aerospace components business, GE Engines.

## Pharmaceuticals

There is a vast and fast-growing global market for patented medicines. Global sales revenue in the sector more than doubled in the 1990s from around $150bn to over $350bn. Despite the overwhelming dominance of the developed countries, in terms of future market growth the developing countries are extremely important for the drugs companies based in the advanced economies, despite their low current levels of expenditure on patented drugs. The East Asian market (excluding Japan) alone is predicted to increase from around $20bn (just 8 per cent of the global total) to $50bn by 2005. A truly global market for patented drugs is forming, which offers unprecedented growth opportunities for firms in this sector. A crucial part of the policy of the advanced economies' policymakers is to establish a 'global level playing field' in products of the 'life sciences' through the TRIPs (Trade Related Intellectual Property Rights) Agreement. Strong enforcement of this agreement among developing countries is a key part of the attempt by the developed country pharmaceutical firms to obtain maximum returns from their huge investment in patented medicines.

A succession of multi-billion mergers and acquisitions transformed the industry. During the late 1990s the leading players in the industry were constantly discussing the possibility of joining forces in order to benefit from scale economies, especially in R&D and marketing. The 'merger frenzy' reached a peak in 1998–2000. From early 1998 until early 2000 around one-half of the world's top pharmaceutical firms announced mergers.

Several of the former leading traditional, focused pharmaceutical companies grew rapidly in the mid-1980s, with merger and acquisition typically playing a major role, frequently involving cross-country activity. For example, by early 2000, the formerly independent pharmaceutical companies Glaxo, Wellcome, SmithKline Beckman (itself the product of several mergers) and Beecham had joined together into a single giant company, to form the largest pharmaceutical company in the world. The first stage in the consolidation process was the formation of SmithKline Beecham in 1989, through a $7.8bn merger of SmithKline Beckman (US) and Beecham (UK). In 1995, with the agreement of the Wellcome Trust (which owned 39.5 per cent of Wellcome's shares), Glaxo launched a successful hostile bid for Wellcome, paying $14.8bn for the company. Despite their great increase in size due to the respective mergers and acquisitions, neither Glaxo Wellcome nor SKB felt that they possessed the necessary scale to compete in the new world of giant pharmaceutical companies. In early 2000, the two companies finally agreed to merge, catapulting the new company into the number one position in terms of sales and R&D expenditure. The new company has 7.5 per cent of the global market for patented pharmaceuticals, with a combined R&D expenditure of around $3.6bn. The new CEO, Jean-Pierre Garnier commented: 'Putting this engine together will produce more drugs. The quality is here, the scale is here ... We will be the kings of science.'

At least as remarkable as the rapid growth of several leading traditional pharmaceutical companies was the revolutionary change in the structure of most of the world's leading chemical companies. Driven by the search for shareholder value, and by the high margins and high global growth prospects for pharmaceuticals, leading chemical companies in the 1990s one after the other shed their traditional chemicals businesses to focus on the 'life sciences', within which pharmaceuticals played a central role. Novartis is a leading example of this form of transformation. In the 1980s, Ciba-Geigy and Sandoz (both of Switzerland) were two of the world's most powerful chemical companies, each of which was particularly strong in specialty chemicals. In 1996 Ciba-Geigy and Sandoz announced a simultaneous merger and demerger that 'changed the corporate landscape for the world's pharmaceutical and chemicals industries'. The main businesses of Ciba-Geigy and Sandoz combined in a $27.5bn merger to form what was then the world's second biggest pharmaceutical company, named Novartis. Ciba-Geigy and Sandoz each spun off their slow-growing, specialty chemicals divisions into a new company, Ciba Specialty Chemicals, in order to 'enhance shareholder value' in the new company, Novartis.

In the early 1990s the pharmaceutical industry was considered to be 'extraordinarily fragmented compared to other global industries'. In 1994 the top ten companies held 28.0 per cent of the total global market. By 1999 the global market share of the top ten pharmaceutical companies had risen to over 43 per cent. Moreover, the degree of concentration in the industry was much greater even than appears to be the case from the aggregate industry data. In the 1990s, leading firms each concentrated on a relatively small number of selected areas in which to focus their huge R&D budgets. This enabled them to establish rising barriers to entry, and became a powerful source of competitive advantage, making it steadily harder for potential rivals to catch up. For example, the newly merged combination of Glaxo Wellcome/SKB has around 7.3 per cent of the world market for patented medicines. However, its global market share rises to 17 per cent for anti-infectives and respiratory medicines. If one looks within sub-categories the market share of global leaders is even higher. Glaxo Wellcome accounts for 49 per cent of the total world market for anti-herpes drugs and 31 per cent of the total global market for anti-asthma drugs.

## Power equipment

The underlying prospects for the world's power generating equipment manufacturers are strong. It is predicted that annual orders for power generating equipment world-wide will grow from around 80 gigawatts in the mid-1990s to around 140 gigawatts in 2010. Of this total increase in demand, around 50 per cent is expected to come from Asia, around 20 per cent from Europe and the CIS, and around 25 per cent from the Americas.

Power equipment manufacture has large economies of scale and scope. The main elements of power stations, boilers and turbines, are of enormous and steadily increasing size. Competitive advantage in this sector depends on several key factors. Leading firms must possess the ability to invest in technical progress in the product and maintain technological leadership globally. They must have the financial strength to withstand technical failures and to provide project funding for acquirers of power equipment. They require a high level of capability in providing service for power units over the whole of their lifetime, and must be able to lower costs of production through effective internal and external business system integration. Pressures on all counts sharply increased in the 1990s.

Up until the 1980s, in the advanced economies, the power equipment business was regarded as strategically important. Each country in Europe had a 'national champion', supported through captive sales to the nationalized electricity industry. The industry changed rapidly in the epoch of globalization. Electricity generation was privatized. The privatized electricity companies were much more price-aware than the old state-owned electricity utilities. This radically altered the nature of the market for power equipment, making it far more competitive. Government support for 'national champions' in this sector fell by the wayside. As industrialization took off in East Asia, demand for power stations surged, and the prospects for global demand were radically altered. Competition among the main manufacturers for these fast-growing and increasingly open markets intensified. These developments set the scene for a radical change in the industry's institutional structure after the mid-1980s.The subsequent decade saw a wave of mergers in the power equipment industry.

In 1987, Asea (Sweden) and Brown Boveri (Switzerland) merged to form ABB. In 1989 GEC (UK) and Alcatel (France) combined their energy and transport interests to form GEC Alsthom (renamed Alstom). By 1995 there were just five main integrated producers of power plants world-wide, General Electric, ABB, Westinghouse, GEC Alsthom, and Siemens. In 1997, the predicted further round of consolidation began with the takeover of Westinghouse's non-nuclear power equipment business by Siemens. Only a few months later, ABB and GEC-Alstom announced that they were merging their power generation businesses. The new chief executive, Pierre Bilger, referred to ABB-Alstom as a 'European champion in power engineering'.

The merger of ABB and Alstom was the final step in the restructuring of the postwar organization of the world's power equipment industry. The former 'national champions' created to provide national self-sufficiency in this industry that was once thought to have been of crucial national strategic importance, have been swept away to be replaced by large global businesses. The top three global power equipment companies, Siemens, ABB-Alstom, and GE, now accounted for around two-thirds of total global output. However, the degree of dominance is even greater than at first sight appears to be the case. The gas-fired power station market is of crucial importance, since it is widely regarded as more environmentally friendly in terms of greenhouse gases than is steam-powered, which principally means coal-driven. The share of the top three companies in this market now amounts to almost 90 per cent of total world orders. The three giants were poised to dominate the world's power station construction in the twenty-first century. They were now far ahead of any developing country's power equipment producers in terms of their size, R&D spending and technical capabilities to provide systems that generate electricity cleanly and safely, business systems skills, capability to organize the 'external firm' of suppliers on a global basis, to earn high quality revenue over a long period from maintenance services, and ability to participate in the financing of power station construction.

## Oil and petrochemicals

After going through profound changes from the late 1970s through to the late 1990s, an even more fundamental change swept the global oil and petrochemical industry in the late 1990s. In August 1998, BP initiated the biggest ever merger in the oil industry by combining with Amoco in a $55bn stock and debt deal. The combined group had revenues of $68bn in 1998, ranking it nineteenth in the *Fortune 500*. Only two months after announcing the merger with Amoco, BP agreed on a $26.8bn all-stock takeover deal with Arco. After prolonged dispute with the regulation authorities, the merger was approved in mid-2000. The *pro-forma* revenues of the combined company in 1998 totalled $82bn, taking BP up to around the fourteenth largest in the *Fortune 500*. Just three months after the announcement of the BP Amoco merger, Exxon and Mobil announced their plans to merge in an $86.4bn deal, at that point the largest merger ever. Exxon was already the world's largest oil and petrochemical producer, with revenues of over $100bn in 1998. Mobil was the world's number four with revenues of $48bn. The new company became the world's third largest by sales revenue, after General Motors and Daimler-Chrysler. The new company's *pro-forma* profits were almost $12bn in 1997.

These massive deals placed intense pressure on middle-ranked companies to increase their scale. Total (France's second biggest oil group) acquired PetroFina (one of Belgium's biggest industrial companies) in a $7bn stock-swap deal and renamed the combined group as TotalFina. In 1997, the combined group had revenues of $47bn, making it the fourth largest global oil company in terms of revenues. Hard on the heels of the announcement of the merger of PetroFina and Total in late 1998, TotalFina launched a hostile $43bn bid for Elf Aquitaine. The takeover was vigorously resisted by Elf Aquitaine, but after months of protracted negotiation, the two companies finally agreed to a friendly merger in early September 1999. On a *pro-forma* basis, the new company would have revenues of almost $80bn, taking it into the *Fortune 500* top 20 companies by value of sales. In late 2000, after prolonged discussions, Chevron and Texaco agreed to a $43bn merger, bringing together the second and third largest US oil groups respectively. The merger will catapult the combined company into the *Fortune 500* top 30 companies by value of sales, and the combined output of oil and gas will be close to that of the 'three sisters' (Exxon, Shell and BP).

The mergers of 1998–99 produced a fundamental change in the competitive landscape. It created a group of 'super-majors'. Their huge size gave them the potential to construct a portfolio of high quality oil and gas reserves distributed around the world, to invest large amounts in R&D to sustain and extend their technical lead over other companies, to develop integrated global marketing capabilities, to invest in large-scale information technology systems that could better integrate their value chain, to develop their global brand, and to purchase inputs more cheaply due to the scale of purchases. The merger frenzy in the world's oil and petrochemical industry between 1997 and 1999 greatly increased the institutional and technical gap between the world's leading companies and challengers from developing countries.

## Motor vehicles and components

The 1990s saw a dramatic opening up of world motor vehicle markets to international competition and internationalization of production. The intensity of interfirm competition increased greatly. Only the lowest-cost manufacturers could survive. Scale became even more important than before in achieving minimum cost. Larger scale, along with effective management, enabled cost reductions per unit in R&D, vehicle development costs, marketing, and procurement. Liberalization of international capital markets combined with much more active institutional investors, meant that poorly-performing automotive firms were mercilessly penalized by the market, further intensifying the pressure to improve performance through cost reduction. The motor vehicle industry entered a phase of large-scale merger and acquisition at the end of the 1990s, including the Daimler-Chrysler merger, the take over of Volvo automobiles by Ford and the purchase by Renault of a controlling share of ownership in Nissan. By the year 2000, the top seven producers each had annual output of over 4.5m vehicles. Together they accounted for two-thirds of global automobile output. The 1990s saw a succession of mergers and acquisitions in the truck industry. The number of truck makers is estimated to have fallen from more than 40 in 1975 to less than 20 in the late 1990s. By 1999, the share of the top five truck makers had risen to 54 per cent of the global market.

The institutional structure of automobile components production has undergone a revolution in the past decade and the transformation appears to be far from finished. Ten years ago a large fraction of components in Europe and the US was produced within highly integrated 'Fordist' firms. Those components that were purchased from outside typically were supplied by a large number of small firms producing mainly for national vehicle makers, with small international sales. Several large changes have occurred simultaneously in the automobile industry, radically changing the components industry. A common element in the transformation in the global components industry has been a relentless pressure from globalizing large automotive assemblers to reduce costs through applying pressure to components makers. This produced a 'cascade' effect flowing down from the automotive assemblers to the first-tier components makers, with consolidation at the assembler level pushing forward consolidation at the level of the components suppliers. The first-tier components makers have only been able to meet this pressure by themselves developing greater and greater scale on a global level. The estimated number of automotive components makers world-wide has shrunk from around 30 000 in 1990 to around 8000 in 2000. The number is predicted to shrink to just 2000 in six to eight years, with around 30 'mega-suppliers' that dominate the industry. The top ten firms in the components industry have annual revenues of between $10–30bn. In 1998, the industry leader, Bosch, spent $2.1bn on R&D. Levels of concentration in different segments of the industry had grown to high levels. For example, by the year 2000, the top firm accounted for one-half of the global market for automobile exhausts, the top two firms accounted for around one-half of the global market for automobile air conditioners, while the top three firms accounted for three-fifths of the global tyre market.

## Steel

The world steel industry had an annual output value of $250bn in the mid-1990s. Steel has a key role in such central economic activities as construction, automobiles, packaging, wire manufacture, mechanical engineering and electrical goods. World-wide steel output grew from 135m tons in 1947 to over 700m tons in 1974. Following the world economic crisis of 1997, global consumption of steel slumped to around 690m tons in the years 1998–99, but should recover to around 760–770m tons in 2005. The long-term forecasts are that world steel output in the first decades of the twenty-first century will be around 800–850m tons. The regional distribution of steel production is shifting fast, and is likely to continue to do so in the foreseeable future. In the advanced capitalist economies, long-term output has more or less stabilized at somewhat above 300m tons per annum. Alongside the stabilization of long-term output in the advanced economies, two dramatic changes took place elsewhere. Firstly, steel output in the former USSR collapsed, its share of world output falling from 21 per cent in the early 1980s to just 10 per cent in 1996. Secondly, steel output in the seven leading producers in the developing world increased fivefold from 1974 to 1996, their share of world steel output rising from just 7 per cent to 30 per cent in the same period. The vast bulk of this increase took place in East Asia.

Steel industry technology has advanced rapidly. In recent years there has occurred an intensification of pressure on the steel industry due to the rapid growth in the use of materials that compete with steel, notably aluminium, concrete and plastics. In response to this intense market pressure, the steel industry has developed new technologies for lightweight steel for use in vehicles and packages, and new types of steel for use in the construction industry. The leading steel industry firms have developed a much closer relationship with their main customers to meet their needs for improved materials at competitive prices.

The traditional steel industry is well known for the powerful economies of scale at the plant level. There are also significant economies of 'scope' associated with multi-plant operation, such as applying R&D and marketing efforts across many products and plants. The most important examples of 'catch-up' in the steel industry in industrializing countries were each based around large firms. In the US, early growth of the steel industry was closely associated with the rise of Andrew Carnegie's US Steel. In 1901 US Steel's share of US output was 66 per cent for crude steel, 60 per cent for steel rails, 62 per cent for heavy structural shapes, 65 per cent for plates and sheets and 78 per cent for wire rod output. Japanese industrialization was closely associated with the rise of Japan Steel. In 1970, New Japan Steel ('Nippon Steel') was established out of the merger of Fuji and Yawata. It accounted for around two-fifths of total Japanese steel output, and was the world's largest steel producer, with over 28m tons in 1997. Posco was founded by the South Korean government in 1968, as a calculated planning move to enable South Korea to supply domestically the steel it needed for its fast-growing shipbuilding, automobile, electronics and construction industries. In the late 1990s it took over from Nippon Steel as the world's number one producer, with a capacity of 28m tons. Posco is not only the world leader in terms of scale, it also has the lowest production costs in the world among large, integrated companies in the sector.

In Europe after the Second World War, steel was regarded as a key strategic sector, and most governments nationalized the industry. By the late 1990s, a wave of privatizations had signalled the end of the epoch of 'national champions' in steel, in which they had been immune from takeover by or merger with foreign steel firms. There followed a succession of large-scale mergers, increasingly across international borders. A small number of globally powerful 'European champions' with global ambitions was formed. In 1999 Corus was formed from the merger of British Steel with Hoogovens (The Netherlands). This created a company with 70 000 employees, a turnover of $15bn and a steel output of over 23m tons, making it the world's third-ranking producer. In 1998 Usinor took over Cockerill-Sambrell (Belgium). This acquisition lifted Usinor's output to around 23m tons, making it the world's third largest steel producer. In 1997, Krupps-Hoesch launched a massive hostile bid for Thyssen. After intense debate, the two companies eventually merged peacefully to form a giant steel and engineering company with 180 000 employees and a turnover of $33bn, making it the largest company in Germany. In 1997, Thyssen Krupps produced over 17m tons of crude steel, making it the fourth largest steel company in the world. In early 2001, it was announced that Unisor was to merge with Arbed (Luxembourg) and Aceralia (Spain). The new entity would 'tower above its nearest competitors', producing 45m tons of crude steel per annum: 'This completely changes the shape of the steel industry in Europe and globally'.

Another move of immense potential significance was announced in 1999 in response to the Asian financial crisis. Posco and Nippon Steel bought shares in each other as part of a scheme to create 'a mutual anti-takeover alliance'. Posco and Nippon Steel have a long working relationship. If the share-swap presages an even deeper alliance between the two giants then it will have enormous implications for the institutional structure of the world's steel industry. In the view of Morgan Stanley Dean Witter, if this alliance occurs, 'the race for regional dominance would appear to be over before most producers realized it had begun'.

At first glance, the global industry still appears very fragmented. Despite the recent emergence of substantial cross-border merger activity, the top ten companies still account for only around 22 per cent of world steel output. However, on closer inspection, the level of concentration is higher than it at first appears to be. Neither China nor the former USSR is yet actively engaged in the global merger and aquisition process in this industry. The world's top five companies already account for 19.1 per cent of the world's total output excluding China and the former Soviet Union, and the world's top ten account for 31 per cent. Moreover, if one analyses different products, then the level of concentration is even higher than appears to be the case from an aggregate analysis. For example, in stainless steel, Thyssen Krupps and Usinor are the world leaders, and account for around one quarter of total world output between them.

At first glance the steel industry presents much greater possibilities for 'catch-up' in developing countries than do high technology industries such as aerospace, industries which have high R&D, such as patented pharmaceuticals, and industries in which massive investments are needed to created a global brand, such as soft drinks. However, there are large difficulties for firms based in developing countries even in this sector. Although technical progress may be slower than in some other industries, there are still important areas, especially high value-added products and processes, such as special steels, in which large technical gaps exist between leading firms in advanced economies and those in developing countries. There have been important advances in recent years in the way in which the world's leading firms based in advanced economies interact with their customers. In the merger and acquisition boom of the 1990s it has been the steel firms within the advanced economies that have taken the lead. Successful advanced 'economy steel' companies have developed a deep understanding of the requirements of globalizing large firms that are large users of steel, such as automobile and beverage companies. In sum, in the highest profit-margin areas of steel production, there is a small group of industry leaders that is emerging to dominate the global market. The industry is fast becoming bifurcated into two sections, one producing low quality, low value-added products, typically for local firms, and the other producing high value-added, high profit margin products for global firms. Developing country firms face extremely severe competition in the latter segment of the steel industry.

# Coal

Coal remains one of the most important sources of primary energy, accounting for 27 per cent of the world's primary energy consumption in 1996. Known reserves are thought likely to last for 250 years at current levels of consumption. Even in the US, coal still accounts for over 24 per cent of energy consumption. In China it accounts for no less than 76 per cent of total primary energy consumption. Despite the rise of environmental concerns in China, in the foreseeable future coal will remain the overwhelmingly dominant fuel for the Chinese power industry, due to its relative abundance and low cost.

International trade in coal has increased rapidly. The amount of coal traded internationally rose from less than 20m tons in 1973, to almost 240m tons in 1995, and is predicted to rise to around over 500m tons by the year 2010, close to 10 per cent of predicted world output. The main driver of demand has been the growth of steam coal for power stations. Asia accounts for 47 per cent of the world's total international coal demand, and the share is predicted to rise to over 60 per cent by 2010: 'Growth in Asian demand has been astonishing. Largely driven by the construction of modern, efficient, environmentally friendly advanced power stations in Japan, South Korea and Taiwan, the Asian market has expanded at a pace which the producers have barely been able to match.' (*Financial Times*). Due to the relative dearth of oil and natural gas in the region, coal remains a highly competitive fuel source in East Asia.

Compared to the institutional changes under way in most other industries, the coal industry still lags behind in terms of global consolidation. However, consolidation is affecting even this industry. Following the trend in other sectors to concentrate on core business, mining companies also disposed of non-core businesses and acquired businesses in the mining sector. Merger and acquisition has been central to the rise of focused global mining companies. In the late 1990s, mergers and acquisitions grew to record levels in the mining industry, reaching $17bn in 1995, rising to a new peak of $26bn in 1998. No firm accounts for more than around 5 per cent of total global coal production. However, following the rapid growth of mergers and acquisitions in this sector, truly global coal companies are emerging. The high value-added international coal trade in high quality steam coal has become a virtual oligopoly, controlled by a small number of powerful international mining companies, such as Rio Tinto, Anglo American and Billition.

Competitive advantage in the global coal industry lies primarily in size and management skills. Size enables global reach and the construction of a set of low-cost coal mines across the world. This reduces risk, and ensures location within or close to each major market. Successful global firms in this sector have the financial resources to purchase mines, invest in the exploration and evaluation of resources, negotiate with governments, deal with complex land rights and environmental issues, and apply best practice across the whole portfolio of mines. They also have some benefits in the global procurement and operation of large quantities of expensive mining equipment and through the use of common marketing channels and expertise. A multinational mining company may be in a stronger position to employ cost-minimizing methods of labour organization than is a large local firm.

## 2.3 The 'external firm': an ever-larger sphere of co-ordination and planning

If we define the firm not by the entity which is the legal owner, but rather by the sphere over which conscious co-ordination of resource allocation takes place, then, far from becoming 'hollowed out' and much smaller in scope, the large firm can be seen to have enormously increased in size during the global business revolution. As the large firm has 'disintegrated', so has the extent of conscious co-ordination over the surrounding value chain increased dramatically. In a wide range of business activities, the organization of the value chain has developed into a comprehensively planned and co-ordinated activity. At its centre is the core systems integrator. This firm typically possesses some combination of a number of key attributes. These include the capability to raise finance for large new projects, and the resources necessary to fund a high level of R&D spending to sustain technological leadership, to develop a global brand, to invest in state-of-the art information technology and to attract the best human resources. Across a wide range of business types, from fast-moving consumer goods to aircraft manufacture, the core systems integrator interacts in the deepest, most intimate fashion with the major segments of the value chain, both upstream and downstream.

The relationship of the core systems integrator with the upstream first-tier suppliers extends far beyond the price relationship. Increasingly, leading first-tier suppliers across a wide range of industries have established long-term 'partner' or 'aligned supplier' relationships with the core systems integrators. Key systems integrators play an active role in 'industrial planning' through their selection of those suppliers that are to be their trusted partners and with whom they agree to establish a long-term relationship. Trust is an important ingredient in these relationships. In some cases, the most fundamental aspects of the relationship are not even defined through written contracts. In recent years, systems integrators have widely established global procurement offices. This reflects an enormous increase in the central planning function of systems integrators. Leading first-tier suppliers use their close relationship with systems integrators as evidence of their long-term business viability in order to support and enhance their business position. Some key aspects of the intimate relationship between systems integrators and upstream firms include the following.

First, leading first-tier suppliers plan in minute detail the location of their plants in relation to the location of the core systems integrator. This can apply as much to a leading vehicle component maker as to a leading packaging supplier to a fast-moving consumer goods firm. It is not uncommon to find the aligned supplier literally supplying key products through a hole in the wall to the systems integrator. Secondly, it is increasingly the case that the aligned supplier produces goods within the systems integrator itself. It is common for leading suppliers of services, such as data systems or even travel agents, to physically work within the premises of the systems integrator. Sometimes there is a large number of employees, perhaps a thousand or more from a given firm, physically within the systems integrator undertaking such specialist functions. Thirdly, leading first-tier suppliers plan their R&D in close consultation with the projected needs of the core systems integrator. An increasing part of R&D is contracted out to small and medium-sized firms. This is typically under the close control of the systems integrator. Fourthly, product development is intimately co-ordinated with the systems integrator. This can apply as much to the development of a new packaging design for a fast-moving consumer goods firm, such as a new design of plastic bottle or can, as to the design of an aircraft engine for a huge airliner. Finally, precise product specifications are instantaneously communicated to the leading suppliers through newly developed information technology. The production and supply schedules of leading first-tier suppliers are comprehensively co-ordinated with the systems integrator to ensure that the required inputs arrive exactly when they are needed and the inventory of the systems integrator is kept to a minimum.

The systems integrator penetrates everywhere in the value chain in order to provide information to minimize costs across the value chain. It has a powerful incentive to ensure that knowledge is shared in order to reduce systems costs across the whole value chain.

Planning by systems integrators extends downstream also. Manufacturers of complex capital goods, from aircraft and power stations to vehicles and earth-moving equipment, are increasingly interested in the revenue stream to be derived from maintaining their products over the course of their lifetime. New information technology is increasingly being used to monitor the performance of complex products in use, with continuous feedback to the systems integrator in order to construct optimum servicing schedules. Through this pervasive process, systems integrators deeply penetrate a wide range of firms that use their products. However, penetration of the downstream network of firms is not confined to complex capital goods. Systems integrators in the fast-moving consumer goods (FMCG) sector increasingly co-ordinate the distribution process with specialist logistics firms in order to minimize distribution costs. They work closely with grocery chains and other selling outlets, such as theme parks, movie theatres, oil companies (petrol stations have become major locations for retailing non-petrol products), and quick-service restaurants, to raise the technical efficiency in the organization of the selling process. The FMCG systems integrators often have their own experts working within the retail chain.

Through the hugely increased planning function undertaken by systems integrators, facilitated by recent developments in information technology, the boundaries of the large corporation have become significantly blurred. The core systems integrators across a wide range of sectors have become the co-ordinators of a vast array of business activity outside the boundaries of the legal entity in terms of ownership. The relationship extends far beyond the price relationship. In order to develop and maintain their competitive advantage, the systems integrators deeply penetrate the value chain both upstream and downstream, becoming closely involved in business activities that range from long-term planning to meticulous control of day-to-day production and delivery schedules. Competitive advantage for the systems integrator requires that it must consider the interests of the whole value chain in order to minimize costs across the whole system.

In the old vertically integrated large firm, employment frequently totalled many hundreds of thousands of people. For example, in 1990, the world's largest capitalist firm by number of employees, General Motors, employed 750 000 people. Among the world's 100 largest international firms (by overseas assets), 51 had more than 100 000 employees. It is widely thought that the average size of large corporations has sharply declined since the late 1980s due to the impact of downsizing and the relentless pursuit of cost reduction. However, this is far from clear. In 1998, among the *Fortune 500* companies (ranked by value of sales), the median firm size was 55 000 employees. There were five firms with over 500 000 employees, and 27 with 200 000–500 000 employees and 88 with 100 000–200 000 employees. What appears to have happened is that the impact of mergers and acquisitions has frequently stimulated an increase in the total number of employees within the entire merged company, alongside considerable corporate downsizing within each of the merged entities. The functions of the core systems integrator have changed radically away from direct manufacturing towards the 'brain' functions of planning the global development of the firm. The proportion of employees working outside the home market has sharply increased. However, the world's leading firms remain very large entities, not only in terms of their revenues, but also in terms of direct employment. Employment remains large, but slow-growing or even declining somewhat alongside rapid acceleration of revenues.

Within the old 'Fordist' vertically integrated large corporation, the different departments had considerable autonomy and the problem of monitoring performance of subordinate units was a serious and widely-discussed issue. Even more difficult were the problems involved in monitoring performance in foreign branches of multinational companies. National branches of major multinational corporations typically developed a high degree of operational autonomy. Leading multinational firms often likened their structure to a feudal system, within which the local chiefs had high degrees of independence. New information technology has drastically increased the possibilities for close monitoring of performance within the firm, even across the entire globe. The 'business unit' structure adopted by many firms typically involves constant monitoring of performance in a way that was quite impossible even a few years ago.

The revolution in the global business system in recent years has meant that a high level of conscious planning of business activity is now undertaken by systems integrators across the whole value chain. A large corporation may have a total procurement bill of several billion, or even tens of billions, of dollars. The total procurement could involve purchases from firms that employ a much larger

number of full-time equivalent employees 'working for' the systems integrator
than are employed within the core firm itself. In addition, there is typically a large
sphere of downstream business activity that is co-ordinated by the systems
integrator. A leading systems integrator with 100 000–200 000 employees could
easily have the full-time equivalent of a further 400 000–500 000 employees
'working for' the systems integrator, in the sense that their work is co-ordinated
in important ways by the core firm. In this sense, we may speak of an 'external
firm' of co-ordinated business activity that surrounds the modern global
corporation and is co-ordinated by it.

The realm of planning and conscious co-ordination extends beyond the
individual large systems integrator. Co-ordination with leading first-tier suppliers
and downstream processes, such as logistics, involves systems integrators from
totally different sectors co-ordinating their business activities with the same
firms. For example, a leading FMCG firm may work closely with leading
aluminium or steel can makers. At the same time, the same aluminium makers
may work in close co-ordination with the world's systems integrators in aircraft
and autos. In the steel industry, a leading high-value-added steelmaker may work
in close co-ordination with, on the one hand, a leading FMCG firm in the supply
of high quality steel cans, and on the other hand it may work in close co-
ordination with a leading global automotive assembler.

An even more dramatic expansion of the realm of planning and co-ordination
by the systems integrators has been the establishment of a wide range of on-line
procurement networks by groups of the most powerful firms within given sectors.
The first sector to announce such a process was the automotive industry. In early
2000, GM, Ford, Renault and Daimler-Chrysler announced that they were going
to establish the world's largest electronic market-place to purchase components
(named Covsint). Between them they purchase directly several hundred million
dollars' worth of components. This announcement was closely followed by many
others, including the aerospace, energy and even the steel industry. The
implications of these developments were enormous, not least for the competition
authorities. They signalled a massive extension of the realm of planning and
conscious co-ordination over business activity.

## 2.4    Inequality in the regional distribution of firms that lead the business revolution

This section examines the enormous regional inequality in the distribution of
firms that dominate the global big business revolution. This massive disparity in
the regional bases of the world's leading firms is a deeply sensitive issue in
international relations. Failure to recognize this disparity, and the way in which
in many respects it has become wider, makes international economic agreements

between developing and advanced economies more difficult to negotiate and implement.

## Dominance of firms based in advanced economies

Regions containing a small fraction of the world's population have massively dominated the global big business revolution. The high income economies contain just 16 per cent of the world's total population. In 1997 they accounted for 91 per cent of the world's total stock market capitalization, 95 per cent of the *Fortune 500* list of companies which ranks companies by value of sales, 97 per cent of the *FT 500* which ranks companies by value of stock market capitalization and 99 per cent of the world's top 300 companies by value of R&D spending. Developing countries are massively disadvantaged in the race to compete on the global level playing field of international big business. The starting points in the race to dominate global markets could not be more uneven. The whole of the developing world, containing 84 per cent of the world's population, contains the headquarters of just 26 *Fortune 500* companies, 16 *FT 500* companies, and fifteen 'competitive edge' companies.

## US leadership of the global business revolution

Not only is there a massive imbalance between the 'starting points' in the great globalization race on the global level playing field, but there is also a deeply uneven distribution of business power within the advanced capitalist economies in the big business revolution. The large firms of the US are dominant in this process.

The global business revolution of the 1990s saw a sharp change in the relative economic fortunes of large firms in different parts of the advanced capitalist system. In the 1980s and early 1990s a large part of business economics was concerned with explaining the relative success of East Asian latecomers. There was a large literature on the apparent disadvantages of the Anglo-Saxon business structure. The capitalist stockmarket-based system was argued to be disadvantageous for long-term growth and competitiveness. The 1990s by contrast has seen a dramatic turnaround in relative economic performance, with a sharp improvement in the relative performance of US firms: 'The US has the lion's share of those corporations equipped to exploit global markets. It also supplies the bulk of the technology that knits those markets together.' (*Financial Times*). The 1990s business revolution demonstrated that the stock market can be perfectly compatible with long-term perspectives. Indeed, it may even be argued that the extraordinary surge in stockmarket valuations for globalizing, downsizing, big businesses, and, especially, information technology companies, demonstrated an irrational excess of optimism about the long-term growth prospects for big businesses in the epoch of globalization.

US-based big businesses have absorbed many of the lessons of the East Asian model, especially those of Toyotist outsourcing. However, they have applied those lessons on a global scale. Moreover, they have been able to apply the outsourced, lean-production structure to the whole value chain, using the technological revolution in information technology that has taken place in the 1990s: 'Throughout the 1990s corporate America, which grew lazy in the 1970s and early 1980s, has been in the throes of a far-reaching restructuring – much of it learned from Japan. Displaying remarkable flexibility, many US industries have regained their competitive edge and this has helped power an extraordinary bull market in equities.' (*Financial Times*).

The leading US-based companies have led the way in the resurgence of big business investment in R&D. In 1997 no less than 135 of the top 300 companies by R&D spending in 1998 were based in North America. The pace of growth of US companies' investment in R&D was much faster than across the rest of the world, rising by 15 per cent in 1997 and 19 per cent in 1998. Moreover, the US dramatically dominated the high-technology sectors. The IT hardware sector is much the most important single category of R&D expenditure, with no less than 57 of the top 300 companies by R&D spending in 1998. Of these, 37 are US-based companies: 'This reflects the astonishing turnaround in confidence among American high-tech companies during the late 1990s. Five years ago they were trembling before the onrushing Asian tigers. Now the US appears to be extending its technological lead over both Europe and Asia in many fields of electronics, engineering, information technology and the life sciences.' (*Financial Times*).

A large proportion of the accelerated flow of foreign direct investment (FDI) was accounted for by a small number of countries and firms. US-based companies have been at the forefront of the acceleration of foreign direct

**Table 2.2 R&D expenditure of the top 300 companies world-wide, 1995 and 1998**

| Sector | Number of companies, 1998 | 1998 ($bn) | 1995 ($bn) | Increase/decrease in R&D expenditure % |
|---|---|---|---|---|
| Total | 300 | 176.6 | 253.7 | 44 |
| of which: | | | | |
| IT hardware | 57 | 41.8 | 70.0 | 68 |
| Software/IT services | 17 | 3.3 | 7.5 | 127 |
| Telecoms services | 9 | 9.0 | 9.8 | 9 |
| Autos | 25 | 31.2 | 43.3 | 39 |
| Pharmaceuticals | 35 | 22.4 | 33.1 | 48 |
| Electronic/electricals | 28 | 22.3 | 26.6 | 19 |
| Chemicals | 31 | 14.5 | 20.7 | 43 |
| Aerospace/defence | 11 | 5.7 | 6.9 | 21 |
| Engineering/machinery | 21 | 4.8 | 6.5 | 35 |
| Oil/gas | 12 | 4.0 | 5.1 | 28 |
| Steel/metals | 9 | 1.2 | 1.1 | −7 |

investment since the mid-1980s. The US was much the most important single source of outflows of FDI, the total climbing rapidly in the early 1990s, as American companies powerfully moved towards globalization. American FDI outflows rose from an annual average of \$25bn in 1986–91 to \$115bn in 1997 and the USA's share of total world FDI outflows rose from 14 per cent in 1986–91 to 27 per cent in 1997. Moreover, the process had a powerful element of cumulative causation, with successful investment generating further investment: around 60 per cent of US 'outflows' of FDI in 1994–95 was financed out of reinvested profits. In the period 1986–91, Japan's outflows of FDI were 28 per cent greater than those of the US, but by 1997 the outflows of direct FDI from Japan had declined to only 23 per cent of those of the US.

In 1996, the US had 28 of the top 100 companies ranked by value of overseas assets. By 1998, North American firms accounted for 37 per cent of the *Fortune 500* ranking of the world's leading firms, ranked by sales value. US dominance of the big business revolution is reflected also in the annual *Competitive Edge* studies published by Morgan Stanley Dean Witter. These studies ranked companies by their capacity to have a sustainable 'competitive edge' in the global economy. Morgan Stanley's objective was to 'identify companies with a meaningful advantage in their global sectors'. Their objective was to assemble 'a comprehensive view of the competitive landscape, country by country, and industry by industry'. They ranked large quoted companies in terms of their competitive advantage in their respective sector. A key issue was global market share, which strongly influences the capability of new entrants to catch up: the higher the share, the more sustainable was the firm's leadership judged to be. In 1998 they identified a total of 238 companies that were 'world leaders'. Of these 134 were North American. Japan had just 18 companies that were identified as 'world leaders'.

In the *Financial Times* ranking of the world's top 500 companies by market capitalization, North America had 254 companies in 1998, in other words it accounted for more than one-half of the total. The USA's dominance of world stock market capitalization is crucially important in the epoch of explosive concentration through merger and acquisition. In a virtuous circle of growth and concentration, firms with high stock market capitalization can more easily take over and merge with those with lower stock market capitalizations. Well-focused mergers further enhance stock market capitalizations, paving the way for further expansion through merger and acquisition. Even the largest European companies have often found it hard to match the merger and acquisition capability this provides for leading US firms.

For Japanese companies, to be seriously lagging in stock market capitalization in this period of explosive restructuring of international big business is a deep disadvantage for the long-term positioning of large Japanese firms in the global economy in the twenty-first century. For the vast majority of firms from developing countries, with trivial market capitalizations compared to the global giants, it is inconceivable that they can participate in the global merger explosion in a serious fashion. They are almost entirely passive observers of the revolutionary reshaping of the world's big businesses.

In recent years in the US, globally successful large firms have tended to outperform the average for the whole stock market, reflecting investor perceptions of the gains that large, well-positioned companies can make from globalization and from 'the exploitation of technologies in which the US at present has unique strength': 'Argument rages about the causes of the US bull market, and whether it is sustainable, but to some extent it must reflect the remarkable US dominance of many cutting edge high technology sectors.' (*Financial Times*).

## 2.5  Revolutionary change in business systems outside the US

### Crisis for the East Asian model

An important part of the global business revolution consisted of lessons learned from East Asia by US and European companies, notably in the organization of outsourced supplier networks. However, the global business revolution of the 1990s went far beyond this concept. In the face of this revolution, the East Asian catch-up strategy for big business faced serious shortcomings. East Asia is now itself in the throes of a deep strategic rethinking, fundamentally reorganizing its business structures in the face of the intense competitive threat posed by rejuvenated, giant US and European businesses and the refusal of the advanced economies to continue to allow them to maintain protectionist barriers for international trade and investment. The epoch of 'free riding on free trade' is over.

In the 1970s and 1980s, large European and US businesses typically pursued diversification as a strategy for growth in mature, and often relatively protected, markets. A key aspect of the big business revolution has been the opening up of global markets, enabling the growth of huge focused, global businesses. East Asian businesses have continued to be highly diversified, and now face severe competition from the restructured global giants of the US and, latterly, Europe.

Diversification has been a key part of the growth strategy of large East Asian privately-owned businesses. In the absence of a core technology or brand name firms in late-industrializing countries have typically entered a wide range of unrelated industries. Of the 35 largest private industrial enterprises in developing countries in 1987, only five were specialized companies. The rest were all diversified conglomerates. In the diversified conglomerate group in developing countries, diversification has been 'a defensive tactic for growth'. Large firms have typically grown behind high protectionist barriers with close links to the government in order to maintain such protection. Such firms are at a large competitive disadvantage on the global level playing field.

A business revolution is being forced upon formerly distinctive business structures. To be successful on the 'global level field' requires a focus on core business and a global capability. The frame of reference for competitive success has become the world's leading edge firms, instead of national or regional leading firms. The global business revolution, in tandem with the Asian crisis, has forced drastic restructuring of East Asian businesses along Anglo-Saxon lines.

## South Korea

Each of the major South Korean *chaebols* was a diversified family-owned conglomerate. With strong state support and encouragement, the leading *chaebols* developed powerful exporting capabilities in items such as motor vehicles, ships, steel, semi-conductors and consumer electronics. However, behind high protectionist barriers and with credit from state banks, the *chaebols* also developed highly diversified businesses, often with low levels of technology and low economies of scale. Samsung is typical of the path of development. It began life in the 1930s as an overseas trading company. In the 1950s it moved into sugar refining and woollen textile manufacturing. In the 1960s it branched into broadcasting, entertainment, hospital administration and paper manufacturing. In the late 1960s it entered electronics and in the early 1970s established petrochemical and shipbuilding businesses. It subsequently entered real estate, semi-conductors, precision machinery, telecommunications, construction, sports entertainment, watchmaking, medical equipment and supplies, data processing and aerospace. The diversification path was driven partly by market imperfections and the unavailability of necessary inputs, but also by 'the lure of profits in unmodernized industries'. Both these possibilities were accentuated by the operation of a highly protected economy.

In 1998, in the midst of the Asian crisis, South Korea's leading *chaebols*, Hyundai, Samsung, LG, and Daewoo, agreed to a government-orchestrated restructuring. Having renationalized the big banks, the government attempted to use credit control as an instrument to impose restructuring upon the *chaebols*. The leading *chaebols* agreed to halve their total number of subsidiaries and participate in a comprehensive asset-swapping exercise that would give a much firmer focus on core business, to gain benefits from economies of scale. The goal was to reduce the number of Korean competitors to just two in critical export industries. After the asset swaps, Hyundai and Daewoo were to be the only car manufacturers, Samsung and LG/Hyundai the only semiconductor manufacturers, and Samsung and LG the only consumer electronics groups. Samsung was to merge its petrochemicals and aerospace divisions with other *chaebols*. Hyundai was to merge its petrochemicals, power generation and railway rolling stock operations with rival *chaebols*. However, the extent of restructuring was much less than had originally been planned. By late 2000,

Daewoo Motor had been officially declared bankrupt, with debts of $10bn, and Hyundai Construction, the heart of the Hyundai *chaebol*, was close to bankruptcy. It was widely thought that these events were the prelude to the deep industrial restructuring that had so far been avoided.

## Japan

Pre-1945 Japanese *zaibatsu* typically followed the diversified conglomerate pattern. For example, the Nissan *zaibatsu* in 1937 operated in mining, automobiles, chemicals, fishing, electronics, agriculture and other sectors. In the postwar period immensely powerful export-oriented firms grew up with government support. However, these leading companies in terms of world markets functioned within the *keiretsu* structure of cross-holdings. Within a single keiretsu, there were typically a wide range of mutually supportive businesses. For example, the Fuyo *keiretsu* contained businesses in trading, chemicals, pulp and paper, petroleum, cement, fibres and textiles, iron and steel, construction, electrical machinery, transportation, property and food. The Fuyo *keiretsu* contains a core of businesses that are globally competitive. However, it also has a whole set of businesses that are simply too small to compete on the global level playing field. They are protected by formal international protection, by controls over domestic distribution channels and by access to credit from within the *keiretsu*. The *keiretsu*'s core companies are disadvantaged to the extent that they source their inputs from small-scale companies within the *keiretsu* rather than from the least-cost global supplier.

The *keiretsu* system allowed allocation of capital within the group with little regard to returns achieved. An analysis by Goldman Sachs shows that Japanese non-financial groups in the *Nikkei 300* collectively failed to achieve a return above their cost of capital after 1990; 'Since that date they have destroyed value of ¥3000bn a year, a cumulative ¥21 000bn, by investing in project and plants that generated negative returns'. As long as the Japanese economy prospered, they could be supported by bank loans from within the group. Once the economy began to falter, that source of capital dried up, and by the late 1990s, the ability of the leading members to support weaker *keiretsu* members was in sharp decline.

Even the large core companies in Japanese *keiretsu* typically also are highly diversified. Mitsubishi Electric, the 25th largest Japanese corporation in 1997, is a vast electrical equipment conglomerate. It produces audio-visual equipment, information systems, semi-conductors, communications infrastructure (for example, fibre optic cables, satellite communications, mass communications systems, wireless telephony equipment), energy systems operations, building systems, home electronics, automotive electronics, industrial and factory automation, elevators, escalators, and air conditioning equipment.

Japan's leading companies face great difficulties in open competition with revitalized US and European companies in a world of fast-declining barriers to trade and investment. The mergers of Daimler and Chrysler, Sandoz and Ciba,

Mobil and Exxon, Amoco and BP left Japanese companies looking 'parochial and underscale'. The global business revolution saw a dramatic turnaround in the fortunes of Japan's leading companies. In 1990, six of the world's top ten companies by market capitalization were Japanese. By 1998, there were none. In 1998, Japan had just 46 companies in the *FT Global 500* list, and only two in the *Global 100*. In 1990, Japan's share of the world's stock market value was 41.5 per cent. By 1998 this had fallen to a mere 10.5 per cent. In 1998, Japan still had 18 of the world's top 50 corporations by value of sales, but had only one company in the top 50 by total profits.

The poor stock market performance of Japan's leading corporations is a major worry for them, since it drastically weakens their capability to undertake stock-market-based mergers with leading overseas companies. While leading US and European companies merge across boundaries and with each other, at high speed, Japan's corporations are being left behind in the whirlwind of large-scale corporate mergers and acquisitions. For example, despite an improvement in its share price in early 1999, Sony's market capitalization in mid-1999 stood at $38bn, far behind its US competitors, making it difficult to use its stock to pay for deals in North America.

There are serious fears in Japan that its high investment and R&D expenditure has been disproportionately channelled into industries of the Second Industrial Revolution: 'Japan leads the way in capital-intensive industries, including shipbuilding, steel, paper and pulp, and heavy chemicals. But it lags behind the US in the high technology and life science industries.' (Katsunosuke Maeda, vice-chairman of Kaidanren).

Downsizing had once been thought of as impossible in Japan's leading corporations, with guarantees of lifetime employment within a firm that functioned as a 'large family'. In 1999 there were signs that radical restructuring had begun to take hold among Japan's leading corporations. Company after company among Japan's corporate elite announced major downsizing programmes. Hitachi announced that it was cutting its workforce by 10 per cent (that is, 6500 workers) and selling off unprofitable businesses. Mitsubishi Electric announced that it was cutting 10 per cent of the workforce (that is, 14 500 employees) and would sell off or shut down those parts of the business that it deemed 'difficult or impossible to return to profitability'. Later in the year, Asahi Glass, NKK, Japan Airlines, Toyo Tyre and Rubber, NEC, Mitsubishi Chemical, and Daimaru, all announced large cuts in staff.

Revolutionary changes in the Japanese banking system precipitated major changes in the *keiretsu* system. In 1999, a series of large-scale mergers took place in the Japanese banking system, viewed as essential if Japan's banks were to compete following the revolutionary mergers in the European and US banking systems. Three huge banking mergers transformed the relationship of the core banks with the *keiretsu* in which they were located. For example, the core bank of the Fuyo *keiretsu*, Fuji Bank, merged with Industrial Bank of Japan and Dai-Ichi Kangyo. Fuji Bank then announced that it was inappropriate for it to continue as leader of the Fuyo *keiretsu*. It made it clear that henceforth it would seek to maximize its return on capital: 'Now our lending criteria are based on rational criteria. We are trying to maximize profits'. Constituent companies within the Fuyo *keiretsu* have responded by turning away from the banks towards the bond and equity markets.

A revolutionary process of international acquisition of Japanese companies has begun. Merrill Lynch has bought the branch network of Yamaichi Securities. GE Capital has acquired the leasing operations of Japan Leasing, Japan's second biggest company in this sector. Travelers is buying Nikko Securities. Goodyear (US) has, effectively, taken over Sumitomo Rubber, Japan's third biggest tyre company. Renault has taken a controlling stake in Nissan Motors. Some Japanese industry officials see the 'surrender into the arms of Renault' as symbolic of 'a fall from grace for Nissan and the entire automotive industry'. One former official from the Ministry of International Trade and Industry called the Renault-Nissan alliance a 'national disgrace'.

The consequences of takeover by major multinational companies have been profound. None has been more significant for the transformation in Japanese corporate culture than Renault's purchase of a controlling share of Nissan. It is highly symbolic because it signifies a fundamental change in the way the Japanese automotive industry is organized. No sector has been more important for Japan's industrial rise than the automotive industry. It was this industry that pioneered the methods of industrial organization that were later to be replicated by large parts of US and European industries.

In November 1999, Carlos Ghosn, appointed by Renault to be CEO of Nissan, announced a drastic transformation of the loss-making company. The plan shocked Japan. The vertical *keiretsu* system resulted in the core firms investing heavily in a wide network of supplier companies. For example, Nissan invested in no less than 1394 suppliers. Ghosn bluntly identified Nissan's vertically integrated *keiretsu* system as a fundamental problem for Nissan: 'About 60 per cent of your costs are in the suppliers. You have to have suppliers who are innovative. You want suppliers offering products to many customers so there is a flow of information about best standards. That won't happen with *keiretsu* companies'. Ghosn announced that he intends Nissan to cut its supplier base from over almost 1400 to just 600.

While the larger suppliers are thought likely to survive, many fear the restructuring will wipe out second- and third-tier parts suppliers that depend heavily on Nissan. Only a handful of Nissan's suppliers are considered by industry experts to be internationally competitive. The close personal relationships between Nissan and its surrounding companies will be decimated at a stroke. The Japanese supplier industry is likely to consolidate rapidly as weaker suppliers are weeded out in the new competitive environment. Giant multinational supplier firms are quickly increasing their role in Japan, including Robert Bosch, Valeo and Visteon. Japanese car makers already purchased $13.3bn-worth of components from US suppliers in the first half of 1999. In order to survive and compete, Japanese car makers will have to establish networks of global suppliers from the world's leading component companies.

Nissan will close five factories. When Ghosn made the announcement to an invited audience, 'a shocked gasp went through the crowd'. Global employment in Nissan is to be cut by 21 000, or 14 per cent, of which 16 500 will be in Japan. Nissan's dealer network will be consolidated with 20 per cent of its dealer affiliates 'eliminated' and 10 per cent of sales outlets closed. Nissan will adopt a performance-oriented compensation scheme, including stock options and bonuses based on achievement.

Taken together, these changes amount to a radical change in the *keiretsu* system. The process of dismantling the *keiretsu* system is far from complete. However, many analysts feel that Japan is in the midst of a fundamental change in its corporate culture, moving from a corporate world based on relationships to one based on the free allocation of capital: 'We are at an historic moment. We are seeing the unravelling of 50 years of history.'

## Continental Europe

The impact of the rise to dominance of the Anglo-Saxon business system is not confined to Asia. The global business revolution has also forced dramatic changes on the business system of Continental Europe, from the Nordic countries through to France, Germany and Italy. By the late 1990s, most large European industrial corporations had wholeheartedly embraced the philosophy of globalization, shareholder value, cost-cutting and focus on core business.

### National champions

A wave of mergers swept through northwestern Europe to produce large-scale 'national champions' to compete in the epoch of globalization and big business. The process was typically supported by national governments, often with a significant shareholding interest, including a golden share, in the companies concerned. Within Italy, France, Germany, Spain and the Nordic countries, a succession of large-scale banking mergers took place within national boundaries in the late 1990s. The extent of cross-boundary mergers was still quite limited. Few observers doubted that the process would rapidly spill over onto the international stage. In other sectors many highly significant intranational mergers took place. These included, in Italy, Telecom Italia's merger with Olivetti rather than Deutsche Telekom, after an epic battle in which the Italian government played an important role. In France, the French government strongly supported the merger of Aerospatiale with Matra, to follow the 'French-French' path to building large firms. In the retail sector, Carrefour's merger with Promodes also helped build a 'French' national champion that could compete in the global arena. In oil and petrochemicals, PetroFina's merger with Elf Aquitaine also produced an essentially 'French-French' solution to the search for global scale. In Switzerland, the merger of Ciba-Geigy with Sandoz, to form Novartis, was widely applauded as a 'Swiss-Swiss' solution to the achievement of global scale. In Britain, the merge of BAe with GEC Marconi's defence arm was similarly applauded by many observers. In Germany, the merger of Krupps and Thyssen produced a 'national champion'.

## European champions

However, a purely national solution to the problem of scale in the midst of the global big business revolution appeared increasingly anachronistic and inadequate as a solution to the fundamental problem of achieving the scale necessary for survival on the global level playing field. Alongside the group of national champions being created in the late 1990s, a far more powerful trend was for cross-boundary mergers, which often involved the very firms that had been initially created as national champions. The pan-European merger movement has caused intense debate within Europe on the significance of nationally-based companies in the epoch of globalization and international consolidation. For example, Sweden was arguably the most successful of the smaller European countries in being home to a group of globally powerful corporations. The roll call of great international companies included Volvo and Saab in motor vehicles, Astra in pharmaceuticals, Electrolux in household appliances, and Ericsson in telecommunications. In 1998–99 a revolutionary change took place among Sweden's mighty corporations: 'Sweden's big companies are no longer quite big enough to survive alone in a globalizing economy. In the past year, the search for economies of scale has prompted a wave of mergers and acquisitions that has caused near panic among those Swedes that cherish national industrial champions ... The Swedish media has reacted with barely concealed hysteria, bemoaning the exodus of national talent' (*Financial Times*).

In industry after industry former 'national champions' are merging across borders to create what are increasingly being referred to as 'European champions'. The epoch has seen the gradual emergence of companies that are truly 'European' champions. In power equipment in the late 1980s, Asea and Brown Boveri merged to form the Swiss/Swedish engineering giant ABB, and GEC (UK) and Alcatel (France) merged their power equipment interests to form Alstom. Even these mighty companies were too small to compete with the global leaders. In 1999, ABB and Alstom merged their power equipment divisions to form a 'European champion' in the power equipment sector (ABB Alstom). In steel, Usinor (France) merged with Cockerill Sambrell (Belgium), and British Steel merged with Hoogovens (The Netherlands), to each create a global giant company. That was followed in 2001 by the announcement of the merger of Usinor with Arbed (Belgium) and Aceralia (Spain). In pharmaceuticals, Sweden's 'national champion' Astra merged with Britain's Zeneca, which had been demerged from ICI. Hoechst, the once-mighty engine of the German chemical industry, abandoned chemicals and transformed itself into a focused life sciences company. France's national champion, Rhône-Poulenc followed a similar path. In 1998 they went even further and announced a merger, to form a huge new 'life science' company able to compete on the global market-place. The new entity, to be named Aventis, was to be a true 'European champion'. In aerospace, the Aerospatiale-Matra merger proved to be only the prelude to an even more significant merger, namely that with Dasa, to create a global giant company, called the European Aircraft, Defence and Space Company (EADS).

## Transatlantic giants

A powerful group of focused European businesses have aggressively transformed themselves through transatlantic mergers. In the early 1990s, Daimler-Benz dismantled its high-technology empire to focus on automobiles. The huge reorganization was capped by the merger with Chrysler US in 1998. In the German financial sector the transformation of Deutsche Bank has also been highly symbolic of the business revolution in that country. Deutsche Bank, the biggest in Europe, has shifted from a mainly domestic orientation, with extensive holdings in the German industrial sector, to a bank that is mainly concerned to compete internationally. In 1990, Deutsche Bank still sat on the supervisory boards of more than 400 companies across the spectrum of German industry. In 1998 it acquired Bankers Trust, the eighth largest US bank, to transform itself into a fundamentally different kind of bank, with its main focus upon international competition. BP underwent a huge transformation in the 1990s. The transformation culminated in the merger with US oil and petrochemical giants, Amoco and Arco. Vodafone exemplified the rapid rise to global power of firms in the fast-consolidating and liberalized telecoms sector. Its acquisition of US-based Air Touch turned Vodafone into one of a small group of giant mobile phone companies.

The most dramatic mergers may yet take place in the aerospace sector. The possibility of BaeSystems and EADS each merging with one of the US giant companies is being widely discussed. Nothing would more powerfully signal the end of the epoch of 'national champions' in 'strategic industries'. No industry is more 'strategic' than aerospace.

These developments were radically transforming the traditional ideas of national industrial policy. What point was there in a national government supporting a particular indigenous 'national champion' if at some point in the future it might be merged with a firm based in another European country, or even in the US or Japan?

## Reinvigorated big business in Japan and Europe?

Successful reform of business systems outside the US and UK could lead to a renewed surge of oligopolistic competition between firms based in different regions in the Triad group of countries (Japan, Western Europe and North America). However, the task of reforming business structures in already highly developed economies is very different from framing industrial policy in a still poor country, such as Indonesia, the Philippines or mainland China. There is a real possibility of business renewal in Japan and Continental Europe, producing a new group of large globally competitive firms that provide a strong challenge to those of the US. The possibility of mounting such a challenge would be much greater if the US stockmarket crashed. However, the tasks facing policymakers in developing countries are quite different, facing a vastly weaker domestic business structure. Whatever their respective weaknesses, Western Europe does possess 169 of the world's *Fortune 500* corporations and 86 of the world's top 300 companies by R&D spend, while Japan possesses 107 of the *Fortune 500* companies and 83 of the world's top 300 companies by R&D spend.

## 2.6  **The third technological revolution**

We have seen already that the revolution in information technology is changing massively the structure of business and daily life. Information technology will be at the heart of the global economy for at least the first few decades of the new millennium. The revolution is changing everything from the nature of the firm to the nature of warfare.

It is widely argued that the explosive rise of knowledge-intensive industries provides great possibilities for developing countries to compete effectively. It is thought that developing countries can 'leapfrog' the advanced economies in these industries. Because these are relatively new industries, many people believe that barriers to entry are low, and that small and medium firms based in developing countries are at a competitive advantage. This possibility is thought to be reinforced by the sheer force of numbers, since large developing countries such as China and India contain a vast pool of educated people who are able to use their human capital to rapidly develop knowledge-intensive industries. It is thought that the 'knowledge-intensive' industries require relatively small amounts of capital compared to the 'old technology' industries, reinforcing the possibility for small and medium firms to compete effectively. Such views have been fuelled by the rapid growth of 'information technology' exports from certain developing countries.

The reality is quite different. Despite its relative youth, this sector has witnessed in the space of just a few years a process of explosive concentration that has already established very large barriers to entry in many sectors. It is firms based in the advanced economies, especially the US, that are far ahead in the high-speed race to develop the new technologies that are pushing the industry forward. It is in this sector more than in any other that the dominant firms based in the advanced economies are desperate to extend their market to the vast developing economies such as Brazil, China and India. There are, undoubtedly, massive gains for developing countries through access to the new technologies. However, through the operation of the free market, the gains may be highly unevenly distributed between businesses and people in high and low income countries. Developing countries need to pay careful attention to the ways in which their own businesses can become a part of the high value-added 'brain' activities within this revolution.

## Central position of the knowledge-intensive industries at the beginning of the twenty-first century

The 'First Technological Revolution' refers to the revolution which began around 8000 BC and 'ground to a halt around 2500 BC'. It involved the development of all the basic agricultural techniques, textiles, pottery and metallurgical industries, the techniques of fermentation, the sailing ship, the wheeled cart, and complex organization of labour, enabling the building of large structures such as the pyramids. The 'Second Technological Revolution' refers to the revolution that began in the Middle Ages in China, Europe and elsewhere, accelerated during the British Industrial Revolution, and continued through different phases right up to the late twentieth century. Samuel Lilley argues that the whole period since the Middle Ages can be seen as having an essential continuity: 'This Second Technological Revolution has been going on continuously from the early Middle Ages up to our time'. This revolution was based around increasingly intensive use of exhaustible resources. The first great natural resources casualty of this revolution was the widespread destruction of forests across China and Europe. The technical progress of the Industrial Revolution itself has been linked closely with the exhaustion of the most fundamental natural resource of the late Middle Ages, wood: 'With increasing population density in Europe, shortage of wood became a major problem. Many of the technological innovations in the eighteenth century were the result of attempts to develop substitutes for wood as fuel and as raw material for industry and construction.' (Esther Boserup).

The 'Third Technological Revolution' refers to the revolution in which technology moves from exhaustible to renewable resources. The beginnings of this revolution could already be seen at the end of the twentieth century in the revolution in information technology and biotechnology. In the long run, it is likely that this revolution will lead to a fundamental change in the pattern of production, employment, consumption and settlement. China has great potential to contribute to this revolution, due to its long tradition of investigation in the biological sciences. Information technology and the 'life sciences' constituted the core of the early stages of this revolution as the world entered the third millennium. The central importance of these two sectors in this revolution is indicated by the fact that in 1998, the 'life sciences' and information technology companies together accounted for 134 of the top 300 companies in the world by R&D expenditure and their combined R&D expenditure totalled $140bn (55 per cent) out of a total of $254bn.

The centrality of information to the global economy in the twenty-first century is reflected vividly in the dramatic rise in importance of the cluster of industries concerned with producing information technology hardware, software, services and content. This sector is the key to the world's socioeconomic 'superstructure' of communications and culture. It is the 'brain' of the global firm in the Third Technological Revolution.

No less than 48 out of the top 100 global companies by market capitalization in 1998 were primarily in this sector or were rapidly moving into this sector as their main business (for example, Siemens, Hutchison Whampoa, Sony, Mannesman). To some degree the massive rise in the stockmarket value of firms in these sectors constituted the classic speculative herd instinct at work. By the end of 2000, the massive inflation in stockmarket valuations of companies in these sectors had subsided substantially. However, to a considerable degree, the rise in their valuations reflected a real underlying phenomenon, namely, the central role that these technologies are playing, and will increasingly play, in the Third Technological Revolution. By the end of April 2000, the combined stock market capitalization of the top ten IT firms stood at over $2800bn, more than the combined GNP of the entire group of upper middle income countries in the late 1990s. On the 'global level playing field' they were able to acquire other firms across the world at a fantastic rate, comprehensively consolidating their position as the first-movers in the construction of the 'brain' of the global business revolution of the early part of the twenty-first century. Even after the decline in values, by the end of the year 2000, they still enjoyed hugely increased valuations compared with a few years previously.

The underlying 'real' nature of the stockmarket phenomenon can be seen vividly in the large rise in the R&D expenditures in these sectors and their sharply increasing role in the overall pattern of R&D expenditure. By 1998, the world's top 300 companies by R&D expenditure included over eighty from the information technology sectors (see Table 2.2, page 124). The IT hardware is much the most important single sector in the total R&D spending of advanced capitalist firms. In 1998, the IT hardware sector accounted for 57 of the top 300 firms by R&D spending, much the most important single sector. Total R&D spending by these firms amounted to over $70bn, two-thirds greater than that of the automotive sector, the next largest in total R&D spending and more than double that of the pharmaceutical sector, the third largest (Table 2.2). IT accounted for 28 per cent of the total R&D spend of the top 300 global firms. The sales revenue of these 57 leading IT hardware firms amounted to $790bn, greater even than Brazil's GNP of $773bn (1997). If IT software and services are included, then the IT sector as a whole accounted for over 34 per cent of total outlays on R&D by the top 300 firms.

Information technology figured centrally among the Morgan Stanley Dean Witter (MSDW) list of the world's top 250 firms in terms of their 'competitive edge', or their ability to 'sustain global advantage over well-financed competitors'. No less than 86 of MSDW's top 250 'competitive edge' firms were in the information technology sectors (Table 2.3).

**Table 2.3** *MSDW 'competitive edge' companies in information technology sectors, 2000*

| Sector | Number of firms | of which US-based |
| --- | --- | --- |
| Media | 14 | 8 |
| Computer and business services | 4 | 2 |
| Data networking and telecoms services | 7 | 4 |
| Enterprise hardware and software | 18 | 13 |
| Internet, PC hardware, software, consumer electronics | 12 | 7 |
| Semi-conductors, components | 18 | 10 |
| Telecoms services | 13 | 6 |
| Totals | 86 | 50 |

## Comprehensive dominance of the Third Technological Revolution by oligopolistic firms from the advanced economies

Firms from the advanced economies are even more dominant in the knowledge-intensive industries than in the traditional industries of the Second Industrial Revolution. The key to progress in this sector, more than almost any other sector, is investment in R&D and in high quality human resources. The sector is advancing technically at such high speed that only those firms which undertake high and effective R&D investment can compete. Despite the relative youth of these sectors, already an explosive process of business concentration has taken place, making it hard for latecomer firms to catch up with the industry leaders. Across all knowledge-intensive industries a small group of companies, all based in the developed countries, controls an ever-growing share of the global market. In 1998, the top ten companies accounted for 32 per cent of the $23bn global market in commercial seeds, 35 per cent of the $297bn global market in pharmaceuticals, 60 per cent of the $17bn market in veterinary medicines, 70 per cent of the $334bn global market in computers, 85 per cent of the $31bn global market in pesticides and 86 per cent of the $262bn global market in tele-communications.

In 1998, the top five companies in the information technology sector, IBM, Lucent Technologies, Compaq, Hitachi and Nortel, spent an average of $4.8bn on R&D, amounting to around 10 per cent of their total revenue. Their combined revenues totalled $240bn, greater than the GNP of Austria ($226bn in 1997). IBM alone has a revenue of $82bn, greater than the GNP of Chile or Egypt ($73bn and $71bn respectively). In 1998 it spent $5.4bn on R&D, greater than the GNP of 46 developing countries included in the main tables of the World Bank's annual report.

Despite the fact that the industry was relatively new, by the year 2000 consolidation had already progressed very rapidly, telescoping into a few years processes that took decades in other sectors. Firms based in developing countries already face serious barriers to entry and growth. A small group of immensely powerful firms has emerged rapidly to dominate key parts of the new information technology sector. These firms have rapidly established powerful barriers to entry at the level of systems integration. Across the industry, from IT hardware, through software, services, telecoms, and even in the Internet, a relatively small group of firms has established a powerful competitive advantage. This derives from their huge expenditure on R&D and large outlays on global brand-building. In the same way as in many other sectors, the leading hardware and software firms, and, increasingly, the content providers, have developed a high capability as 'system integrators'. They have constructed an 'external firm' consisting of a large number of small enterprises that undertake a variety of subcontracting functions for the core systems integrators, including R&D, components manufacturing and local program-making.

At the end of the 1990s, a series of colossal mergers transformed these sectors. We have seen that in the *FT's Year 2000* ranking of the world's top companies by market capitalization, no less than 48 of the top 100 companies were in the information sector. The massive stock market valuations of information companies enabled them to merge with or take over rivals or complementary companies that enhanced their competitive position. The pace of consolidation was fantastic. The explosion of merger activity was taking place both horizontally and vertically. Processes of industry consolidation that took decades in other sectors are happening at incredible speed in this sector. By the late 1990s, in sector after sector within the IT industry, from IT hardware through to media, a relatively small number of giant players had emerged to dominate their respective sector. Moreover, a powerful process of vertical mergers had begun to take place leading to the emergence of super-giant IT companies that spanned more than one area of expertise.

The information technology revolution was comprehensively dominated by firms based in the advanced economies. Only one of the top 48 information technology companies in the *FT Top 100* firms by market capitalization is from a developing country. Not one of the IT firms in the top 300 companies by R&D spending in 1998 was from a developing country. Within the MSDW 'competitive edge' firms in the information technology sector, only seven out of 86 firms were from developing countries, and the number falls to just two if Taiwan and Korea are counted as 'developed' countries.

Among the oligopolistic firms based in the advanced economies, those based in the US are especially powerful. Of the 48 information technology firms in the top 100 firms by market capitalization no less than 26 are from North America, compared with just 11 from Europe and eight from Japan. Among the top 55 information technology firms in the world's leading firms by R&D expenditure, 36 are US firms, and, even more strikingly, among the top 17 IT software firms by R&D expenditure, 16 are US firms, an extraordinary degree of dominance of the 'brain' of the information technology revolution. Within the MSDW list of the world's leading companies in terms of 'competitive edge', no less than 50 out of the 86 information technology firms are from the US (see Table 2.3, page 137).

## Global level playing field

A key part of the WTO negotiations during the Uruguay Round of the GATT and a central issue for the future development of international economic relations under the WTO is the rules governing competition in knowledge-intensive industries. The issue has been a central one in the intense negotiations between China and the US about China's entry to the WTO (see below). The world's leading firms based in the advanced capitalist economies have invested vast sums in R&D and systems capability. They are deeply interested in the degree to which they are allowed to compete openly in the fast growing markets of developing countries, of which China is by far the most important. Two landmark agreements have already signalled the future path that firms based in the advanced economies wish to use as the basis for the rules governing future international development of this crucial sector of the world economy. These are the TRIPS (Trade-Related Intellectual Property Rights) Agreement and the World Telecoms Agreement.

## TRIPS

We have seen that a small number of companies now accounts for a large segment of global market share in the knowledge-intensive industries. Moreover, we have also seen that they account for a very large share of the top 500 corporations ranked by market capitalization and for a very large share of the top 300 companies by R&D expenditure. Global demand for the products of these sectors is growing at high speed. Their dominant position in the world stockmarkets is closely related to the high value-added and high profit margins that can be achieved in these sectors. In the *Fortune Global 500* ranking of corporations by returns on revenues, eight of the top ten companies are in the information technology, telecommunications and life sciences, and 26 of the top 50 are in these sectors. Among 31 sectors, the average return on revenues in 1998 was 2.8 per cent. The leading sector was pharmaceuticals with 18.4 per cent and the second highest was telecommunications with 10.2 per cent. Their high profitability is closely related to their dominant position in R&D. Firms from high income countries account for 97 per cent of all patents held world-wide. In 1995 more than one-half of total global royalty and licensing fees were paid to the United States, mostly from Japan, the UK, France, Germany and the Netherlands. In 1993 firms from just ten countries accounted for 84 per cent of global research and development, controlled 95 per cent of the US patents of the past two decades and captured more than 90 per cent of cross-border royalties and licensing fees.

In their catch-up process, Japan and first-tier Asian NICs greatly reduced the costs of catch-up by the weak enforcement of intellectual property rights in the region before the mid-1980s. However, in 1994, the WTO drew up the far-reaching TRIPS agreement. This drastically increased the level of international control over technology transfer. The TRIPS agreement affects such diverse areas as computer programming, circuit design, pharmaceuticals and transgenic crops. Although each country administers intellectual property right law at the national level, the TRIPS agreement imposes minimum standards on patents, copyright, trademarks and trade secrets. These standards are derived from the legislation of the advanced economies, applying the form and level of protection of the industrialized world to all WTO members. This is far tighter than the existing legislation in most developing countries. Most developing countries in the WTO have been given until 2000 to adjust their laws, and even the least developed have been given only until 2005.

The TRIPS agreement is vital for the world's leading corporations in the knowledge-intensive industries, if they are going to be able to extend the benefits from their technology to markets in developing countries as these expand. They provide an all-embracing legal form of protection for firms based in the advanced economies, that enables their technology to constitute a real barrier to competition from firms based in developing countries, and ensures that they are able to earn the same profit margins from sales in developing countries as they earn from sales in the advanced economies.

## World Telecoms Agreement

In February 1997, the WTO concluded the World Telecoms Agreement. Colossal US government effort over three years of 'gruelling negotiations' was put into brokering this incredibly complex deal. The historic agreement was signed by almost 70 countries, the notable exceptions being China and Russia. It will usher in 'an era of free competition, low prices and cross-border investment'. Poor developing countries will benefit from access to capital with which to construct telecommunications facilities, which will in turn have powerful positive externalities in stimulating market development.

However, the gains for a small number of competitive telecommunications companies in the advanced economies are likely to be vast. The telecommunications market is huge. World-wide industry revenue grew from around $440bn in 1990, to around $830bn in 1996, and rose to over $1200bn in 2000. Neil Macmillan, who chaired the negotiations, commented bluntly: 'The developed countries will get the lion's share of this market'. Charlene Barshevsky, then US trade representative designate, commented: '[This Agreement is] a triumph for the American way ... US companies are the most competitive telecommunications providers in the world; they are in the position to compete and win under this agreement'. The British and US negotiators 'know that their countries have the advantage of the experience of more than a decade of competition – and are best placed to benefit from liberalization.' (*Financial Times*).

The principal beneficiaries from the telecoms agreement will be the giant carriers, such as AT&T, SBC Communications, Deutsche Telecom, Worldcom, and France Telecom. The vast bulk of the equipment that they use will be produced by the leading companies based in the advanced economies, such as Cisco, Lucent, IBM, Hitachi, Nortel, Ericsson and Nokia. The global fibre optic links will be owned by companies like Global Crossing. The main software systems and IT services will be provided by the leading companies based in the advanced economies, such as Microsoft, Oracle, and SAP. The main Internet companies through which people communicate with the world-wide web will be based in the advanced economies, including companies such as Yahoo!, Lycos, Goo (NTT) and Excite. The main entertainment companies that provide services through the telecoms service companies will be firms that are based in the advanced economies, such as Walt Disney, AOL-Time Warner, Vivendi-Seagram, News Corp., and Viacom. There are large opportunities for small and medium-sized firms in the IT sector based in developing countries to participate in the lower reaches of the global IT value chain, as outsourced providers of a wide array of products in software, hardware and services. However, there are very few, if any, firms based in developing countries that have the capability to compete directly with the global giants in this fast-consolidating industry. The 'global playing field' is hugely uneven.

## Competitive capability of firms based in developing countries

In most areas of IT, companies based in developing countries have hardly begun to develop. In the telecoms service sector the enormous size and business capabilities of the leading service providers, mean that local players would find it extremely difficult to compete on the global level playing field. Most of the remaining powerful telecoms companies in developing countries are almost all either state-owned or strongly protected by government legislation.

In the hardware segment, there are few significant challengers in the developing world to the established giants of the advanced economies. Even the remaining 'national champions' in the telecoms services sector in developing countries have no alternative but to mainly buy equipment from the advanced economies.

The main area of potential competition is in software. India is much the most successful developing country in the software industry. India contains six of the world's top software development centres according to a study by the Carnegie Mellon Software Engineering Institute. India's exports of software products and services has grown at high speed, reaching $3.9bn in 1999, out of a total turnover of $5bn. The industry's 'phenomenal' growth has had a far-reaching impact, 'causing upheavals within corporate India, as owners of big corporations are finding that their tiny software subsidiaries are worth more than the parent company'. Companies such as British Airways, Swissair, and GE Capital are setting up online back office, data processing and support centres in India. Two Indian information technology companies have listed on Nasdaq, 'a sign of the industry's growing confidence and international ambitions'. By mid-1999 India had over 860 software exporting companies. Its share of the world market for software was reported to have reached 20 per cent. Two hundred and three companies out of the Fortune 500 have 'outsourced their software needs from Indian companies'. India's high quality elite-based scientific education has been an important factor in developing Indian firms' competitive advantage in this sector. A further crucial advantage compared to other developing countries has been the wide education among the Indian intellectual elite in the English language.

However, there are still major shortcomings even in the Indian software industry compared to the global giants. The industry has very limited domestic demand compared with exports. Domestic demand amounts to only one-fifth of the total value of sales in the sector, reflecting the low income level and low level of access to information technology within India.

India's software exports are strongly oriented towards the lower value-added segments of the industry, in which competitive advantage relies principally on cost. A major boost to the industry was undertaking contract work for the 'year 2000' problem for the multinationals. The industry relies very heavily on performing low-value added outsourcing work for US-based multinationals. The industry's total annual sales amount to around $6bn, including hardware, software and services. This is in total only a small fraction of the revenues of a single one of the world's largest IT companies, such as IBM. The average revenue of the top 25 companies in the sector in 1999 was predicted to be only around $150m. The revenues of a single large US information company are typically many times greater than the revenue of the entire Indian software industry.

The market capitalization of the largest Indian software company, Wipro, in mid-1999 was $6.5bn, compared to hundreds of billions of dollars for the industry's leading players. It is predicted that Indian software companies will start acquiring US-based companies. If Indian government regulations are relaxed, then it is predicted that Indian-based companies may be able to spend $3bn in acquiring US-based companies in 1999–2000. Such sums are trivial besides the vast transactions that are reshaping the entire industry. The total stock market capitalization of the Indian IT sector peaked at $104bn in February 2000, still only a fraction of a single one of the world's leading firms in the sector. Moreover, by mid-year, the value had tumbled by more than one-half, leaving the entire sector with a market capitalization only around one-tenth of that of Cisco Systems. The level of investment in R&D is minuscule compared to the world's leading companies in the sector.

The domestic Indian market is incredibly backward compared to that of the advanced economies, greatly weakening the domestic companies' international competitiveness. A crucial part of the success of the US-based firms is the virtuous circle of high incomes, high expenditure on information technology, massive outlays on R&D, huge institutional investment boosting stock market valuations, which provides the basis for further concentration and stock market appreciation. By contrast, developing countries have much more limited domestic purchasing power and a correspondingly more weakly-developed domestic information technology infrastructure (Table 2.4). The level of penetration of personal computers, mobile phones and the Internet is still trivial compared to the level of the advanced economies. Moreover, the international language of telecommunications is English and a large fraction of the population of developing countries cannot speak English. In India, for example, 'only one in twenty people has a sufficient command of the English language to participate in the new software meritocracy'.

**Table 2.4** *Selected indicators of information and telecommunications development by country level*

| Country/ country group | Per 1000 people (1997): | | | | Internet hosts ** /10,000 people (Jan 1999) |
|---|---|---|---|---|---|
| | TV sets | Telephone main lines | Mobile telephones | Personal computers | |
| LIEs * | 59 | 16 | 1 | negl. | 0.2 |
| MIEs | 272 | 136 | 24 | 32 | 2.4 |
| HIEs | 664 | 552 | 188 | 270 | 470.0 |
| India | 69 | 19 | 1 | 2.1 | 0.13 |
| China | 270 | 56 | 10 | 6.0 | 0.14 |
| US | 847 | 644 | 206 | 407 | 1131.5 |

*Source:* World Bank, 2000: pp. 226–7.
*Notes:* * Excluding India and China. ** Internet hosts are computers directly connected to the world-wide network. Many computer users can access the Internet through a single host. LIEs: Low Income Countries.
MIEs: Middle Income Countries. HIEs: High Income Countries.

A major problem for the Indian software industry is that a large number of its software engineers have emigration as their main goal, with the US as the main chosen destination. US software firms have already recruited a large number of software engineers from India, often going direct to Indian campuses to lure the best software engineers directly upon graduation. Indians are reported to account for around 38 per cent of the total number of software engineers in the US's Silicon Valley, as well as heading some of the most successful new ventures. The US government has lifted its visa quota for software engineers from 115 000 to nearly 200 000. Nearly half the current quota is taken up with Indians. The extent to which India's 'software migrants' will return to India is an open question. There are large gains for India in terms of remittances, ideas and incentives to acquire education, but the degree to which it is rational for the migrants to return to India to establish local software firms is uncertain.

There are obvious benefits for developing countries in opening their countries up to the world's most advanced information technology. Investments in this sector bring large positive externalities. This sector holds the key to economic progress in the early part of the next millennium. However, the brutal reality is that in all parts of the industry, from software through to services, the leading firms of the advanced capitalist economies have established an unassailable lead, in which there are already massive barriers to entry for firms based in developing countries. There are innumerable opportunities for firms based in developing countries to enter the lower end of the value chain. However, there are very limited possibilities for them to compete and win on the global level playing field against the leading systems integrators.

## 2.7 The global revolution in financial services[2]

### Deregulation

Since the breakdown of the Bretton Wood System in the 1970s, financial liberalization has affected most countries. In the US in the mid-1970s, many countries started to gradually reduce controls over interest rates and exchange rates, and international differences in tax rates were reduced. Deregulation accelerated in the early 1980s after a surplus of capital was generated by the world oil crises of 1973–75 and 1979–82. Most Western governments further deregulated their national financial markets. In the US, government-imposed ceilings on interest rates were formally ended in 1983. The first major regulatory breaches of the rules governing the ability of financial institutions to start diversifying into other fields took place with the Garn-St Germain Depository Institutions Act of 1982 and the Supreme Court decision on regional banking in 1985. In the UK, the 'Big Bang' took place in 1986. Fixed commission rates on bond and share transactions were abolished. The old distinction between jobbers and brokers was discarded and the Stock Exchange was opened up to full ownership of member firms by outside institutions. These changes constituted a revolution in terms of the structure, speed and manner of conducting financial activity. They greatly increased the international mobility of capital and the volatility of international financial markets.

In the 1990s, financial deregulation went even deeper. In Europe and the US, some of the main restrictions on cross-border and cross-sector financial

---

[2] This section is based on the research of Wu Qing, Judge Institute of Management Studies, University of Cambridge.

transactions were removed completely. In the early 1990s, deregulation, such as the Single Market Programme in the European Union in 1992, and the Riegle-Neal Act of 1994 in the US, made cross border M&A much easier and cheaper. Cross-border financial activities, including syndicated credits, securities issuance and M&A advice, increased sharply from 1992 to 1998. In the late 1990s, there began a 'campaign of financial modernization'. It included the Big Bang of 1998 in Japan and the Gramm-Leach-Bliley Act of 1999 in the US. These far-reaching changes further liberalized the financial industry. They stimulated a new wave of M & A, based not only on cross-border transactions, but increasingly involving cross-sector transactions.

## Impact on the industry

The deregulation, together with explosive changes in information technology, are comprehensively transforming the financial services industry towards globalization, innovation, integration, concentration and Americanization.

### Globalization and cross-border transactions

The globalization of the world economy since the 1980s has created a huge demand for worldwide financial services, and great opportunities for financial institutions to expand globally. Simultaneously, deregulation, particularly the erosion of the geographical entry restrictions, made it possible for aggressive financial institutions to become global.

Internal expansion by financial institutions has not stopped. However, in the 1990s mergers and acquisitions became the major growth path for financial services firms. From 1989 to 1999, there were estimated to be 3844 mergers and acquisitions in the global banking industry, with the acquiring institutions purchasing more than $3 trillion in assets. Merger and acquisition among big banks increased drastically. By 1998, there were 406 banking institutions involved in mergers, with total assets of $1087bn. As a result of M&A among financial firms, the number of banks in most countries fell significantly. In the late 1990s there was not only a large jump in US domestic M & A, but also a substantial increase in cross-border M & A. In the mid-1990s, M&A activity among European financial institutions took off.

During this wave of M & A, most of the big financial institutions, such as Citigroup, Bank of America, Chase Manhattan, Deutsche Bank, UBS, HSBC, Merrill Lynch, Morgan Stanley, ING, and AXA, achieved or enhanced their leading position in the global market. Today, about one-third of the world's largest financial institutions operate in three or more continents. Citigroup now has branches, subsidiaries or offices in more than 100 countries, while Merrill Lynch has 900 offices in 43 countries with a leading market position on all the key exchanges. AXA employs 140 000 people in 60 countries. HSBC is a striking example of growth from a leading regional position to a leading global position, through relentless cross-border acquisitions in the late 1980s and early 1990s. By the late 1990s, HSBC had become one of the biggest and most profitable banks in the world.

The banks that have led the globalization process argue that cross-border expansion is necessary in order to achieve economies of scale and scope in the global competition. A major motive is to be able to provide a global service to customers who themselves increasingly operate on a global basis, as well as acquiring new customers in other countries through international M & A. A further driving force is the need to distribute the risk internationally. The dramatic developments in IT radically increased the possibility of operating a bank on a global scale.

## Consolidation: cross-sector transactions

Traditionally, in most countries the financial services industry was divided into commercial banking, investment/merchant banking and insurance. The main exception was Germany, which operated with a universal banking system.

With the development of information technology and financial innovations (see below), especially securitization, the boundaries between different sectors (that is, commercial banking, investment banking and insurance) have become blurred. Traditional banks face severe challenges from other parts of the industry. Deregulation lowers the barriers to entry. Competition within the industry has greatly intensified. Some traditional commercial banks and insurance companies found themselves disadvantaged in the competition. In order to reduce costs and improve efficiency, many financial sector firms expanded their business not only in terms of size, but also in terms of scope, by moving into other sectors than that in which they had formerly operated. In the 1980s and early 1990s, some big European financial institutions diversified their business through M & A. These included Deutsche Bank's acquisition of the UK Merchant bank, Morgan Grenfell; Credit Suisse's acquisition of the US investment bank First Boston; UBS's acquisition of the UK merchant bank Warburg; and ING's take over of the UK merchant bank Barings.

In the US, the most important mergers and acquisitions took place either within the commercial banking sector (such as, BankAmerica/Nations Bank/ Barnet Bank, Chase Manhattan Bank/Chemical Bank, Bank One/First Chicago NBD) or within investment banking (such as, Morgan Stanley/Dean Witter Discover, Salomon Brothers/Smith Barney). This was mainly because of the Glass-Steagall Act of 1933, which separated the banking, securities and insurance business. However, with the extensions of deregulation in the 1990s, the scope of major mergers widened. Some big banks tried to convert themselves into multi-business banks. For example, Citibank had dreamed of being a financial conglomerate since the 1980s. J P Morgan made great efforts to convert itself into an investment bank after 1989, when it became the first American commercial bank that was permitted to become involved in investment banking. After the late-1980s, the US Federal Reserve gradually loosened the limitation on the proportion of revenues from securities. This move stimulated further legislative reform.

In 1998, the merger of Citicorp, a leading commercial bank, with Travelers, a big insurer with an investment banking subsidiary, Salomon Smith Barney, directly led to the enactment of the Financial Modernization Act of 1999 (Gramm-Leach-Bliley Act)(GLB), which abolished the Glass-Steagall Act. This law created a new type of financial firm called a financial holding company (FHC), which is allowed to undertake almost any business in financial services. The Chairman and CEO of Chase Manhattan, Mr Harrison, commented: '[A]s we get into convergence, where traditional companies partner with dot.com companies, we'll be able to do a lot of things that will stretch the definition of banking and commerce'. Under the new law a FHC could own up to 100 per cent of any of type of company (Financial Services Modernization Act of 1999), so theoretically, a FHC could own any business 'from toothpaste to technology'. It is not expected that FHCs in the US will become multi-industry conglomerates, or quickly convert into a US version of German universal banks. However, it is more likely that highly integrated businesses (retail and wholesale financial services, banking and securities and insurance service) will be adopted by most of the FHCs.

The GLB Act has had a revolutionary impact on the global financial services industry. It meant that the biggest financial industry in the world, that of the US, with the world's largest financial institutions, was liberalized completely. One of the most important results will be to permit even greater concentration in the global industry, dominated by US financial services firms (see below).

## Innovation – financial engineering and e-banking

One of the important consequences of deregulation is financial innovation, which is spurred on by intensifying global competition. The financial engineers, a new generation of bankers, are creating a wide range of new financial products. The development of technology, particularly IT, has greatly accelerated the pace of innovation and made the innovations easier to deliver. From the 1980s, transactions in derivatives and securitized financial assets became key products in the financial market. There were no longer clear dividing lines between raising money for corporations through commercial paper or through share issues, through long-term or through short-term instruments, depending on regulation and requirement. Instead debt has become interchangeable, 'an endless stream flowing one currency to another and from one type of paper to another without difficulty'. Since 1987, when Citibank and J P Morgan experienced debt problems in emerging markets, securitization has grown rapidly in the global market. In addition, the separation between securitized mortgage loans, unit-based insurance contracts, and mutual funds has declined. Customers' demands for diversified financial assets have grown. In order to maintain their competitive advantage, big firms, especially the investment banks, needed to invest huge amounts in R&D. It is now commonplace for Wall Street investment banks to hire a large number of PhDs in Mathematics and Physics.

In the late1990s, with the high-speed development of IT, e-commerce became a new way of doing business in every sector. Unsurprisingly, the financial services industry, especially the big firms, adopted it quickly and applied it widely to their business. Internet and Intranet information systems enable financial services firms to reduce dramatically their management and operation costs. IT has been a powerful instrument for developing competitive advantage and expanding market share for the successful financial services firms. It is the easiest, most cost-effective and rapid way to become a global operator. Some firms were even 'born global'. For instance, E*Trade created a global brand and established operations in 33 countries in only three years, while Merrill Lynch needed more than thirty years to achieve a similar coverage.

The development of IT along with lowered entry barriers makes it easier for non-financial industries, particularly retailers, to diversify their business and penetrate the financial services market. For example, Marks & Spencer, Tesco and Virgin have expanded into banking and financial services. The use of 'cash-back' from supermarkets has increased sharply. This has pushed the big financial institutions such as J P Morgan, Citigroup, and Chase Manhattan, to strengthen their online services. Recently, the top three investment banks, Merrill Lynch, Goldman Sachs and Morgan Stanley Dean Witter, launched an electronic bond trading system called BondBook. HSBC and Merrill Lynch invested $1bn to set up an online joint venture, which is expected to share their customer network and technology. Moreover, the innovation is not only in the instruments used, but also in the organization itself. In the last few years, many leading financial firms (such as Goldman Sachs and J P Morgan) have radically changed their institutional structure to adapt to the changing world.

## Intensified competition

Deregulation, especially the collapse of the 'wall' separating different financial sectors, removed the barriers preventing banks from entering the securities and insurance industry, as well as those preventing securities and insurance firms from entering other sectors. This means that there will be more players in each of the formerly separated sectors. Therefore, there will be more intense competition across the whole financial services industry. In the US, only four months after the enactment of the Gramm-Leach-Bliley Act, 117 banks, large and small, applied for and received permission from the Federal Reserve to convert from bank holding companies to FHCs. They included both giant banks like Citigroup, Chase Manhattan, J P Morgan, Bank of America and HSBC, as well as small ones like Acadiania BancShares of Lafayette, LA, and Yarville National Bancorp of Hamilton, NJ. Under the umbrella of FHCs there are increasing numbers of financial institutions diversifying their business and supplying a wider range of financial services. It can be expected that there will be more and more financial firms moving from their current category of 'commercial and savings', or 'insurance', or 'securities' to the 'diversified financials' category in the *Fortune 500*.

New entrants are not only coming from other branches of the financial services industry, but also from other industries. As we saw above, with the development of IT and the deregulation of financial services, the distribution channels for financial services are changing dramatically, and the barriers to entry are falling. Rival firms from the non-financial sectors, which are diversifying their businesses or converting themselves into firms focused on financial services, are penetrating the financial services market through their existing customers' network, or using their competitive advantage in brand, capital or technology. The most striking example is GE Capital, but other firms, such as GMAC, Tesco Finance and Virgin Money, have also followed this path. In addition, there are entirely new categories of financial services firms, such as the new e-bancasurances and online-financials.

Not only are there more threats from new entrants, but also the competition between existing rivals has intensified. Citigroup's successful business model has stimulated more and more cross-border and cross-sector M & A. This has created intense competition between the giant financial conglomerates.

## Concentration and Americanization

In today's intensive competition in global financial markets the mantra has become 'bigger is better'. World-wide deregulation, especially the repeal of the Glass-Steagall Act, made it possible for the American financial giants, such as Citigroup and Chase Manhattan, to expand their cross-sector business. It also made it possible for those banks that have struggled for years to convert themselves into different types of firms, to achieve their objective. The consequence is increased industry concentration. Each of the world's top five banks in *The Banker*'s list of the world's top 1000 banks has been involved in mergers or acquisitions during the past three years. As well as innumerable take-overs of small financial institutions by large ones, most of the top banks have been involved in mergers with other giant banks. Since the late 1980s, the number of banks has fallen substantially. In the US, the number declined from 36 000 in 1980 to 22 000 in 1997. The share of the top ten banks in total assets rose from 14 per cent to 28 per cent in the same period. In Western Europe, the number of banks fell from 9500 in 1980 to 7000 in 1997. However, up until now, the biggest mergers and acquisitions have tended to be between financial institutions within the US or within a given European country, rather than cross-border and cross-sector transactions.

With the accelerated deregulation and intensified competition in recent years, especially the enactment of the GLB Act, a new wave of M&A has started world-wide. In the first three quarters of the year 2000 alone, there was a wave of giant deals, most of which were cross-border and cross-sector transactions, undertaken by the global giants to enhance their global leadership position. These included

Citigroup's takeover of Schroders, the biggest UK merchant bank, and Chase Manhattan's acquisition of Flemings, one of the last remaining UK merchant banks, and its subsequent merger with J P Morgan.

Today, as in many other sectors, a large proportion of the leading firms in financial services are US-based. There is a striking development of global business between leading financial services providers and globalizing large corporations. The top five M&A advisers are all US-based firms. Four of the top five international equity bookrunners are US-based firms. Three out of the top five firms in the issuance of international convertibles are US-based firms. Three out of the top five syndicated credit arrangers are US-based firms. In terms of market share, from North to South America, from Europe to Asia, the ranks of the top firms in equities, bonds, syndicated loans and M & A, are dominated by US firms, such as Citigroup, Bank of America and Chase Manhattan in commercial banking, and Goldman Sachs, Merrill Lynch and Morgan Stanley Dean Witter in investment banking. Even in Japan, the top bookrunner in equities and the top advisers in M&A are US-based firms such as Citigroup and Merrill Lynch. MSDW estimate that in the global equity business, the top three firms (namely, MSDW itself, Goldman Sachs and Merrill Lynch), which are all US-based, accounted for 36 per cent of the global equity market business in 1999, up from 31 per cent in 1998. They estimate that these same firms accounted for between 34 per cent and 42 per cent of global M&A deals, compared with an estimated 27–40 per cent in 1998.

In the global *Fortune 500* for the year 2000, 15 of the world's 50 most profitable (total profits) firms are in the financial services sectors. Of these, nine are US-based firms. Four out of the top five are US-based firms. Four of the top ten most profitable commercial banks are US-based. Out of the top five of securities firms by sales revenue, four are US-based. All of the six 'diversified financials' in the *Fortune 500* are US-based companies. Within the financial services industry, only the global insurance market is not dominated by US institutions. However, analysts predict that even this will change in the near future: 'Most of the major insurance companies are European. But the big US investment banking houses will inevitably play a leading role in this sector. They have the financial muscle and the market strength.' The trend towards concentration is likely to intensify with the deregulation of US financial services. It can be expected that, in the future, a handful of US-based financial conglomerates will dominate the financial services industry and supply a full-range of products as 'one-stop-supermarkets' operating across the world.

There are hardly any developing country firms among the world's leading financial services companies: out of a total of 128 financial services firms in the *Fortune 500*, just six firms are from low and middle income countries.

# Conclusion

## The challenge for developing countries

All previously successful latecomer, industrializing countries have used some form of industrial policy to construct large, indigenous globally competitive firms. A major policy challenge for developing countries in the early twenty-first century is to determine the degree to which it is either feasible or desirable to construct indigenously owned large businesses, which can challenge the global giants. Does the global business revolution signal the end of state-led industrial policy to construct large, globally competitive firms in latecomer industrializing countries?

## Big business is central to capitalism

The normal path of development in advanced capitalist countries has been for oligopolistic business organizations to stand at the centre of the system. Since the 1980s there has occurred a big business revolution. Under the impact of increasingly important institutional investment, large capitalist firms have drastically reorganized. They have downsized employment, focused on core business, selling off large segments of assets not relevant to the core activities. They have globalized at high speed, even though large parts of the developing world have received relatively small amounts of FDI. The degree of concentration by sector has risen dramatically. If we examine subcategories of markets, then it becomes clear that the level of global concentration has risen drastically. This fast-moving change cannot be captured by aggregate data for individual capitalist countries, which is still the most frequently-used basis of analysis. To understand the true extent of influence of big business within advanced capitalism it is necessary to examine global market share by sub-categories of markets. It is necessary also to analyse the relationship of the core globalizing systems integrator with the myriad of firms that are dependent upon it. The role played by big business is even more important in the late 1990s than it was at any previous point in the history of capitalism. Large capitalist firms now stand at the centre of a vast network of outsourced businesses which are highly dependent on the core big businesses for their survival. Using new information technology, the core firm links together on a global scale a large number of related businesses.

## Benefits of globalization and big business

The growth of global big businesses alongside the liberalization of global markets has brought many gains. Big businesses have played a central role in generating high rates of investment and in stimulating technical progress. Oligopolistic competition can be at least as intense as small-scale competition. In the big business revolution the degree of oligopoly has reached a new level of development. The top three or four firms in sector after sector are now engaged in competition of unprecedented intensity. They are investing ever-increasing amounts in R&D, information technology and marketing systems, and procuring ever-increasing quantities of inputs across the global economy. In sector after sector, from aircraft to coal, ferocious price-cutting battles are taking place.

Firms are fighting intensely to improve product quality and lower system costs across the whole value chain, including the entire supplier network. Globalizing large firms have brought to bear intense pressure which cascades down through the first-tier suppliers to the myriads of small and medium-sized local businesses that supply the first-tier components and subsystems suppliers. This process drives forward technical progress, product quality, and management skills across the value chain.

Across the world, individual consumers and firms can have access to lower cost and higher quality products, benefiting from the massive investment in research and development by the global oligopolists and their increasingly powerful first-tier suppliers. They can benefit from the ferocious price competition and pressure to provide high quality products that has developed among the leading companies across the world. Not only the price of primary products has fallen, but also the price of a wide range of complex manufactured goods and services. The real price of IT goods and services is falling at high speed, producing enormous developmental benefits. The simultaneous increase in the degree of oligopoly and the intensity of competition among large corporations and their associated 'external firms', provides a deep challenge to traditional neoclassical views of competition, which identify the degree of 'competition' with the number of firms in a given market. The epoch has provided a strong support to the non-orthodox, 'Schumpeterian' view of the nature of competition.

## The gap between big business in the advanced economies and the businesses of developing countries is wide

It is much harder today for a developing country to establish a business that can compete with the most advanced capitalist big businesses than was the case only a decade ago. In the new world of global oligopoly, for a long period ahead, the 'distribution of the gains' will be highly uneven in terms of the geographical distribution of the core big businesses and powerful second-tier suppliers, that are emerging as the global winners. The world of the 'global level playing field' is likely to result in competitive success for those large firms that already have a head-start in the global competition. It has been suggested that the 'global level playing field' is the 'protectionism of the strong'. There is little doubt in the minds of the proponents of the 'global level playing field' that the main beneficiaries among large firms will be those that are based in the advanced economies. Their shareholders are mainly from the advanced economies. As late as the early 1990s the senior managers of the world's leading multinationals still came preponderantly from the company's home country.

We have seen that in terms of several different criteria, relatively large firms from developing countries are almost insignificant within the global business revolution. Large firms from developing countries, which contain 84 per cent of the world's population, account for just 5 per cent of *Fortune 500* companies, 3 per cent of *FT 500* companies, and a mere 1 per cent of the world's top 300 firms by R&D expenditure. Morgan Stanley Dean Witter's selection of the 250 leading 'competitive edge' companies includes just 19 from the whole of the 'emerging market' world. Of these there are six from the whole of Latin America, three of which are from Brazil and three from Mexico. The whole of the rest of Latin America has none. The entire area of South Asia has just one representative. The whole of non-Japan Asia has twelve. There are none from Eastern Europe, the former Soviet Union, the Middle East or Africa. In other words, in the view of the most brutally honest evaluation available, almost the entire developing world has virtually no representation in the list of the world's most competitive companies. The race for position in the coming struggle for the world's global market-place begins with the runners in a most uneven position.

## Sustainability of the gap

Barriers to entry are different in different sectors (Table 2.5, overleaf). It is hardest to catch up in the most technically complex sectors, and the ones with high R&D outlays. Such sectors in which catch-up is especially difficult include pharmaceutical products, defence and aerospace, and complex machinery, such as power equipment, construction machinery, large machine tools, farm machinery, and aircraft engines. Morgan Stanley estimate that it will take well over 20 years for an 'aggressive and well-financed competitor' to establish a similar business to the global leaders in the aerospace and defence industry. They believe that it would take an average of 14 years in the heavy machinery sector and 11 years in the pharmaceutical and medical products sector (Table 2.5). However, there are also wide gaps in firm capability in the consumer goods sector. The barriers to entry are especially high in the branded consumer goods sector. The catch-up possibility is especially small as the firms that establish first-mover advantage in the early phase of the epoch of high globalization will be in an extraordinarily strong position to shape the habits of consumption for a long period ahead.

The possibilities appear to be easiest in 'mid-tech' industries rather than low-tech consumer goods or high-tech products. Industries such as steel, chemicals, automobiles and transport equipment appear to offer the best opportunities for emerging big businesses in developing countries to catch up. However, within these sectors, there are big differences in catch-up possibilities. Within these broad categories, the sub-sectors in which it is easiest to catch up are basic 'commoditized' goods in which the basic technology is relatively old and non-

**Table 2.5** *Average sustainability of MSDW stocks by sector\**

| Sector | Average Sustainability (years) |
|---|---|
| Aerospace/defence | 23 |
| Capital goods (complex machinery) | 16 |
| Consumer goods | 14 |
| Paper and packaging | 12 |
| Pharmaceutical and medical products | 11 |
| Building products | 10 |
| Banking and financial services | 9 |
| Electric utilities | 9 |
| Energy | 9 |
| Mining | 8 |
| Media | 8 |
| Chemicals | 7 |
| Lodging | 7 |
| Retail | 7 |
| Transportation | 7 |
| Automotive | 6 |
| Insurance | 6 |
| Steel | 6 |
| Tyres | 5 |
| Technology | 4 |
| Apparel and footwear | 2 |
| Telecommunications | 2 |

Note: * Defined as the number of years it would take an aggressive and well-financed competitor to establish a similar business.

proprietary, and in which margins and value-added are low. These include products such as coal, low grade tyres, construction steel, chlorine, ethylene, aspirin, vitamin C and nylon.

Even within these sectors in which there is on average a lower degree of sustainability for leading edge companies, there are still huge and growing barriers to entry in the high value-added, high R&D subsectors. Moreover, even within 'traditional', commoditized sectors there are massive technical advances in process technology, which greatly reduce costs of production and increase profitability. High value-added creates high margin pricing, which creates high profitability, which allows further enhancement of competitive advantage through investment in R&D. There are few hiding places from the intensifying global competition.

# The challenge for China

Part 1 of this book analysed the internal reasons for the special difficulties China faced in trying to build globally competitive giant corporations. At least as important as the special difficulties that confronted China on the internal front in implementing a successful industrial policy, is the fact that China's attempt to build large globally competitive firms coincided with the most revolutionary epoch in world business history, possibly even including the Industrial Revolution. The period during which Japan and South Korea were putting into place their industrial policy to build global giant corporations was a much less dynamic one in terms of the structure of the large capitalist firm.

China faces many of these external challenges in a common position with other developing countries. However, China is in many senses a giant. It has huge potentialities for market growth and a vast sea of high quality and fast-growing human resources. It has an intense sense of its special place in world history. It has high administrative capabilities. It is locked in an uneasy relationship with the global superpower, the USA. Nor is its relationship with Russia, Europe, Japan or its other East Asian neighbours without tensions. These forces provide both a spur and a potentiality to construct a successful industrial policy to build large indigenous firms that can compete with firms based in the high-income countries. They provide greater possibilities for China to construct a successful industrial policy to build large, competitive firms, than exist for other developing countries. However, the global business revolution has greatly increased the difficulties that confront Chinese policymakers in this endeavour.

**Part 3**

# China enters the WTO: Choices and prospects

# 3.1 Can large Chinese firms compete on the global level playing field?

Part 1 analysed the ways in which China's policymakers and managers attempted to build large firms in different sectors that could challenge the global giants. In the course of two decades of struggle, China's large enterprises changed greatly, achieving evolutionary institutional change in key aspects of their business organization. As was seen in Part 2, during the same period the world's leading businesses underwent high-speed, revolutionary transformation. As the epoch of the 'global level playing field' moves ever closer, it becomes increasingly necessary for China's reforming large enterprises to benchmark themselves realistically against the global giants. The historic agreement of 15 November 1999 between the US and China on China's accession to the WTO (see below, Section 3.3), makes that task even more urgent. This section examines the capability of China's national champions to compete on the 'global level playing field'. It uses firm-level case studies, as well as secondary sources to examine the IT and financial services sectors.

## Case studies

### AVIC

In the 1970s there was a wide gap between China's aerospace industry and the world's leading companies. In this, the most 'strategic' of all Chinese industries, the gap between China's 'national champion' and the global giant companies widened drastically after the 1970s. The extent of the gap is revealed by the fact that the entire Chinese civilian aircraft fleet, with the exception of a small number of domestically-made turbo-props, is imported. We have seen that China's attempt to build its own indigenous large aircraft, the Y-10, failed. China's attempt to partner the multinationals in co-designing and building a large civilian aircraft failed. China's subcontracting for the multinational giants remains at a pathetically low level compared to the levels of Japan or South Korea. Even China's domestically-made turbo-prop is only able to make a few export sales through the use of key imported components, reflecting the backward nature of its aero-engine and avionics industry.

At least as revealing about the failure to make any inroads on the world's leading corporations is the fact that the Chinese military has been forced to rely more and more heavily on imports, and domestic production under licence, of fighter planes from the former USSR. China's airforce is now almost wholly dependent for advanced fighters on Su27's bought from the former USSR. The number either already produced or on order is now well over one hundred, and rising. Moreover, China is negotiating for the purchase of the more advanced Su30's.

The core aerospace business of AVIC in the late 1990s was extremely small, on a par with a medium-sized company such as Vickers (UK) (see Table 3.1). Moreover, AVIC contained the full range of aerospace activities, including engines and avionics as well as airframes. AVIC had been turned into a vast empire of diversified businesses, totally unable to compete directly with the global giants in aerospace.

**Table 3.1** *Selected indicators of the competitive capability of leading Chinese companies compared with the global giants: aerospace*

| Company | Revenues $bn | Post-tax profits $m | Employees 000s | R&D $m |
|---------|---------|---------|---------|---------|
| Boeing ('97) | 45.8 | (178) | 239 | 1 830 |
| Lockheed-Martin ('97) | 28.1 | 1 300 | 190 | 1 060 |
| BAe ('97) | 10.4 | 681 | 44 | 690 |
| AVIC ('97) | 3.1 | 72 | 560 | n.a. |
| of which: aerospace | 0.7 | – | – | – |

*Notes:* Figures in brackets indicate losses.

The 'reform' of AVIC in 1999 had no immediately comprehensible rationale. Instead of one huge diversified conglomerate with no capability to compete with the multinationals, it created two smaller, and even less internationally competitive conglomerates. The reform could have separated the vast civilian from the aerospace business, but was unable to do so because this would have provoked much opposition from the subordinate entities who stood to lose many of their most profitable activities. It could have separated engines and avionics from the airframe business, but it didn't. It could have separated military from civilian aerospace, but it didn't. If its main goal was to develop its capability as a subcontractor, then it might have allowed strong subordinate production units such as Shanghai, Xian, Chengdu and Shenyang to become independent companies that could compete for business with the multinationals, but it didn't. In sum, the prospects for AVIC on the 'global level playing field' are bleak.

Alongside the halting, uncertain reforms in the Chinese aerospace industry has gone the most revolutionary epoch in the history of the world industry. By the late 1990s, after an unprecedented epoch of merger and acquisition, only a tiny handful of firms dominated the entire world industry in both civilian and military aircraft. The epoch of 'national champions' had vanished, to be replaced by 'regional' European champions contesting with the massive US-based firms for the entire world's market. Moreover, the process was becoming even more internationalized by the beginning of a possible revolutionary period of massive transatlantic mergers and acquisitions, affecting even the formerly sacrosanct military aerospace sector. These changes placed China's halting efforts at industrial policy at an even greater disadvantage on the global stage.

## Sanjiu

Sanjiu is exceptionally interesting from the point of view of industrial policy and catch-up, since it had the backing of the People's Liberation Army. This provided many difficulties, but also conferred some important advantages, such as access to markets and the possibility of taking over other enterprises in the sector. As we saw in Part 1, Sanjiu developed a modern business system. It had the benefit of a powerful leadership team, and an outstanding chief executive officer. Sanjiu developed a powerful brand within China. It had an acute sense of the importance of product quality and modern production systems. It had a professional management team, with a deep awareness of global trends in the pharmaceutical industry. It was one of the earliest Chinese firms to develop a modern marketing system.

**Table 3.2** *Selected indicators of the competitive capability of leading Chinese companies compared with the global giants: pharmaceuticals*

| Company | Revenues $bn | Post-tax profits $m | Employees 000s | R&D $m |
|---|---|---|---|---|
| Merck ('97) | 26.03 | 8069 | 54 | 2760 |
| Novartis ('97) | 22.34 | 6166 | 87 | 2620 |
| Glaxo Wellcome ('97) | 17.38 | 4626 | 53 | 1870 |
| Sanjiu ('97) | 0.67 | 98* | 13 | n.a. |

Notes: * Pre-tax profits.

However, despite these great strengths and business achievements, Sanjiu faces enormous difficulties in competing directly with the multinationals (Table 3.2). China's pharmaceuticals industry is highly fragmented. China has thousands of small-scale pharmaceuticals producers that will face large difficulties on the 'global level playing field'. The largest companies, such as Sanjiu, occupy only a tiny fraction of the national market. Even the leading pharmaceuticals companies, such as Sanjiu, are tiny in scale compared to the global giants. R&D is crucial to the ability to compete with the multinational giants. Even one of China's leading pharmaceutical companies, such as Sanjiu, has a minuscule research capability compared to the global leaders. Zhao Xinxian, Sanjiu's chief executive officer recognizes explicitly that his company cannot contemplate direct competition. The alternative routes within the pharmaceuticals sector are, firstly, to produce out-of-patent, low value-added medicines, with low rates of profit. Several of China's large state-owned enterprises have a considerable capability in this area. However, none of the global giant companies relies on this as their path to growth and high levels of profits.

The second path, and that which Sanjiu has chosen, is to focus on traditional Chinese medicines. Sanjiu's chosen route is especially interesting as it raises the issue of the degree to which Chinese firms can compete with multinationals without engaging in head-to-head competition. This path enabled Sanjiu to expand rapidly within China, rising quickly to become one of the top two pharmaceutical companies. However, Sanjiu has found it very difficult to grow in China apart from its main product, *Sanjiu Weitai*, the stomach medicine. On international markets, despite passing FDA health requirements, it is also difficult for it to grow. The overseas Chinese community is not sufficiently large to provide for sustained long-term growth. The extent of prescription of Chinese traditional medicines by Western doctors is still small. Moreover, lacking a patent, there is nothing to stop Western pharmaceutical companies producing the product and using their massive marketing structure to sell traditional Chinese medicines such as *Sanjiu Weitai*, should they find the market growing more rapidly than at present. Sanjiu would find it hard, or simply impossible, to compete with such a strategy. Moreover, there is nothing to prevent the multinationals from adopting such a strategy even within China, if they find the profit margin sufficiently attractive.

Therefore, Sanjiu's ability to compete directly with the multinationals is virtually non-existent. It is a highly successful business that has performed extremely well in an important niche market, which is essentially a branch of the food industry, rather than a true medicine. However, this market, which avoids head-on competition with the multinational giants, has only limited long-term growth prospects. This fact explains to a large degree, Sanjiu's decision to enter a wide range of businesses other than pharmaceuticals. At one point it had a huge range of largely unrelated businesses, including even automobile production. Even after it had drastically reduced its portfolio's range, it still had a wide range of activities. However, these were mainly in food and drink, which are reasonably closely related to Chinese medicine. Sanjiu's main assets are now its high quality managerial personnel, its brand and its marketing skills. These may enable the company to remain a reasonably successful food and drinks conglomerate for a certain period of time. However, they do not suggest that Sanjiu will be able to compete with the multinational giants of the pharmaceuticals industry.

The 1990s saw a revolutionary change in the structure of the world pharmaceuticals industry. The global industry was massively transformed by a sequence of massive demergers and mergers. One after the other, the global giants of the chemical industry demerged their pharmaceuticals businesses. These de-mergers were followed by a sequence of massive mergers. By the late 1990s, a small group of colossal pharmaceuticals companies had emerged. They undertook vast, multi-billion dollar R&D expenditure. They developed a huge capability to develop drugs through clinical trials and to market their portfolio of drugs through common channels. They also had the financial resources to withstand the failure of a large fraction of their R&D investment and the possible disasters of drugs that turned out to be harmful to health. This global revolution made the emerging Chinese 'national champions' appear even more puny by comparison.

## Harbin Power Equipment Company

Compared with other developing countries, at the end of the 1970s China had a relatively advanced power equipment industry. It had three major producing units, with around three-quarters of the domestic market between them. At the beginning of the reform process, these three entities were under a single central source of control. Under reform, these enterprises faced two decades of rapidly-growing demand, providing an important opportunity for catch-up. Under these circumstances, As we saw in Part 1, China's leading producers made considerable progress. Harbin benefited greatly from a government-orchestrated programme of technical transfer, enabling it to upgrade its technical capability significantly. If the three main Chinese producers had been able to effect a merger, they would have formed a genuinely large-scale entity, even in global terms. Not only was the Chinese market one of the world's fastest-growing, but also a large fraction of Chinese equipment is coal-fired, so that China might have built a considerable capability in this branch of the industry.

However, China's industrial policy did not follow this path. Instead, China's policies of enhancing the independence of subordinate operational units allowed the separate units to become increasingly autonomous. Both Dongfang and Shanghai Electrical Corporation were allowed to establish joint ventures with multinational companies. In addition, many smaller Sino-foreign joint ventures were established. Harbin's own attempt to form a northeast China electrical company, uniting its interests with those of neighbouring electrical equipment producers, foundered on the separate ambitions of the electrical equipment manufacturers. Moreover, even Harbin itself did not constitute a unified modern corporation. It consists of three main separate entities each with their own strong traditions. The 'unification' to form Harbin Power Equipment Company (HPEC), was principally as a vehicle to gain permission for flotation. Even after flotation, the separate entities within HPEC had a wide range of independent functions.

The increasing independence of the power generation sector from the equipment manufacturing sector sharply changed the competitive landscape of the Chinese power equipment industry from the mid-1990s onwards. Foreign-invested and wholly domestically owned power stations increasingly looked towards buying equipment with the lowest costs, including costs of maintenance, with high levels of reliability and the ability to meet increasingly stringent anti-pollution regulations, irrespective of the manufacturer's country of origin. In this sector, China still has significant industrial policy measures, including restrictions on foreign investment in both the equipment and the generation sector, limitations on the size of power plant imported, and domestic content requirements. Even with these measures, the share of multinational companies rose sharply, through import and domestic production in joint ventures, reaching around one-half of annual installed capacity by the mid-1990s. Most significantly, the entire first tranche of equipment for the massive Three Gorges Project, comprising fourteen 700mW units, was awarded to multinational companies.

Despite considerable progress, China's domestic industry in the late 1990s remained institutionally fragmented. The fragmentation even penetrated its leading companies, including the separate sub-units within HPEC. Alongside the growth of autonomy at the enterprise level within China, the global 'battle of the giants' was reaching the endgame, with just three giant companies dominating the world market, emerging from the former diverse structure of separate national champions within each advanced country. As a separate entity, it would be extremely hard for HPEC, China's leading firm, to compete even within China with the global giants on the 'global level playing field' (Table 3.3). China's main producers other than HPEC were increasingly being integrated into the global sub-contracting system of the multinational giant companies. Despite the considerable progress, even in this sector, the institutional and technical gap between China's leading companies and the world leaders has enlarged during the reform period.

**Table 3.3** *Selected indicators of the competitive capability of leading Chinese companies compared with the global giants: power equipment (1998)*

| Company | Revenues $bn | Post-tax profits $m | Employees 000s | R&D $m |
|---|---|---|---|---|
| Siemens | 57.95 | 990 | 376 | 5 008 |
| : power division | 6.39 | n.a. | n.a. | n.a. |
| ABB | 29.72 | 2 500 | 208 | 2 368 |
| General Electric | 100.47 | 9 296 | 293 | 1 930 |
| : power division | 8.47 | 1 306 | n.a. | n.a. |
| Harbin (HPEC) | 0.35 | 9 | 27 | 3 |

## CNPC and Sinopec

The Chinese oil, gas and petrochemical industry is highly important in a global perspective. China has risen to become a major player in the world energy economy. During the reform years the Chinese industry has made major technical advances. Large institutional changes have taken place. The industry has absorbed modern management techniques. It has raised substantial capital on international markets through a series of H-share flotations. A sequence of huge, multi-billion dollar international joint ventures has been agreed. With greatly increased autonomy for the production units, real competition began to develop among domestic producers.

However, despite these significant advances, important difficulties remained unresolved for the industry, rendering it at a considerable disadvantage in the global competition. As we have seen, at the institutional level, the industry remained torn by the tension between trying to create powerful, autonomous enterprises and trying to construct globally competitive, giant multi-plant firms. For most of the reform period, production units gained increasing autonomy. However, the central authorities within the industry placed limits on the degree of autonomy. Powerful subordinate enterprises, such as Daqing and Shanghai Petrochemical Company, were not allowed to undertake large-scale mergers with other domestic enterprises, lest they challenge the authority of the ministry and/or holding company. Belatedly, in the late 1990s, the central government undertook a comprehensive change of direction. They attempted complete reorganization of the industry, integrating the upstream and downstream components of the sector, with the aim of greatly enhancing the authority of the central bodies so as to create two truly integrated, globally competitive firms. This is a huge task, since the embedded vested interests at the level of the production enterprises are large. It will require a major struggle to truly centralize control within the sector.

Apart from the institutional issue, major technical problems still exist for the industry. China's reserves have not proved as prolific nor as well-located as was once hoped. Offshore oil reserves have proved disappointingly small and are typically located at considerable depths. China's onshore oil reserves are mainly located in relatively distant areas in China's central Asian republics, notably Xinjiang. These are of uncertain amount and typically are at great depth. Both the costs of raising and transporting the products are high. In the downstream part of the industry, China's major companies have a proliferation of high-cost, small-scale refineries. They have only a relatively small share of petrochemical output from high value-added, high profit margin products. The downstream distribution system is backward compared to the global giants, lacking high value-added products, such as environmentally-friendly varieties of petrol, lacking modern logistics systems and without a high quality global brand. The Chinese industry is still highly protected through tight restrictions on foreign direct investment, with projects typically requiring many years of negotiation before obtaining approval, major restrictions on the openness of bidding for major oil and gas exploration and development projects, and through labyrinthine controls on the distribution system for oil and petrochemical products.

Alongside China's halting, uncertain reforms has gone a revolution in the world's oil and petrochemical industry. A handful of companies in the advanced economies now occupy the commanding heights of the industry (Table 3.4). They possess large, high quality reserves, distributed around the globe. They have integrated oil refineries and petrochemical plants. They have high levels of R&D, and a portfolio of globally leading, high value-added, products in the petrochemical and oil products sectors. They have a sophisticated logistics system and global brand names. China's partially reformed national champions, CNPC (PetroChina) and Sinopec are still far from the completion of a massive process of institutional restructuring. The weakness of the Chinese industry on the global level playing field was sharply revealed by the withdrawal of CNOOC's hoped-for $2.5bn IPO in October 1999. Although there were disadvantageous short-term factors, at least part of the reason for the failure of the offering was the investors' perception of the institutional weakness of China's oil and petrochemical companies in the global competition. In the year 2000, PetroChaina and Sinopec together raised $6.5bn from their IPOs, and in early

**Table 3.4  Selected indicators of the competitive capability of leading Chinese companies compared with the global giants: oil and petrochemicals**

| Company | Revenues $bn | Post-tax profits $m | Employees 000s | R&D $m |
|---|---|---|---|---|
| Exxon/Mobil ('97) * | 182.36 | 11 730 | 123 | 720 |
| Royal Dutch/Shell ('97) | 128.14 | 7 760 | 105 | 770 |
| BP Amoco ('97) | 123.30 | 8 540 | 123 | 390 |
| CNPC ('98) | 32.6 | 107** | 1 540 | n.a. |
| Sinopec ('98) | 34.0 | 194** | 1 190 | n.a. |

Notes: * Proforma. ** Pre-tax profits.

2001, CNOOC finally launched its IPO, raising $1.4bn. The total for the three IPOs, around $8bn, was only around one-half of the amount originally hoped for. Moreover, a crucial factor in the success of the flotations was the fact that around one-third of the floated shares were bought by the global giants, Exxon Mobil, Shell and BP Amoco.

## Yuchai

China entered the reform period with a highly fragmented automobile industry. The degree of fragmentation increased in the early years of reform as a large number of new domestic entrants entered the fast-growing industry, which was protected from international competition and had a high degree of local protection. We saw earlier that the government built its industrial policy around support for a small number of domestic producers, who were encouraged to compete with each other in the fast-growing domestic market. Three powerful production units within the old planned economy were selected to form the core of the reformed industry, namely Shanghai Auto, Yiqi (Number One Auto) and Erqi (Number Two Auto). Large-scale foreign direct investment in automotive assembly was closely guided to these plants. The auto components sector was even more fragmented than the auto assembly sector. In the late 1980s there were more than 1600 components makers, and more than 200 enterprises manufacturing internal combustion engines. In this sector also the government tried to support the growth of a small number of powerful enterprises that could compete with the global giant companies.

Yuchai began as one of the large number of state engine manufacturers. It grew at high speed, stimulated by the rapid growth in the market for medium-duty trucks. Its growth was due to a number of astute management decisions. These included the purchase of second-hand equipment from abroad, clever product choice and development, a keen sense of the importance of brand and advertising, including a deep understanding of the importance of product reliability and product guarantees, and early development of a sophisticated, national marketing system. Yuchai was a pioneer in all these developments and reaped the benefits

**Table 3.5  Selected indicators of the competitive capability of leading Chinese companies compared with the global giants: auto components**

| Company | Revenues $bn | Post-tax profits $m | Employees 000s | R&D $m |
|---|---|---|---|---|
| Bosch ('98) | 28.61 | 446 | n.a. | 2 020 |
| Denso ('98) | 13.76 | 461 | 57 | 1 350 |
| Caterpillar ('98) | 20.98 | 1 513 | 86 | 838 |
| Cummins Diesel Engine ('98) | 6.27 | (21) | 28 | 255 |
| Detroit Diesel ('98) | 2.16 | 30 | 7 | 98 |
| Yuchai ('98) | 0.14 | 15* | 9 | n.a. |

Notes: Figures in brackets indicate losses. * Pre-tax profits

of its first-mover advantage. Yuchai's ambition was to form a pillar of the development of the Chinese components industry. Its chief executive officer hoped to develop Yuchai into a Chinese version of the US companies Detroit Diesel or Cummins Diesel Engine, both large-scale global diesel engine makers (Table 3.5).

In order to accomplish this goal, Yuchai needed to be able to develop the engine business by taking over other powerful diesel engine makers, and securing a long-term market with the main truck makers, namely Yiqi and Erqi, which between them occupy 90 per cent of the Chinese medium duty truck market. The chief executive officer of Yuchai persistently lobbied the central government to support Yuchai as China's 'national champion' in the diesel engine sector, having already demonstrated its managerial and technical capabilities. However, as we have seen, Yuchai's main consumers, Yiqi and Erqi decided that they would prefer to retain their own engine making capability within the company, and internalize the profits from the diesel engine business. They were able to lobby the central government successfully to allow them to retain their independent capability in diesel engines. Indeed, Erqi had established a major joint venture with Cummins Diesel to develop its technical capability. By the late 1990s, despite having demonstrated immense entrepreneurial capability, Yuchai faced a bleak market prospect.

Despite rapid growth and institutional change, the Chinese automotive industry remained at a severe disadvantage compared to the global giants at the end of the 1990s (Table 3.6). In the auto assembly sector, even its leading producers remained small-scale compared to the global giants. For example, Shanghai Auto, in the late 1990s, the country's largest auto company, with around 60 per cent of the national market, produced only around 200 000 vehicles per year. This compared with over 5m vehicles for GM, almost 4m for Ford and 3.5m for Toyota. The company's domestic success was entirely due to its joint venture with VW. Shanghai Auto is closely integrated within the VW global system.

The global automotive assembly industry is in the process of high-speed concentration, with large-scale mergers, including the Daimler-Chrysler path-

**Table 3.6**  *Selected indicators of the competitive capability of leading Chinese
companies compared with the global giants: auto components*

| Company | Revenues $bn | Post-tax profits $m | Employees 000s | R&D $m |
|---|---|---|---|---|
| GM ('98) | 161.3 | 2960 | 600 | 7 800 |
| Ford ('98) | 171.2 | 23 160 | 364 | 7 500 |
| Daimler-Chrysler ('98) | 154.6 | 5660 | 300 | 5 800 |
| Yiqi ('98) | 4.4 | 21* | 156 | n.a. |
| Erqi ('98) | 2.6 | (5) | 134 | n.a. |
| Shanghai ('98) | 4.8 | 594* | 60 | n.a. |

*Notes:* Figures in brackets indicate losses. * Pre-tax profits.

breaking merger. In the auto components industry also, the late 1990s saw an explosion of mergers and concentration, as well as the demerger of the auto component giants Delphi (from GM in 1999) and Visteon (from Ford, in 2000). Alongside the continued explosive growth through merger and acquisition of the leading tyre companies (Bridgestone, Goodyear and Michelin) other specialist components makers are merging at high speed in order to meet the globalizing needs of the world's biggest motor vehicle assemblers. The world's leading auto components companies, such as Cummins Diesel Engine, have already entered China in force, incorporating local joint venture partners into their global system. The capability even of the most successful of China's independent first tier auto components makers, such as Yuchai, to compete on the global level playing field is very limited indeed. Had the central government supported Yuchai's bid to be the core national champion for China's diesel engine sector, then there might have been a serious possibility of challenging the global giant diesel engine companies. It decided otherwise.

## Shougang

China's steel industry boomed during the economic reforms. During this period, Shougang rapidly increased its output. As we saw in Part 1, it undertook a wide-ranging programme of modernization, technical upgrading, and diversification into activities that might support its further expansion. It developed a significant export capability in both steel and steel plant construction. Its computerization skills developed sufficiently for it to win an important competitive contract to design and install the control systems for a leading US steelmaker. Both Shougang's plans for expansion and its management style bore a close resemblance to those of South Korea's Posco steel company.

Despite these important advances in Shougang's institutional and technical capability, Shougang faced severe limitations on its capability to compete on the 'global level playing field' (Table 3.7). In the first place, although its output grew rapidly, a large part of the growth was in low value-added, low quality steel, such

**Table 3.7**  *Selected indicators of the competitive capability of leading Chinese companies compared with the global giants: steel*

| Company | Revenues $bn | Post-tax profits $m | Employees 000s | R&D $m |
|---|---|---|---|---|
| Nippon Steel ('98) | 21.59 | 90 | 28 ('95) | n.a. |
| Posco ('98) | 9.72 | 680 | 23 ('94) | n.a. |
| NKK ('98) | 14.15 | 849 | 18 ('95) | 190 |
| Usinor ('98) | 10.65 | 373 | 58 ('95) | 180 |
| Shougang ('98) | 2.16 | 25* | 218 ('97) | n.a. |
| Baogang ('98) | 3.12 | 265* | 35 ('97) | n.a. |

Notes:  * Pre-tax profits.

as construction steel. In the late 1990s, after two decades of rapid growth, high quality steel still accounted for only 15 per cent of its total output. Shougang's sales value in 1997 amounted to $2.2bn, compared with $11bn for British Steel, $12bn for Usinor and $25bn for Nippon Steel. All four of China's top producers together, namely Shougang, Angang, Baogang and Wugang, had a sales revenue of $9.0bn, still well below that of the main European and East Asian producers, reflecting, to a considerable degree, their high proportion of low quality, low value-added products. Shougang found it hard to extricate itself from a vicious circle. The fact that it principally produced low quality steel meant that it was mainly in competition with small-scale local producers contesting with them for local markets. The low value-added produced low profit margins, which in turn limited Shougang's capacity to modernize through investment in R&D and new products. In the late 1990s Shougang was anxious to develop joint ventures with leading Western companies in order to acquire technology in high quality steels, such as those for large-scale modern buildings.

We saw in Part 1 that Shougang's plans to double its capacity by building a completely new steel plant at Qilu in Shandong province were overturned by the central government after the retirement in 1995 of its chief executive officer, Zhou Guanwu. At a stroke, this bureaucratic decision rendered irrational a large part of Shougang's diversified expansion, since many of its acquisitions had been intended to support the construction of Qilu. Without Qilu, these served little purpose for Shougang. Using the modern Kaiser Steel Plant, which Shougang had bought cheaply in California, Shougang might well have been able to make a high level of profits in a new plant with much lower manning levels than at the main site. This might have formed the basis for a serious challenge to the multinational giant companies.

Alongside the blockage placed on Shougang's expansion, the global industry began to enter a period of large-scale institutional and technical change. In the US, a new form of large steel firm based around mini-mills began to develop, of which Nucor is the leading example. A truly global steel company, Ispat, based in London, with a collection of steel plants across the world, rapidly came to prominence. Within Europe a series of large-scale cross-border mergers transformed the industry. By the year 2000, a small group of 'European champions' had emerged in the industry, led by Arbed, Thyssen-Krupps, Usinor and Corus (the merger of British Steel and Hoogovens). Each of these firms had global reach, with plants across the world, and a high capability in specialist, high quality, high value-added steel. They were able to supply the global needs of large firms in such industries as packaging, automobiles, complex machinery, high quality construction, and white goods. The leading companies established close ties with their multinational customers in order to met their global needs for high quality steel.

Baogang (Shanghai) is the only large Chinese steel company that, by the late 1990s, had established a capability to compete on the 'global level playing field' with the world's fast-transforming steel companies. Its greenfield site, strongly supported by the local Shanghai government, without a large body of existing employees and with the benefit of a booming local market for high quality steels, had developed into a potentially competitive firm able to compete on the 'global level playing field'. In contrast, other leading steel firms in China remained heavily dominated by low quality products. As import controls were reduced in the 1990s, China's imports of steel rose substantially. These principally consisted of high quality products, reflecting the weakness of domestic firms in these areas. For example, in 1996, China still imported one-half of its consumption of car sheets, 70 per cent of its tin sheets, and 80 per cent of its cold rolled stainless steel sheets.

China's leading steel firms may well be able to compete at the low value-added end of the market. However, the steel market is becoming increasingly segmented. In the high value-added and high profit part of the industry, which is closely linked with the needs of globalizing large firms, only Baogang can feel some degree of confidence that it is able to directly compete with the emerging global giants of Europe and the established giants of Asia in Japan and Korea. Shougang, like other large traditional Chinese steel firms, will find it difficult to compete directly on the 'global level playing field' in high quality steel. Moreover, as China's international markets for steel are further liberalized, Shougang will face intensified competition from other countries' producers of low value-added steel, such as the former USSR.

## Shenhua

In the midst of a vast sea of coal producers, the Chinese government has supported the construction of a potentially globally competitive large coal company. As we have seen, the government used powerful measures of industrial policy to support the growth of a large modern 'high-quality coal company'. A primary objective is that this company can supply Chinese power stations with high quality coal that can reduce the environmental damage of burning coal to generate electricity. A subsidiary, but also important, goal is to create a firm that can compete with the global giant corporations in this sector, especially in supplying the fast-growing markets of northeast Asia, but also in supplying large modern coal-fired power stations on the Chinese coast. It has supported Shenhua's development through the grant of property rights to the vast coal reserves under the Ordos Plateau, as well as through the direction of large preferential loans. Following closely the model of the world's leading coal producers, Shenhua is building a dedicated railway line to ship coal 800 km from Shenhua to a dedicated port facility on the coast. Starting from scratch, Shenhua has very low manning levels compared to old-established state-owned mines, which gives it a large advantage compared to domestic competitors in relation to wage costs, welfare burden and ability to organize a highly qualified and highly motivated workforce.

Despite these positive aspects of Shenhua's development, it confronts many difficulties in battling with the global giant companies. Shenhua's property rights over the associated railway and port facilities are ambiguous. It is uncertain how secure will be Shenhua's long-term right to use the facilities exclusively. Nor is it clear how the long-term charge for using the facilities will be set. Shenhua operates in a fundamentally different environment from that of the multinational coal companies. The main source of domestic and international competition for the latter is other modern coal companies. However, Shenhua faces a fierce battle with other domestic producers as well as an increasing battle with the multinationals. Shenhua must compete with small-scale local producers that pay subsistence wages to workers in conditions that have not been seen for over 100 years in the advanced economies. The small producers are heavily supported by their local governments in their battle for survival with the large coal companies. Shenhua must compete also with heavily subsidized state-owned enterprises. Not only does Shenhua face severe domestic competition, it has also had to accept a major reorganization of its business structure, being forcibly merged by the central government with five large state-owned enterprises. This has drastically altered Shenhua's character. Three of the mines are in a terminal state of decline and heavily loss-making. Instead of being a company with 7000 employees, Shenhua overnight became a company with 80 000 employees.

Alongside the rise of the Chinese coal industry has gone a powerful reshaping of the coal industry in the outside world. The world coal industry is becoming rapidly segmented. A large part of the industry is still producing with traditional methods within developing countries. In Europe, the industry has rapidly declined, as power stations have shifted heavily to oil and gas. However, a powerful group of modern, high quality coal companies has emerged. They are supplying the modern coal-fired power stations in the US and East Asia. Increasingly, they are supplying the power stations of developing countries, as the power generation industry is privatized, and operators seek the lowest-cost source of high quality coal. The emerging global giants, such as RWE, Billiton, BHP and Rio Tinto, are able to compete successfully in these markets by benefiting from having large deposits of high quality, mainly open-cast mines, through the provision of coal that is washed and graded, through centrally purchasing large amounts of modern large-scale equipment, and through supplying coal reliably through a tightly integrated transport system. Shenhua's ability to compete with these companies is weakened greatly by the problems it faces in domestic competition and by the enforced merger with the five state-owned mines.

## Information technology

### China's competitive capability in the IT industry

Most analysts believe that, unlike the 'old technology', the IT sector offers a true 'global level playing field' in which 'everyone is starting at the ground floor' (Laurence Lau). The Internet is a 'democratic equalizer'. In this sector 'each firm pinches only a small piece of the action'. Competition is 'all very open', allowing start-up Chinese firms to compete and win. The IT sector offers China an opportunity to 'leapfrog the Second Technological Revolution', which dominated the twentieth century, and rapidly become a leader in the new technologies of the Third Technological Revolution in the early twenty-first century. This view presents deep problems. These problems are especially significant in view of the central role of information technology in the negotiations for China to join the WTO.

### Old versus new technologies

Throughout this book, I have emphasized that the boundaries of 'old' and 'new' technology are blurred. Every single sector of business activity from aerospace and electrical engineering, to coalmining and soft drinks, is being revolutionized by the new information technologies. This was forcefully symbolized by Jack Welch's response to a reporter at a meeting with journalists after he announced GE's takeover of Honeywell in October 2000. She enquired why he was buying an 'old technology' company rather than one in the information technology sector. He exploded, saying that she showed total ignorance of the real nature of technical progress in the modern world. GE was at the forefront of high technology as was the company it was proposing to take over, Honeywell.

### IT hardware

China's leading IT hardware firms developed rapidly in the late 1990s. However, the prospects for even the most successful of these were highly uncertain if China strictly applied the WTO Agreement.

By 1998, China's leading computer maker, Legend, had captured 11 per cent of the total domestic PC market, ahead of IBM (8 per cent), Hewlett-Packard (7 per cent) and Compaq (5 per cent). By the middle of 1999, its share of the domestic PC market was reported to have exceeded one-fifth. It had established itself as much the most powerful indigenous PC maker, with a serious domestic brand, with a high quality manufacturing and marketing capability. However, Legend remained heavily reliant on several forms of protection. For example, it gained the sole distribution rights to Toshiba notebooks, which occupied 27 per cent of the Chinese domestic notebook market in 1997. It had a wide network of customers among China's state enterprises, to which it was extremely hard for multinational firms to gain access. Finally, it was heavily protected through a 15 per cent import tariff and a 17 per cent value-added tax. Like China's other leading IT hardware companies, Legend remains a minnow in international terms (Table 3.8). Their sales revenue, profits and R&D are tiny. In direct competition with the world's leading systems integrators in this field, it is hard to imagine that they could be successful.

**Table 3.8** *China's leading IT hardware firms in international comparison, 1998*

| Company | Revenue ($bn) | Profits ($m) | R&D spending ($m) |
|---|---|---|---|
| Legend | 1.0 | (28) | 1* |
| TCL | 1.3 | (49) | – |
| Huawei | 0.7 | (156) | 120 |
| IBM | 78.4 | 10 200 | 5 100 |
| Hitachi | 71.8 | 2 000 | 4 400 |
| Hewlett-Packard | 45.3 | 4 200 | 3 200 |
| Lucent | 29.1 | 2 500 | 4 900 |

Notes: *Legend's reported R&D spending in 1998 totalled just 9.3m Hong Kong dollars. In 1998 Legend had 120 R&D engineers. Figures in brackets indicate pre-tax profits.

Even before the conclusion of the WTO agreement, China's leading telecoms equipment manufacturers faced severe competition from the global leaders. Huawei is China's leading maker of networking equipment. Its business grew rapidly in the late 1990s as the telecoms revolution took hold in China. Huawei developed a high quality manufacturing capability and brand reputation. By the late 1990s it had established a domestic market share of one-fifth in 'network switches'. However, its development was crucially related to government support, especially through restrictions on the import of networking equipment. At the end of the 1990s, despite rapid growth, Huawei still remained a small firm, with very limited R&D and tiny profits. Compared to the global giants in the field, such as Cisco or Lucent, it stood little chance of winning in direct competition, without considerable state support.

Despite state support for selected domestic firms, the multinationals made rapid headway in the Chinese market for networking equipment in the 1990s. The leading multinationals frequently circumvented import restrictions by setting up production facilities in China, agreeing to transfer technology to joint venture partners as a condition for access to the domestic market. Cisco is the Chinese market leader in networking equipment. It sold more than $250m-worth of equipment to China Telecom in the late 1990s, mainly to upgrade the latter's fixed line network for Internet use, and will supply a further $200m-worth of Internet equipment to China Telecom's Guangdong subsidiary to build its Internet. China Unicom's newly-built long distance network contains 23 circuit switches, all from Lucent. Its data and Internet Protocol networks contains 90 asynchronous transfer mode switches, all from Lucent. Its routers and other Internet protocol equipment are from Cisco.

The lion's share of China's fibre optic transmission trunk, built in the 1990s and the backbone of China's telecoms system, was constructed by a group of international industry leaders, namely Lucent, Alcatel, Nortel and Ericsson, with fierce competition for the large contracts. By 1998, Lucent had established six joint ventures in China, and had become the leading maker of fibre optics in the country, accounting for a reported 24 per cent of the domestic market.

In wireless communications equipment, the world's leading players, Nokia, Ericsson, and Motorola, together account for 80 per cent of the Chinese domestic market, produced mainly from local plants within China. Facing import restrictions, the global giants set up large-scale production facilities in China. For example, Motorola increased domestic output to 4.9m phones in 1998, doubling in just one year to 9.8m in 1999. By 1998, Motorola had invested over one billion dollars in China, with plans to increase this to $2.5bn by the year 2000. Its production centre in Beijing had 10 000 employees by 1998. Its investments included construction of its largest wafer fabrication plant outside the US. China is either the first or the second largest market for the world's three major producers of handsets.

Not only do the three global giants supply the handsets to China, but they supply also a large part of the base stations and switching equipment for the wireless network. In the late 1990s, NEC reportedly supplied 40 per cent of the total SDH microwave networks in use in China. NEC's investment in China had already reached $1.5bn by 1998.

Indigenous Chinese-owned mobile phone suppliers have not been at all competitive so far, lacking the economies of scale or the technology of the global leaders in the most technically advanced, and high value-added, aspects of the industry. The leading domestic firms, such as Konka, face a severe battle in attempting to compete with such powerful companies. The Chinese state attempted to nurture domestic competitors through various measures of industrial policy. It set quotas on the import of telecoms equipment for each of the leading global firms in the sector. The size of the quota was linked to a company's performance in localizing production and transferring technology to Chinese companies. In 1999, the government announced plans to impose production quotas as well as import restrictions on foreign manufacturers of mobile phones. An official spokesman said: 'The government policy is to encourage development of the national mobile phone industry'. It is already extremely difficult for the leading domestic firms to compete in this area, and after China joins the WTO, it will be much harder if the Agreement is observed strictly, since it prohibits the Chinese government from directing telecoms operators about the sourcing of their equipment. Moreover, there is great ambiguity about the meaning of 'local' firms, in this as in other sectors. In the telecommunications hardware industry the term 'local' has frequently been interpreted as including local production by multinationals.

In the not-too-distant future, China will introduce Third Generation (3G) mobile telephones, which will be a crucial aspect of the entire IT revolution. The established giants of the mobile phone industry have already invested huge amounts in becoming the global industry leaders in this technology. It will be very difficult indeed for China's fledgling indigenous manufacturers to compete as systems integrators in this field.

China's low income level means that the penetration rate of PCs is very low compared to Western markets. China has just six PCs per thousand people, compared with over 400 per thousand in the US. The total number of PCs is 7m, compared with 110m in the US alone. A major avenue for the development of the Chinese IT industry is through set-top boxes. China has 270 TV sets per thousand people, with a total of 335m sets, meaning that most households have a set. Therefore, the most rapid way forward for the Internet in China is via the TV. However, this requires considerable investment in the technology of the 'set-on-box'. Microsoft has realized the enormous potential this provides for its technology. It has used its colossal R&D capability, with a total spending of almost $3bn per annum, to rapidly develop this technology (called Venus) and is the market leader, having launched the product in March 1999.

## IT software

It is extremely difficult for firms based in developing countries to compete directly with the industry leaders in this sector. They can have important roles as sub-contractors. It is this that largely accounts for the rapid growth of Indian software exports in recent years, as discussed above. While the number of India-based software firms has increased fast, few of them are able to challenge the global leaders in the higher value-added segment of the business. India is by far the most advanced of the low-income countries in the development of its software industry. Even India faces major difficulties in establishing large domestic firms that compete with the global giants of the industry. However, China still lags far behind India in the development of the software industry. The total output value of the entire Chinese software industry in 1999 was just $2.2bn, only 0.42 per cent of the global industry and only around one-third of the size of the Indian industry.

## Telecoms services

Telecoms services appears to offer somewhat greater possibilities for building large indigenous Chinese firms. Most importantly, this sector is far less dependent on large-scale R&D spending than other IT sectors. In 1999, there were just nine telecoms service companies among the world's top 300 firms by

R&D spending, compared with 55 IT hardware and 21 software companies. The IT hardware firms spent a total of $59bn on R&D, compared with $8bn by the software firms and just $7bn by the telecoms firms. In the 1990s, China rapidly expanded its telecoms system.

By the late 1990s, Chinese telecommunications were growing at high speed. By 1999, China had 109m fixed line subscribers, 43m cellular subscribers, and 3.8m internet users. China had become a key part of the global battle in telecoms services. It was already the largest single market in the world for mobile phones. In 1994, the Chinese government announced its intention to establish a group of globally competitive telecoms firms. By the late 1990s, the Chinese government had broken up the monopoly of the former Ministry of Posts and Telecommunications, and established six major telecommunications carriers (Table 3.9). Much the most important of these were the two entities which emerged directly from the Ministry, namely, China Mobile and China Telecom. China Telecom is still wholly state-owned with almost 100 per cent of China's fixed-line telecommunications. In 1999 it had a total sales revenue of $19bn, close to that of Telefonica (Spain) or MCIWorldcom (USA).

**Table 3.9** *Major Chinese telecommunications players in each sector, 2000*

|  | Market players | Market share % |
| --- | --- | --- |
| Local services | China Telecom, China Unicom | China Telecom: 99 |
| Long distance services (incl. Internet Protocol Phone) | China Telecom, China Unicom, China Jitong, China Netcom | China Telecom: 99 |
| Mobile services | China Mobile, China Unicom | China Mobile: 88.6 China Unicom: 11.4 |
| Paging services | Guoxin Paging, China Unicom, and 1600 other players | Guoxin: 59 Unicom paging: 5 |
| Data communication services | China Telecom, China Unicom, China Jitong, China Netcom, China Mobile |  |

China Mobile was formerly a branch of China Telecom, but it was allowed to become an independent company in the late 1990s. In 1997, China Mobile floated in Hong Kong 25 per cent of the equity value of its mobile assets in the provinces of Guangdong and Zhejiang. The IPO raised $4.5bn, at that point a record in Asia for an IPO. China Mobile (Hong Kong) raised a further $2.6bn through an international share issue in 1999. This financed the acquisition of the parent company's mobile phone assets in Fujian, Jiangsu, Henan and Hainan provinces. By the end of 1999, China Mobile (Hong Kong) had a total of 15.6m subscribers. China Mobile occupied an 87 per cent market share in the provinces in which it operated. These provinces had a total population of 320m. By late December 1999, China Mobile (Hong Kong) had a market capitalization of over $92bn, ranking 51st in the *FT 500*.

China Unicom was established in 1993 as a state-owned entity intended to provide competition for the incumbent, China Telecom. It was licensed to operate in all segments of the telecoms industry. It rapidly increased its mobile phone business, with a total of 4.2m subscribers at the end of 1999, and its market share stood at 14.2 per cent. China Unicom was given permission to float 25 per cent of its equity on international markets. Despite its relatively small size, the flotation attracted intense interest, and raised \$4.9bn. The flotation was seen as 'a play on China's red-hot cellular industry'.

Superficially, China has been successful in establishing global giants in the telecoms sector. However, large challenges remain for China telecoms firms on the 'global level playing field'.

Each of the main telecoms service providers is under heavy bureaucratic control. China Telecom is a wholly state-owned enterprise. A great deal hinges on the way in which China's bureaucracy responds to the challenge of globalization in this sector. China Unicom's parent company has 15 major stakeholders, all state-owned enterprises of one variety or another. China Mobile (Hong Kong) is still 75 per cent owned by China Mobile, which is, in turn, owned by the Ministry of Information Industries (MII). This is, in turn, the largest single shareholder in China Unicom, China Mobile's main 'competitor'. The Chinese government is in the process of 'severing the MII's ties with the commercial interests', and allowing an autonomous and professional business structure to develop within China Mobile. The composition and background of the board of directors of China Mobile (Hong Kong) casts considerable doubt on how far this process has advanced. In sum, it is not clear whether the 'firm' is China Mobile (Hong Kong), the parent company China Mobile, the provincial subsidiaries of China Mobile, or the MII.

Despite the successful flotations of both CTHK and China Unicom, the operational mechanism of these telecoms companies is far removed from that of the giants of the global telecoms industry, such as SBC or Vodafone AirTouch Mannesman (VAM). Their bureaucratic management methods and complex structure of ownership by different state interest groups, is far removed from even the partially privatized telecoms giants, such as France Telecom, NTT and Deutsche Telecom. Instead, they still have as a main goal the preservation of monopoly rents for their respective interest groups, both from other domestic entities, as well as from the multinational giants.

Even if China is successful in delaying and restricting the access of the multinational telecoms firms, it faces serious medium-term challenges through 'encirclement' by giants that are far larger, and faster-growing than indigenous firms. At some point, it will have to directly confront this challenge. The incumbent telecoms giant, China Telecom, faces domestic 'encirclement', in the sense that the rate of growth of mobile telephony is far faster than the fixed line business. Already it is facing the challenge of telephony provided by cable TV companies. However, the entire indigenously-owned industry faces a much deeper problem of encirclement from the global giants.

The global telecoms giants of Europe, the US and Japan are building their

**Table 3.10  China Telecom, China Mobile (Hong Kong) and China Unicom**
**compared to other leading telecoms firms (unit: $bn), December 1999**

| Company | Market capitalization | Revenue | Pre-tax profits |
|---|---|---|---|
| NTT Mobile | 366 | 30 | 3.4 |
| Vodafone (VAM) | 291 (April 2000) | 26 (pro-forma) | 3.0 (pro-forma) |
| NTT | 275 | 94 | 12.6 |
| Deutsche Telecom | 210 | 37 | 5.1 |
| AT&T | 164 | 53 | 8.3 |
| British Telecom | 151 | 28 | 7.0 |
| SBC | 150 | 50 | 10.9 |
| MCI WorldCom | 141 | 18 | (1.6) |
| France Telecom | 131 | 25 | 3.7 |
| Bell Atlantic | 90 | 32 | 5.0 |
| Bellsouth | 84 | 25 | 5.5 |
| Telefonica | 81 | 18 | 2.5 |
| TIM | 71 | 6 | 2.3 |
| Telecom Italia | 70 | 24 | 4.9 |
| Telstra | 69 | 12 | 3.5 |
| GTE | 64 | 25 | 6.4 |
| China Telecom | – | 19 | – |
| China Mobile (Hong Kong) | 92 | 5 | 1.1 |
| China Unicom | 34 | 2 | 0.3 |

companies on a truly global basis, while China's telecoms companies must prepare themselves for the coming battle using only their domestic market as the base for the competitive struggle, lacking the capability of directly competing in the international arena. There is an unprecedented process of merger and acquisition among the firms based in the advanced countries. Very rapidly, a group of super-giants is developing, that will soon dwarf even the present giant companies. Moreover, the global giants are fast moving into the developing countries. Already, almost the entire Latin American market is controlled by multinational operators. Furthermore, the telecoms business in the advanced economies is growing at high speed, with enormous income to be derived from the move into higher value-added services as broadband develops in the near future.

Fast as the Chinese market is growing, it is far smaller than that in which the global giants operate. Although China has a huge number of people within its still highly protected telecoms market, the size of the market is limited by the country's poverty. In 1998, China's average *per capita* income in the cities was just $650 and in the countryside was only $260. Even the top decile of income earners in the cities, who totaled around 40m people, had an average *per capita* income the equivalent of just $1300. Some analysts believe that the rate of growth of China's telecoms market will slow down considerably. Moreover, the revenue per subscriber is low by international standards and falling. In part, this is the successful result of competition. However, it is also strongly related to the country's poverty. In 1999, China Unicom, for example, derived 63 per cent of its operating income from pagers. China Unicom's revenue per subscriber for paging services is only $2 per month, compared with $20 for cellular phones. The market for local mobile phones with no roaming capability is fast-growing, but provides low revenues per subscriber. Such business forms a weak base from which to challenge the global telecoms giants.

One option is for the leading Chinese players themselves to try to become part of the international merger and acquisition process. However, the large share of state ownership drastically limits the capability to use their stock market valuation to merge with foreign operators. Deutsche Telecom, DoCoMo and Singapore's Singtel, have each encountered serious barriers to international acquisitions due to their state ownership, since private telecoms firms do not wish to have any serious element of control in the hands of foreign governments. However, each of these operates in a relatively transparent way, with comprehensive autonomy for the management. China's telecoms firms have the difficulty of a much less transparent and more bureaucratic background than their international, majority state-owned competitors. In addition, China's telecoms firms have the huge obstacle that for many advanced economies, telecoms is still a highly sensitive sector from a national security perspective. It is most unlikely that the governments of high income countries, or even southeast Asian countries, would allow a Chinese majority state-owned telecoms firm to merge with a domestic telecoms company. Morever, in terms of acquisitions, China's telecoms firms are severely constrained by their relatively small revenue base. China Mobile (Hong Kong) currently has annual revenues of less than $5bn. Even if it took over the mobile phone operations in the seven other provinces planned for the near future, it is hard to imagine that its revenues could exceed $10bn in the foreseeable future, far behind those of DoCoMo or Vodafone Mannesman, which are directly comparable.

Even China's fast-growing Internet sector may also face problems of 'encirclement' due to the relatively small size of the Chinese market. There are enormous prospects for market growth in China. However, the reality is that to-day, access to the Internet is still extremely limited. In early 1999, China had just 0.14 Internet hosts per 10 000 people, compared with 470 per 10 000 in the high income economies and 1131 per 10 000 in the US. PC penetration rates are still tiny. Moreover, only around one-fifth of PCs are on a network. Most PCs in China are used for routine office tasks, like typing, spreadsheets or making graphic presentations. Only a few employees in any given office have access to the Internet from work. Moreover, the low incomes of most Chinese people means that their capability to spend heavily on the diverse offerings available via broadband are relatively limited.

A deep constraint on the development of the Internet market, and the business capabilities of those indigenous firms trying to build Internet businesses, is the limited degree of connection with the global Internet. This results partly from the attempt to restrict access to global ideas that are unpalatable to the leadership. China has attempted to develop a 'Chinese-only' version of the Internet, walled off from the rest of the world. In its attempt to control the content that is transmitted through the Internet, and monitor the activities of dissident movements, such as the Falun Gong, the government has attempted to enforce tight controls over the use of encryption. It has forbidden the use of foreign encryption products, upon which so much of the Internet hardware and software depend.

A second constraint on Internet growth in China is the relatively low level of development of the international connections of Chinese Internet services. China's total bandwidth for the five major ISPs connected with the rest of the world is only 355 megabytes. By comparison, Taiwan, with one-fiftieth of China's mainland population, has a total international data communications bandwidth of 37 gigabytes, or one hundred times that of the mainland. The city of Hong Kong alone has 233 megabytes, while just one major multinational company, Intel, has 256 megabytes of bandwidth for international connectivity. A third problem for the development of the Internet is the high cost of Internet connections, reflecting the attempt by China's leading telecoms companies to use their monopoly position to extract monopoly rents from the connection to the Internet. Unlike in the US, local calls in China are billed according to connection time rather than flat monthly fees.

Thus, despite the rapid growth of the Internet in China, the base from which domestic Internet companies are trying to build their businesses is much weaker than that which faces Internet companies in the advanced economies. Internet companies based in the advanced economies are starting the 'global race' with access to a vastly greater, more open and less regulated market than their erstwhile competitors in China. In an industry in which speed is crucial in building new global businesses, such a disadvantage is crucial. The world leaders have already built global brands and a global business system that surrounds China.

In sum, China's aspiring globally competitive Internet companies will face severe competition from the established global giants. These are rapidly changing their shape, and daily becoming more global and more powerful, developing their technical capabilities and their global brand name. Already, China's domestic companies lag far behind in this battle. There is a high incentive to use remaining monopoly controls to establish passive ownership positions in joint ventures with the global giants, rather than attempt to compete with them head-on. There is already a tremendous disparity in the basic elements of competitive edge in this sector between China's fledgling companies and the global giants.

The WTO Agreement (see below) provides a framework in which the doors are opened to joint ventures in the telecoms sector on a widespread basis from the moment that China joins. The global giants provide enormous attractions for different players in the Chinese telecoms industry. In the long-term, without an extremely clear-sighted government industrial policy, it is hard to imagine how any domestic telecoms company will compete with the global giants. However, while the market is in the process of liberalization, there are very strong financial incentives for the different players to enter joint ventures. Through access to international capital they can enhance their position in the domestic struggle. The different interest groups that are the ultimate owners of the wide variety of telecoms service providers, actual or potential, have powerful incentives to enter joint ventures. It is not necessary for the multinational telecoms companies to establish monopoly ownership of any individual joint venture in order to rapidly take control of the Chinese market. All that is necessary is application of the WTO Agreement which allows the multinationals speedily to establish joint ventures across the whole spectrum of the telecoms businesses. Through a succession of minority or 50/50 joint ventures with a variety of different indigenous entities, the multinationals can develop national businesses that are far larger and more powerful than any individual Chinese joint venture partner. This is exactly the process that has happened in sector after sector, 'eating China piece by piece'.

There is a serious danger that China Telecom will be by-passed by a wide variety of nimbler businesses that can offer numerous services as well as voice communication through broadband. In the ferocious struggle with other domestic entities that may team up with multinational giants after China's entry to the WTO, China Telecom at the national or local level may find it impossible to avoid 'partnership' with the global players if it is to survive.

There are just two mobile phone licensees, China Unicom and China Mobile. It is possible that China Telecom will be added to that list. There will be intense pressure from different interest groups to establish more mobile phone licences. Joint ventures do not need to be only established with the central authority of each telecoms entity. It is logically possible that different subsidiaries within China Mobile, China Telecom and China Unicom may establish international joint ventures.

It is highly uncertain what will happen to the licences for 3G mobile phones. There are enormous benefits for individual indigenous interests to join with the global giants in bidding for 3G licences, not least their experience in developing 3G networks in other parts of the world.

There are currently seven major licensed Internet backbone providers in China. These are ChinaNet, Golden Bridge network, China Education and Research Network, China Science and Technology Network, China Unicom Network, China Netcom Network and China Mobile. China has currently awarded five Internet protocol (IP) phone licences. These have been issued to China Telecom, China Unicom, Jitong, China Netcom and China Mobile. Any of these could in principle team up in a joint venture with the global telecoms giants.

China has a vast network of 1300 cable TV companies. In the urban areas almost every household is connected to cable TV. More households have cable TVs than have a telephone. Most cable companies are independent legal entities, having been developed with local capital. Already there is, literally, warfare between the local cable companies, wishing to provide telephony services through their cable network, and the telecoms companies, wishing to provide non-telephony services through their fibre optic network, such as video and data services. Despite a formal government prohibition, preventing cable TV and telephone companies from offering each others' services, in practice it has proved hard to stop the respective sectors using their networks to compete with the other sector. In the battle for the broadband market there is a high incentive for local players to link up with the multinational giants. At the moment only around 10 per cent of the national cable network is fully interactive offering two-way communication. Both camps will need substantial foreign capital and technology to upgrade their networks to make them fully interactive.

Once any entity establishes a joint venture with a leading multinational in this field, there is an unstoppable cumulative effect upon the incentives of other entities to do likewise. There are extremely powerful reasons for seeking a joint venture partner in the struggle for the domestic market. The global giants bring huge capital resources to bid for telecoms licences, such as 3G mobile phones. They have access to the resources necessary to rapidly expand the network. They have powerful global brands, a global network of advertising revenue, and rich content for multi-media, broadband provision. They possess huge global procurement to leverage cost reduction and unique, customer-specific technologies. They have the ability to provide global services to global business customers, and they have superior management skills, especially those acquired through the development of broadband in other parts of the world.

An alliance with a global giant offers the possibility for large revenue streams as a passive partner, essentially deriving 'rentier' income from the business relationship. The main goal for the multinational giants will be in the high value-added markets of relatively affluent urban dwellers and international businesses in major cities. One analyst commented: 'The focus is going to be on high value-added multinationals. I don't think people are interested in wiring villages in Hunan'.

In late 2000, AT&T became the first foreign company to be allowed to offer telecoms services in China. It established a joint venture with Shanghai Telecom, a subsidiary of China Telecom, to supply high-speed data services in Shanghai's huge Pudong business district. In early 2001, Rupert Murdoch's News Corp announced that it had taken a minority stake in China Netcom. China Netcom has 8500 km of fibre optic cable connecting 17 Chinese cities. It represents 'China's most advanced telecoms infrastructure'. Analysts believe that 'News Corp may be hoping to circumvent strict legal limits on foreign participation in China's cable TV market by delivering video over a telecoms network'.

## Financial services[3]

A severe challenge awaits China's financial services sector. The first problem is the simple gap in scale between domestic and global financial institutions, in terms of capital, assets and profitability. At the end of 1999, the equity capital and

---

[3] I am indebted to Wu Qing, Judge Institute of Management Studies, University of Cambridge, for compiling the information in this section.

**Table 3.11** *Top four foreign and domestic commercial banks (1999)*

| Rank | Institution | Revenues $m | Profits $m | Assets $bn | Equity $m | Employees | Profit per employee $000s |
|------|-------------|-------------|------------|------------|-----------|-----------|---------------------------|
| G1 | Citigroup (US)* | 82 005 | 9 867 | 716.9 | 49 700 | 176 900 | 55.8 |
| G2 | Deutsche Bank (Germany) | 58 585 | 2 694 | 841.8 | 23 200 | 93 232 | 28.9 |
| G3 | Bank of America (US) | 51 392 | 7 882 | 632.6 | 44 432 | 155 906 | 50.6 |
| G4 | Crédit Suisse (Switzerland) | 49 361 | 3 475 | 451.5 | 20 378 | 63 963 | 54.3 |
| D1 | ICBC | 20 130 | 498 | 427.5 | 21 918 | 549 038 | 0.9 |
| D2 | BOC | 17 632 | 534 | 350.7 | 17 921 | 208 792 | 2.6 |
| D3 | ABC | 14 127 | −110 | 244.1 | 16 273 | 500 000 | −0.2 |
| D4 | CCB | 13 392 | 598 | 265.8 | 12 907 | 324 000 | 1.8 |

*Notes:* * The table puts Citigroup, which was grouped in diversified financials, in this group. ICBC = Industrial and Commercial Bank of China; BOC = Bank of China; ABC = Agricultural Bank of China; CCB = China Construction Bank.

assets of the Industrial and Commercial Bank of China (ICBC), the biggest financial institution in China, were $21.9bn and $42.8bn respectively, while those of Citigroup were roughly double in respect to both indicators (Table 3.11). However, the revenue of Citigroup was four times greater than that of ICBC. In terms of profits, the gap is even more dramatic. In 1999, the profits of ICBC were $498m, compared with $9.9bn for Citigroup, twenty times those of ICBC. The scale of Bank of America was not far behind that of Citigroup.

In the insurance sector, the gaps are even bigger (Table 3.12). In 1998, the equity capital, assets, revenue and profit of People's Insurance Company of China (PICC), the biggest firm in the sector and former monopolist, were $972m, $5.4bn, $3.9bn and $101m respectively, while those of ING were $34.1bn, $46.4bn, $5.6bn and $2.9bn respectively. ING is not even one of the biggest insurance companies in the world. Other insurers (also financial conglomerates)

**Table 3.12** *Top three foreign and domestic insurance companies (1998)*

| Rank | Institution | Revenues $m | Profits $m | Assets $bn | Equity $m | Employees | Profit per employee $000s |
|------|-------------|-------------|------------|------------|-----------|-----------|---------------------------|
| G1 | AXA (France) | 87 645 | 2 155 | 508.6 | 16 395 | 92 008 | 23.4 |
| G2 | Nippon Life (Japan) | 78 515 | 3 405 | 23.3 | 10 559 | 71 434 | 47.7 |
| G3 | Allianz (Germany) | 74 178 | 2 382 | 383.7 | 28 854 | 113 584 | 21.0 |
| D1 | PICC | 3 858 | 101 | 5.3 | 972 | 84 657 | 1.2 |
| D2 | Pacific | 2 832 | 19 | 2.0 | 366 | 9 690 | 2.0 |
| D3 | Ping An | 2 409 | 42 | 3.4 | 446 | 110 595 | 0.4 |

*Note:* PICC = People's Insurance Company of China.

such as AXA, and Allianz are even bigger than ING in terms of revenue and profit. The gap between them and PICC is even greater. Moreover, the rest of the insurance companies in China are much smaller than PICC. They are minnows in international terms.

In investment banking, the gap is simply vast (Table 3.13). In 1998, the total equity capital and assets of all 90 securities firms in China added together was about $4.0bn and $45.0bn respectively, while those of MSDW alone were $17.0bn and $376.0bn (about four times and eight times respectively those of the whole of China). The equity and assets of Guotai and J & A (the newly merged and the biggest securities company in China), were only 2 per cent and 0.8 per cent of those of MSDW. The gap in revenue and profits is vast.

**Table 3.13** *Top four foreign and domestic investment banks (1998)*

| Rank | Institution | Revenues $m | Profits $m | Assets $bn | Equity $m | Employees | Profit per employee $000s |
|------|-------------|-------------|------------|------------|-----------|-----------|---------------------------|
| G1 | Merrill Lynch (US) | 33 962 | 1,259 | 299.8 | 10,132 | 63,800 | 19.7 |
| G2 | MSDW | 31 126 | 3 281 | 376.0 | 17 014 | 45 712 | 71.8 |
| G3 | Goldman Sachs | 22 478 | 2 428 | 217.4 | 6 310 | 13 033 | 186.3 |
| G4 | J. P. Morgan* | 18 110 | 2 055 | 260.9 | 11 439 | 15 512 | 132.5 |
| D1 | Guotai | 325 | 75 | 1.5 | 192 | 2 800 | 26.7 |
| D2 | China South | 288 | 10 | 1.9 | 171 | 2 500 | 4.0 |
| D3 | Shenyin Wanguo | 258 | 44 | 2.1 | 265 | 3 000 | 14.7 |
| D4 | China | 230 | 12 | 1.9 | 138 | 3 100 | 3.9 |

Note: *The table puts J. P. Morgan, normally regarded as a commercial but now actually an investment bank, in this group. The data is based in 1999.

The relatively small scale of the China's financial services sector means large competitive disadvantage with the global leaders in terms of unit costs, expenditure on R&D, IT systems and brand building, risk management, product development and diversification, and ability to attract the best staff and to provide services for global clients.

The narrow business scope is becoming a more and more significant shortcoming of China's financial services industry. The newly enacted Chinese Securities Law of 1998 adopted the approach of the US's Glass-Steagall Act, strictly separating the securities, banking, insurance and trust businesses. In the year 2000 the separation was in the midst of being implemented. For example, the Big Four commercial banks and PICC, had transferred their securities arms from the bank-owned trust and investment companies to the Ministry of Finance, so as to form a new state-owned securities company. All of the trust and investment companies owned by the Big Four and their branches had also become independent.

As we have seen, this is precisely the opposite direction from the global trends. Most of the EU countries traditionally did not have sectoral restrictions, and in recent years tended to apply the German universal banking model. The US, as the inventor of the separation policy, and its follower, Japan, have repealed the laws separating business in the different sectors. We have seen that this has enabled the US to produce giant financial conglomerates such as Citigroup and Chase Manhattan. By 1999, non-interest income (mainly from investment banking-related business rather than conventional commercial banking) had become the largest single element in the revenue of the biggest American banks. Some big investment banks (such as Merrill Lynch) have established diversified financial services networks, and big insurance companies, both in Europe and the US, have become multi-sector financial services suppliers.

While the financial giants are increasingly enjoying economies of scale and scope and becoming stronger, weak domestic Chinese firms are specializing and downsizing, and becoming weaker in terms of global competition. In the fast-moving world of IT, not only is the financial industry constantly innovating, but also the needs of its customers are growing and diversifying. The global financial conglomerates, which are able to provide 'one-stop shopping' for financial services, have big competitive advantages compared with China's narrowly-focused banks, brokers and insurers.

Not only is the scale of assets and capital of Chinese financial firms much lower than that of the leading global firms, but, crucially, their profits are much lower. The income and profit per employee in China's financial institutions is negligible compared with the global giants. In the year 2000, for the first time all of the Big Four Chinese state-owned commercial banks appeared in the *Fortune 500*, in which firms are ranked by sales revenue. In the commercial banking category, none of the Big Four ranks in the top ten. However, in terms of the number of employees, the Big Four Chinese banks are all in the global top four. Their level of productivity per employee is extremely low. For example, Industrial and Commercial Bank of China (ICBC) and Agricultural Bank of China (ABC), two of the biggest financial institutions in China, each had about 500 000 employees. In 1999 ICBC's profits per employee were about $900, while ABC had losses per employee of $200. In the sharpest contrast, Citigroup and Bank of America had 177 000 and 156 000 employees respectively, with profits per employee of $55 800 and $50 600 respectively.

There is also a huge gap in the Return on Equity (ROE) and Return on Assets (ROA) between the domestic and global institutions. The fact that Chinese financial institutions have a huge number of employees, with low productivity and high costs, as well as large numbers of retired employees, and without a developed system of social and commercial insurance, intensifies their disadvantage compared with the global leaders. The productivity gap in the securities sector is somewhat less severe than that in the banking and insurance sectors (Tables 3.11–13). However the scale of the leading domestic securities firms is far too small to be able to compete head-on with the global leaders.

Moreover, most big securities firms have a problem of 'financial triangular debt' which needs a huge amount of provision and reduces profits significantly.

The quality of assets of Chinese banks has been a big problem for years. The central or local governments have routinely interfered in the operation of China's banks, especially the Big Four, despite serious attempts to establish operational independence. Sometimes apparently commercial activities have been converted into 'political' or 'social' ones, such as lending to the many State-owned enterprises that are on the edge of bankruptcy, recruiting redundant government employees and retired soldiers. The problem of 'quality' relates not only to their assets management and business operation, but also to their corporate governance and ownership.

## Conclusion

China began liberalizing the post-Mao economy in the late 1970s. The early versions of the contract system in industry were introduced in 1979, of which that at Shougang was the most important and symbolic. Therefore, one can say that China's industrial policy has been in operation for two decades. A consistently stated goal has been to construct globally powerful companies that can compete on the 'global level playing field'.

During a similar period in Japan's development, from the 1950s to the 1970s, Japan's industrial planners supported the growth of a series of globally powerful companies. After two decades of industrial policy in Japan, the country possessed a whole corps of globally competitive companies. By the late 1980s, it had twenty of the largest one hundred corporations in the *Fortune 500*, including Toyota, Hitachi, Matsushita, Nissan, Toshiba, Honda, Sony, NEC, Fujitsu, Mitsubishi Electric, Mitsubishi Motors, Nippon Steel, Mitsubishi Heavy Industry, Mazda, Nippon Oil, Idemitsu Kosan, Canon, NKK, Bridgestone, and Sumitomo Metal. These companies developed through extensive support from state industrial policy, including tariff and non-tariff barriers, restrictions on foreign direct investment, preferential purchase policy by state-owned utilities, government defence procurement contracts, government-subsidized R&D, government-sponsored rationalizations of different industries, and a 'flexible' competition policy that encouraged the growth of oligopolistic competition.

From 1980 to the late 1990s, China's gross domestic product grew at over 10 per cent per annum. By 1998, China was the world's seventh largest economy in terms of gross domestic product valued at the official rate of exchange and the second largest valued in 'purchasing power parity dollars'. After twenty years of industrial policy in China, employing many similar measures to those used by Japan, and with a similar explicit policy goal, major changes have taken place in China's large, state-owned enterprises. The leading enterprises have grown rapidly in terms of value of sales. They have absorbed a great deal of modern technology, learned how to compete in the market-place, substantially upgraded the technical level of their employees, learned wide-ranging new managerial skills, gained substantial understanding of international financial markets, and become sought-after partners for multinational companies.

Despite important progress, none of China's leading enterprises has become a globally competitive giant corporation, with a global market, a global brand, and a global procurement system. China has just five companies in the *Fortune 500*. It does not have one company in the world's top 300 companies by R&D expenditure. Mainland China does not have a single company in the *FT 500*. Nor does China have any representatives in MSDW's list of the world's top 250 'competitive edge' companies.

The competitive capability of China's large firms after two decades of reform is still painfully weak in relation to the global giants. This is extremely marked in the high-technology sectors, such as aerospace, complex equipment such as power plants, pharmaceuticals, and in 'mid-technology' sectors such as integrated oil and petrochemicals and auto components. However, even in sectors with apparently less advanced technology, such as steel and coal, there is a significant gap with leading global companies in the high value-added segments of the market. The gap in IT hardware and software, and in the financial services is huge. Even in telecoms services, China's large indigenous firms have significant competitive disadvantages. In these senses, China's industrial policy of the past two decades must be judged a failure. The reasons for this failure are partially internal and partially external. Part 1 analysed the internal reasons for failure. Part 2 examined the external reason for failure, namely the global business revolution.

The brutal reality of this situation left China's policymakers in a deep dilemma at the end of the 1990s. If China had not opened itself to the international economy through trade and foreign investment after the 1970s, then its economic progress would have been much slower. China has huge advantages as a late-comer, with access to massive pools of global capital and technology. However, at the level of the large firm, it faces greater challenges than have confronted any previous late-comer country. The pace of change in global big business has massively outpaced that of China's large enterprises. No other late-comer countries have had to confront such a difficult external environment in relation to competition at the level of the large firm. For the first time, in sector after sector, a small number of truly global corporations accounts for a large fraction of total world sales. China is joining the global level playing field at the point at which the degree of unevenness of business capability has never been greater.

At the end of the 1990s, the differential rate of change in business structures and technological capability between China and the outside world presented a massive challenge to China's industrial policymakers. Would a further ten years using the same measures as in the past two decades be able to ensure that China's large firms caught up with the global leaders? Was it possible that after a further ten years China's large firms might be even further behind than they are today? In the face of such ferocious competition, was there any set of industrial policies that could enable China to establish a large group of globally competitive firms?

It is extremely difficult for Chinese policymakers to confront such possibilities. However, the blunt reality is that it may no longer be possible for industrial policy to build powerful competitive large firms based in even the largest and most powerful of the developing countries. If this were indeed to be the case, then it would require immensely subtle international relations to accommodate to this new reality. It would require a radical redrawing of the ambitions of large developing countries, especially, but not only, China. It would require separating the goal of catch-up at the firm level from the goal of catch-up by means of advancing national output, structural change, wage employment and the standard of living.

Even for advanced European countries, it was, and still is, very difficult to accept that former 'national champions' may be unable to compete on the global level playing field as individual players. Whereas individual European countries may have to accept the demise of their national champions, the continent as a whole is breeding a group of regional champions and transatlantic champions. For China, a huge civilization with a proud economic and political history, it is very difficult to accept that it may be unable to emulate Britain, the US, Japan and Korea in building national champions through industrial policy. However, for there to be an alternative, there has to be a coherent and realistic strategy. It is a great challenge for Chinese policymakers to identify what such a strategy could be in the face of the incredible pace of global change in the nature and business capability of large firms. It is better to 'seek truth from facts' than to live with illusions.

It can be argued that there is no point in trying to fight a battle that cannot be won: 'If you outnumber the enemy by ten to one, surround them; by five to one, attack them; by two to one, divide them. If you are equally matched, be good and skillful in battle. *If the enemy forces outnumber yours, retreat.*' (Sun Wu, *The Essentials of Warfare*). It may be the case that the heroic age of building national champions through state-supported industrial policy is over. If this is indeed the case, the idea will not have been defeated by the triumph of small-scale perfectly competitive firms. Rather, it will have been defeated by the full flowering of global oligopolistic capitalism.

As the 1990s drew to a close, China needed to choose between extremely difficult alternatives in its industrial policies. It stood between the devil and the deep blue sea, between a rock and a hard place. Intense debates took place over this issue. Should China strengthen its industrial policy of building global giants? Did China possess the political commitment and bureaucratic capability to reconstruct its failed industrial policy? Even if it had the capability to do so, was there any longer any point in trying to support the 'national team' when the pace of change in the global corporation had so far outstripped that in China?

## 3.2 **Strengthening China's industrial policy?**

Faced with the widening gap between the business capability of China's leading firms and the global giant companies, China reached a hugely important turning point in the late 1990s. Reflecting on the failures of industrial policy over the previous decade and a half, China's policymakers could have chosen to learn from the past failures and attempt to strengthen and improve their industrial policy. This would have been consistent with China's approach towards experimentation in its reform programme, with the incremental transition towards a market economy and with gradual, controlled integration with the world economy. Many policymakers and industrialists supported such a path.

China's strategic options for restructuring its large state enterprises had been narrowed by the late 1990s. Although the room for manoeuvre had been greatly reduced, there were still choices that planners could have made that might have enabled a group of large, globally competitive Chinese firms to emerge. China's aspiring global corporations faced a far more difficult international business environment than that which confronted Japan and the Four Little Tigers during a comparable stage in their catch-up efforts. However, China has the potential advantages of a huge, unified, ancient culture. It contains over one-fifth of the total world population. This is a mighty political force capable of being mobilized in support of such an endeavour. In addition, it has a domestic market that already is one of the world's largest and most dynamic, and that is potentially the largest of any country. These factors provided great potential 'leverage', if China's policymakers were willing to use them in pursuit of a reinvigorated industrial policy. The following are some of the suggestions that were made in these debates.

### State-orchestrated mergers

One option was to merge the domestic 'giant' companies into just one or two giant firms within each sector. Japan pursued this route in the 1930s by state-led mergers of several leading steel firms to produce Japan Steel, which had a virtual monopoly over the domestic steel market prior to 1939. The state also encouraged the growth of just two giant automotive firms in the 1930s, Toyota and Nissan, which accounted for 85 per cent of total production by the late 1930s. The Korean government allowed Posco to develop in a massively protected domestic market without any significant competition for a long period. In early 2000 the Brazilian state allowed the formation of the giant domestic beverage company, Ambev, produced by a merger of the two leading domestic brewers, Brahma and Antartica: 'The prospect of creating a Brazilian beverages multinational helped win regulatory approval for the merger, despite the fact that the new group will have about 65 per cent of the beer market. In a country with few internationally-known national champions, the national champion argument drowned out potential threats to competition in the domestic market.' (*Financial Times*).

Many of Europe's leading private or quasi-private companies of the 1990s emerged from similar structures. In the 1960s Britain merged many different steel, aerospace and automobile firms to form, respectively, British Steel, British Aerospace and British Leyland. In the former two cases these were to form the basis for highly successful private enterprises. It is almost certain that they would not have become successful without the initial merger imposed by the British government. Other Western European countries followed similar industrial policies (for example, France's Usinor Steel Company was formed in this fashion).

As in other countries that pursued this strategy, this path opens up the possibility of domestic monopoly and requires skilful regulation to prevent low levels of efficiency. Due to the relatively small size of the domestic market, such mergers could still result in entities that are relatively small by world standards, given the massive growth in size of the world's leading system integrators. Such mergers do not directly address the problem of poor corporate governance. Nor do they solve the problem of backward technology. However, they provided a more realistic foundation for competition with the global giants than did the previously fragmented industrial structure.

## Increased autonomy for powerful emerging corporations

In Europe in the 1980s and 1990s, a succession of former state-owned 'national champions' were transformed into autonomous, competitive transnational corporations. These included ENI, Repsol, BP, and Elf Aquitaine in oil and petrochemicals, Usinor and British Steel in the steel industry, Volkswagen and Renault in the automotive industry, and Aerospatiale, Rolls-Royce and BAe in the aerospace industry. The typical pattern was for the appointment of a strong, market-oriented chief executive officer who was subject to strict performance criteria. The CEO was authorized to change business practices radically, gradually privatize ownership rights, and develop an international capability, especially through mergers and acquisitions.

We have seen that in China in the 1990s, there emerged numerous powerful enterprises. They developed a deep sense of corporate identity and ambition. They were led by ambitious and effective chief executive officers. These included Shougang under Zhou Guanwu, AVIC under Zhu Yuli, Shanghai Petrochemical Corporation under Wu Yixin, Daqing under Ding Guiming, Shenhua under Ye Qing, Yuchai under Wang Jianming, and Sanjiu under Zhao Xinxian. Each of these leaders had a clear understanding of the nature of global competition. Each of them was ambitious to turn their firm into a true global competitive business. However, the enterprises' superior authorities were nervous at the loss of power that might result from these enterprises taking an increasingly independent path.

The degree to which these enterprises were allowed to reduce the state's ownership share was tightly controlled. Not all of them were permitted to raise funds from the stockmarket and none was permitted to reduce the state's share below 50 per cent. Each of them had severe bureaucratic barriers placed in the path of their domestic expansion, and more than one had severe bureaucratic constraints on their international expansion. They each faced serious bureaucratic constraints on large-scale domestic mergers and acquisitions.

If the central government was willing to provide strong support for emerging autonomous enterprises, then the respective corporations would be much better able to raise funds from domestic and international stock markets. Instead of the disappointments of China's international flotations, China's leading corporations might be able to enjoy strong stock market performance, which facilitates further international expansion. It would also demonstrate the benefits of improved corporate governance to aspiring large corporations. The Argentinean oil and petrochemical company YPF and the Brazilian aerospace company Embraer both demonstrate that possibilities do exist for selected firms based in developing countries to absorb international capital and begin to grow in international markets.

## Government procurement contracts

To this day, state procurement contracts remain an important and highly controversial instrument of industrial policy in advanced capitalist economies. State procurement contracts were an important mechanism of state support for the emerging national champions in aerospace, telecoms equipment and power equipment. China's use of this instrument was relatively limited, and weakened significantly as the influence of market forces grew stronger over the course of the reforms. In the aerospace sector, the central authorities were able to do almost nothing to support the growth of a domestic aircraft industry by ordering domestic airlines to purchase short-haul jet aircraft from the McDonnell Douglas/Boeing or AE-100 ventures. In the power equipment sector, the state's ability or desire to influence the purchases made by power stations declined substantially over the course of the reforms. Increased use of this instrument still remained a logical policy choice for China's leaders at the end of the 1990s.

### Using global competition

We have seen that China was a major location for multinational investment by large global corporations. These were mainly in joint ventures. However, the very intensity of global competition between giant corporations threw up possibilities for a different strategy that might have been pursued by Chinese industrial planners. In the 1990s intense global oligopolistic competition in each sector produced firms based in the advanced economies that were technically strong, and which had a strong modern management system, but which fell behind in the global oligopoly race. They lacked the global scale necessary to compete. Such companies included Westinghouse and Mitsubishi Electric in the power equipment sector; Fokker in the aerospace sector; Sumitomo, Pirelli and Continental in the tyre sector; Volvo, Nissan, Mitsubishi, Daewoo and even Fiat in the automobile sector; Scania, Volvo, MAN and Paccar in the truck sector; Detroit Diesel in the diesel engine sector; Bethlehem Steel, YKK and Cockerill Sambrell in the steel sector; Astra, Rhône-Poulenc and Hoechst in the pharmaceuticals sector; Repsol, Arco and ENI in the oil and petrochemical sector; and Alcatel and Marconi in the IT hardware sector. In addition, there were a few thrusting new players from other developing countries which lacked the scale to grow into global giants on their own. Such firms included Embraer (Brazil) in the aerospace industry; Hong Kong Telecom and Singapore Telecoms in the telecoms sector; YPF (Argentina), Reliance (India) and Petrobras (Brazil) in the oil and petrochemical sector.

If the Chinese government had been sufficiently purposive about industrial planning, in the way that Japan or South Korea had been, then it is logically possible for a full-scale merger to have been negotiated between selected large Chinese companies and the respective global partner. Without such a merger, the foreign partner anyway faced the prospect of extinction through bankruptcy or merger with another giant capitalist company. The terms of the merger with the Chinese company could have been constructed in such a way to provide better earning prospects for the foreign shareholders through access to the huge and fast-growing Chinese market. It would have provided the vista of secure long-term rentier income for the foreign shareholders.

The weak multinational would have been offered a minority share in the new entity, but would be ceded full management control. The Chinese partner's equity share would come from a combination of bank loans, stockmarket flotation, asset contribution and a value placed on privileged access to the Chinese market for a specified period of time. The new entity would have been given both this privileged access and various supportive policies. For example, in aerospace, a certain proportion of Chinese airliners would be allocated to the new firm established between the Chinese and the multinational, after which point protection would be steadily reduced, and it would have to sink or swim in open competition. The foreign management would be ceded full management authority to run the business in order to make a profit for the Chinese and foreign shareholders.

Thus in the aerospace industry, Xifei (Xian Aerospace) might have partnered Fokker, and Chengfei (Chengdu Aereospace) might have partnered Embraer. In the automobile industry, Yiqi might have partnered Daewoo, and Erqi have partnered Mitsubishi. In the auto components industry Yuchai might have partnered Detroit Diesel. In the pharmaceutical industry, Sanjiu might have partnered Astra and Huabei have partnered Rhône-Poulenc. In the steel industry, Shougang might have partnered Cockerill Sambrell, Angang partnered YKK, and Wugang partnered Bethlehem Steel. In the oil and petrochemical sector, Daqing might have partnered ENI, SPC partnered YPF and Yanshan partnered Arco. In the telecoms industry, Guangdong Telecom might have partnered Hong Kong Telecom. In the IT hardware industry, Huawei might have partnered Alcatel or Marconi. Numerous such options still existed at the end of the 1990s.

The key purpose of such international mergers would be 'to liberate the large state enterprises from bureaucratic control, using the management methods of large global corporations' (Wang Xiaoqiang).

## Supporting non-SOE national champions

A small group of relatively strong domestic non-SOE firms emerged in the late 1990s. Leading examples of such firms included Haier and Meidi in consumer electronics, Legend in personal computers, Huawei in IT hardware, Baiyunshan in pharmaceuticals, and Jianlibao in soft drinks. These firms were typically led by charismatic CEOs, such as Liu Chuanzhi at Legend and Zhang Ruiming at Haier. They emerged typically in relatively low technology sectors and were able to establish a degree of domestic brand recognition, and in some cases began to penetrate the lower value-added segments of international markets. They employed modern methods of business management. They raised funds from the stockmarket. They used stock options to stimulate employee enthusiasm. They established genuinely autonomous businesses free from detailed interference from the state. They competed ferociously with the multinational corporations.

These companies often received favourable treatment in the international press. They were sometimes written about by international business schools. For example, the Harvard Business Schools produced a much-read case study on Haier. They were lauded by the populist neoclassical economists within China as examples of the achievements that Chinese firms could make if left to compete on their own on the global level playing field, unaided by state intervention. They were held up as examples of the new shoots that could burst into life once the old world of the state-owned enterprises was destroyed.

However, a closer look at these firms reveals that they typically benefited from a protected domestic market, and from state support through soft loans, state procurement, and protected marketing channels. Despite their enormous achievements, without exception these firms were far behind the global leaders in terms of revenue, R&D expenditure, marketing expenditure and global market share. They were all anticipating serious competitive challenges after China's accession to the WTO. Without continued state support, they were most unlikely to be able to build on their considerable entrepreneurial achievements, and mount a serious challenge to the global giants in their respective sectors. Nurturing such already demonstrated 'green shoots' through industrial policy measures was an obvious path to pursue. Such measures included continued protection, continued soft loans, state support for their R&D, and state support for them in their efforts to expand through merger and acquisition.

The mythology surrounding these companies attributes their relative success to their 'success in market-place competition' not to government support. The blunt reality is that, in most cases, relative success required both high entrepreneurial achievements as well as state support. Private discussion with the strategic officers of some of the leading non-state firms reveals great concern about the challenges that await them if China fully applies the WTO Agreement. The leaders of these firms are only too aware of the difficulty they will face in genuinely open competition with such firms as Cisco and Nortel, Coca-Cola and PepsiCo, Whirlpool and Electrolux, IBM and Dell.

## State support for technological upgrading

The most successful examples of high-speed technical upgrading in developing countries have taken place through powerful direct and indirect state support. Taiwan provides a vivid example of this form of partnership in a developing country. To this day, almost two-fifths of US technical progress takes place through direct state support for R&D, funded by US taxpayers. In 1994, this totalled no less than $36bn, around the same size as the entire national product of Malaysia. One can only wonder at the impact on China's technical progress of such a vast infusion of state support for R&D.

In the early days of the reforms, China's central planners enacted a highly successful programme of technical transfer, including a large-scale programme in the power equipment industry. At that point it appeared as if the central planners might mimic the role of MITI in Japan. In fact, as the size of the Chinese market in aerospace, power equipment, autos, pharmaceuticals, high quality steel, oil and petrochemicals, and telecoms equipment grew ever larger, so the degree of state intervention to ensure technical transfer as a condition of access to the Chinese market became weaker. Instead of a centrally co-ordinated activity, linking procurement, market access and ownership in a rational, explicit and transparent fashion, the technology transfer requirements from multinational companies became increasingly decentralized and unco-ordinated. There is no reason in principle why state co-ordinated technical transfers should not be revived and greatly strengthened, 'trading market for technology' on a large scale.

## Conclusion

A key aspect of following such a path was the necessity to create a credible threat of international competition that was sufficient to stimulate change, but not to create international competition that was so severe as to prevent any realistic chance of competing with the global giants. Joining the WTO on terms that paid due recognition to the reality of China's impoverished status as a developing country was one such possibility. A long transition period to accepting the full impact of WTO rules would have been one part of such a programme. Following such a path of substantially reorganized industrial policy alongside the credible threat of incremental reduction in protection for Chinese large firms would have constituted a coherent path for industrial policy to follow. It would not have involved rejection of the importance of market competition. It would have involved further experimentation and learning from previous policy mistakes. It would have been realistic about the magnitude of the task facing China.

## 3.3    China joins the WTO: abandoning industrial policy?

In November 1999, China and the US signed the historic agreement under which China would be permitted to join the WTO. The US negotiating team was led by Charlene Barshefsky, who had also led the US team in the prolonged negotiations for the World Telecoms Agreement in 1997. The Agreement was of great importance for US foreign policy and inspired intense national debate. President Clinton was heavily involved in the campaign to persuade the US people of the benefits for the US that would flow from the Agreement.

The US-China Agreement formed the bedrock of the terms under which China was to be formally admitted to the WTO. This was not only a decision of great importance for China, but also for the whole developing world, and, indeed, for the development of global capitalism. Many people interpreted the decision as a recognition that the gap between China's leading firms and those of the advanced economies had widened beyond the point of realistic catch-up. Through this decision China was bowing before the extraordinary force of global oligopolistic capitalism. Under the terms of the Agreement, China agreed to dismantle almost the entire range of mechanisms that has formed the core of industrial policy in the past two hundred years as a succession of countries has supported the growth of domestic large corporations. China has accepted that there will be enormous changes in its dealings with the global market-place. Within the WTO it will be extremely difficult for China to limit access to its domestic market.

The US-China Agreement is the most detailed agreement yet signed by any country on its entry to the WTO. The US-China WTO Agreement in itself constitutes a massive programme of economic system reform. Nine hundred Chinese laws will need to be changed and/or adapted for China to enter the WTO. The US is providing 'extensive legal and technical assistance' with a view to 'helping China in making its laws comply with WTO obligations in an effort to ensure that Beijing lives up to its obligations' (*Financial Times*). China has been granted only a five year adjustment period before it must implement in full the rules of the WTO. Many important changes will have effect from the day that

China joins the organization. Most of the significant changes will have been completed within only three years of China's entry. Moreover, there will be strong incentives for multinational businesses to push their participation in the Chinese economy beyond that which is permitted legally in anticipation of a future more liberal regime which will retrospectively sanction the quasi-illegal advances they have made. This has already been widely observed in the shape of the large-scale illegal entry of foreign capital into the Chinese telecoms industry through the 'China-China-foreign' formula.

For almost two decades the Chinese government experimentally charted its own internally-directed reform programme. With the entry to the WTO under such detailed, internationally-set conditions, China would voluntarily give up its autonomy in charting the complex path of economic reform.

## General measures

China has agreed to reduce the average level of industrial tariffs from 24.6 per cent to an average of 9.4 per cent by 2005, with a wide range of detailed commitments to lower tariffs on other products. China will make substantial tariff cuts immediately upon accession, with further cuts phased in, two-thirds of which will be completed within three years and almost all of which will have been completed within five years.

WTO rules prohibit quotas and other quantitative restrictions. Frequently, the Chinese government requires a variety of conditions to be fulfilled in order for foreign investment or imports to be approved. It has agreed that immediately upon entry to the WTO it will observe the WTO's rules on Trade-Related Investment Measures (TRIMS). China has agreed that the government (at central, provincial and local levels) will not condition import licences, quotas, tariff-rate quotas, or any other means of approval of importation, or the right to import or invest upon any kind of agreement as to whether a Chinese company is able to supply the given product, or on any kind of performance criterion. It has agreed that it will not enforce existing contracts that impose these requirements. Quotas currently apply to a wide range of products. Most quotas will be eliminated immediately upon China's accession to the WTO. Most of the remainder will be eliminated by 2003, and they will be entirely phased out by 2005.

China has agreed to eliminate local content requirements for foreign investment and imports immediately upon entry to the WTO. China has agreed to eliminate technology transfer requirements and offsets as a condition for investment or importation immediately upon entry. These include requirements to conduct R&D within China. The terms and conditions of the contract are to be agreed only between the respective business entities, without any government involvement. China has agreed to increase the guarantees of protection for any intellectual property that is transferred, and to eliminate requirements mandating that the Chinese partner in a joint venture gains ownership of trade secrets after a certain number of years. China has agreed to eliminate export performance and trade balancing requirements as conditions for foreign investment immediately upon entry to the WTO.

China has agreed to implement the TRIPS agreement of the WTO immediately upon accession to the WTO. China has agreed to eliminate over a three year period the current tight restrictions on the right of foreign firms to import and operate independent distribution networks for either imported or domestically-produced goods. China's distribution commitment is comprehensive. It covers commission agents' services, wholesaling, retailing, franchising, sales away from a fixed location, as well as related activities, such as inventory management, repair and maintenance services. These rights are critical restrictions on the competitive capability of foreign firms operating in China: 'As in the case of trading rights, the rights to distribute our products is critical to our ability to export successfully to China' (Barshefsky).

China has agreed to apply WTO rules to state-owned enterprises and to extend these rules to state-invested enterprises, that is, companies in which the state has an equity interest. Under these commitments, China's state-owned and state-invested enterprises are required to buy and sell based on commercial considerations, such as quality and price. China has agreed to provide foreign firms with the opportunity to sell products to state-owned and state-invested enterprises. China has agreed that purchases and sales of goods by state-owned enterprises, for commercial resale or for use in the production of goods for commercial sale, must not be considered for government procurement and are to be subject to WTO rules. China has agreed that the US can determine whether government benefits to a given sector, such as equity injections or soft loans, have been provided using market-based criteria rather than Chinese government benchmarks.

The implications of these general features of the WTO Agreement are enormous. They would have great implications for firms in sectors as diverse as power equipment and coal. We have seen that multinational firms have already developed strong positions in the Chinese power equipment market. Under the terms of the WTO Agreement, the key instruments of industrial policy in this sector would be illegal. Low-interest loans to support technical modernization at Harbin would be illegal. Using the Three Gorges turbine purchases from multinationals to require subcontracting of components from domestic firms and technical transfer to domestic firms would be illegal. Using government procurement contracts to purchase from domestic firms in 'unfair' competition with multinationals would be illegal. Using rights to establish a joint venture as a condition of technical transfer, such as at Shanghai Electrical Company, would be illegal.

The terms of the WTO Agreement would have large implications for the Chinese mining industry. The world's leading international mining corporations have already developed large markets in East Asia and are deeply anxious to increase their access to China's huge potential market. In the coal industry, which has grown at high speed, the leading international firms would now be able legally to bid to supply high quality coal to China's fast-growing modern power plants. It would be illegal for the contracts for these to be awarded on other than commercial criteria. The leading coal companies have been involved in protracted negotiations to establish joint ventures with China's leading coal companies. So far, none has been established on a permanent basis. Under the terms under which China has entered the WTO, the multinational coal companies could no longer be forced into joint ventures if they did not wish to do so. China's aspiring global leaders, such as Shenhua, have received large-scale state support in the shape of low interest loans and other assistance, such as access to rail transport and internal port facilities at prices that are far below international transport prices. Much of this is illegal in terms of WTO rules. Moreover, a large fraction of the industry only survives thanks to low-interest loans from state banks, especially the Construction Bank. Such subsidies to state enterprises are technically illegal under the terms of China's entry to the WTO.

## Terms of the Agreement in specific sectors

### Automobiles

China's tariffs on automobiles currently stand at 80–100 per cent, depending on the category of vehicle. China has agreed that by the year 2003 they will have fallen to 38–43 per cent, and will continue to fall to 25 per cent by the year 2006. Tariffs on auto parts will fall from an average of 23 per cent to 10 per cent. Quotas will be phased out by 2005, with an initial level of $6bn (above the actual level of imports in 1999), growing by 15 per cent per annum until their final elimination. China has agreed that former tight restrictions on distribution of automobiles and parts within China will be eliminated three years after accession to the WTO. Foreign firms will be allowed to engage in a full range of auto-related services within three years of joining the WTO. Upon accession, non-bank financial institutions will be allowed to provide finance for buying automobiles without any market access or national treatment limitation. China has agreed to end equity injections or soft loans to the automotive sector using anything other than market-based criteria. China has agreed to end all local content rules after it enters the WTO, and not to enforce existing agreements in this regard. It has agreed that it will not condition imports or investment approvals in the automotive sector upon technology transfer or on conducting R&D in China.

The terms of the WTO Agreement would have a large effect on this industry, on both the assemblers and the components suppliers. Multinationals would no longer be required to participate in joint ventures in the assembly and components industry if they did not wish to do so. They would no longer be required to transfer technology as a condition for establishing a joint venture. China's high tariffs would be eliminated. The leading multinationals that do not yet have large production bases in China might well choose to export to China from their bases elsewhere in Asia, such as Thailand, South Korea and Japan, rather than expand production directly in China. China's government departments and state enterprises would no longer be able to procure their fleets of saloon cars and trucks 'unfairly' from domestic firms such as Yiqi and Erqi. Multinationals would be legally able to capture market share through ownership or franchised operation of dealerships and provision of finance for vehicle purchase.

## Oil and petrochemicals

Tariffs on chemical imports will fall from 15 per cent to 7 per cent by 2005. Quotas will be virtually eliminated immediately upon accession. China has agreed that within three years of its accession any entity will be allowed to import chemicals (except chemical fertilizers) into any part of China. Foreign firms will be allowed to engage freely in the full range of distribution services. Importation or foreign investment approval in the chemicals sector will no longer be conditional on export performance, local content or similar requirements. For crude oil and petroleum products, China will allow foreigners to provide wholesale services within five years from the date of admission. For processed petroleum products, retail services will be permitted within three years from the date of accession. Crude oil will not be excepted from China's retail commitment, so it will be treated as any other product.

Under the terms of the WTO Agreement, multinationals will no longer be barred from the most lucrative downstream markets, the area in which the competitive advantage and the weakness of the Chinese companies is most marked. It will no longer be possible for multinationals to be required to enter joint ventures as a condition for operating in China. Any joint ventures in which they participate cannot any longer be made conditional on a transfer of technology to the Chinese partner. The multinationals will be able freely to procure their equipment from wherever they wish. They will be allowed to source their raw materials from wherever is most economically advantageous to them. The Chinese government will no longer be allowed to provide soft loans to help the domestic firms to modernize. The multinationals will be able freely to import oil, gas, oil products and petrochemicals from wherever is most efficient.

## Civil Aircraft

Currently, the right to import civil aircraft is restricted to a small number of entities with government approval. China has agreed that within three years, any entity can import civil aircraft into any part of China. Within three years also, foreign firms will be allowed to engage in the full range of distribution services for civil aircraft in any part of China. The Chinese government has agreed to eliminate equity injection or soft loans to the aircraft industry. It has agreed to end local content requirements, domestic R&D requirements and technology transfer requirements for the import of civil aircraft or for investment approvals in the civil aircraft industry. Importation of aircraft or investment in the sector will no longer be conditional on offset arrangements.

The WTO Agreement means that China would be unable to use its huge imports of aircraft to require multinational companies to transfer technology to China's aircraft and components industry, to set up joint ventures with them, or to provide subcontracting work for China's ailing aerospace enterprises. It would be unable to provide soft loans to the industry to help build business capability in key parts of the industry that might have a hope of becoming globally competitive, such as second- or third-tier suppliers in the aerospace components industry. China's rumoured attempt to support the development of a 70–80 seat commercial aircraft along the lines of Embraer or Bombardier could not be supported by government soft loans or by procurement requirements from domestic airlines without running the risk of prosecution by the WTO.

Some indication of the possible consequences of such a path was provided by the case of the Brazilian aircraft manufacturer, Embraer. In April 2000 the WTO ruled on the case of alleged illegal Brazilian government support for Embraer, the Brazilian national champion in the aircraft industry. Canada filed the complaint, alleging that Brazil had granted subsidies worth $3.7bn to Embraer in the form of export financing from Proex for the export of 900 aircraft already contracted for delivery. This unfairly disadvantaged the Canadian-based firm, Bombardier, which is Embraer's main competitor. Embraer argued that the subsidies were merely in order to equalize domestic and international interest rates for export finance. However, the WTO panel ruled that the subsidies went far beyond this 'legitimate' purpose. The WTO decision was regarded as 'a heavy blow for Embraer, which has become one of Brazil's most successful companies since it was privatized in 1994' and made record profits in 1999 (*Financial Times*). Once the panel ruling is adopted, Canada will be entitled to negotiate compensation from Brazil or ask the WTO for authorization to impose retaliatory trade tariffs on trade equivalent to the losses from Brazil's 'illegal actions'.

## Pharmaceuticals

China has agreed to reduce the average tariff on pharmaceuticals from 10 per cent to 4 per cent, commencing with the date of accession, to be completed by 2003. China's agreement to implement the TRIPS agreement on intellectual property rights immediately upon accession is of special importance for the pharmaceuticals sector, in which the profits of multinational firms are intimately related to the ability to enforce intellectual property rights. Other developing countries, notably India, have been much more cautious about the degree to which they agree to implement the TRIPS agreement on entry to the WTO. Rights to import and distribute pharmaceuticals are currently tightly controlled by government approvals, constituting an important source of protection for China's fledgling pharmaceuticals firms. China has agreed to phase in the elimination of these requirements over three years. After this period foreign pharmaceuticals firms will be able to import and distribute their imported products freely to any part of the country, including both wholesale and retail distribution.

Under the terms of China's entry to the WTO the Chinese government could not try to nurture a group of 'national champions', such as Sanjiu, through 'non-market' mechanisms. China's aspiring global giants in this sector cannot hope to grow through cloning Western patented drugs. The Agreement means that the protection provided for domestic producers through restrictions on access to the domestic distribution system will disappear. It means that global pharmaceuticals firms will be able to advertise freely in China and establish their own distribution systems. It means that it will be illegal to require joint ventures to transfer pharmaceuticals technology and/or agree to transfer pharmaceuticals patents within a certain period of time. It means that the global giants will be able freely to import their products, drastically reducing the incentive to produce locally.

## Steel

China has agreed to reduce its tariffs on steel and steel products from the current level of 10.3 per cent to 6.1 per cent by the end of 2002. The right to import steel is still restricted to a small number of entities that have been approved by the government. Over a period of three years from the date of China's accession to the WTO these restrictions on the import of steel are to be eliminated. Over the same period restrictions on the right to distribute steel within the domestic economy will also be phased out. Steel is of special importance in relation to so-called 'dumping'. China has agreed that for twelve years after China's accession to the WTO, the US should be able to retain legislation which prohibits 'import surges' in steel. Moreover, it has agreed that the US's legislation known as Section 201 should remain in place to control surges in the import of steel and other products from China. The Chinese government has agreed to give up the right to allocate equity injections or provide soft loans to the steel industry.

China's entry to the WTO on the terms agreed would have a substantial effect on the steel industry. Despite the large fall in tariffs on steel imports, China still has extensive non-tariff barriers in this industry. These would no longer be legal. All China's large steel producers, with the partial exception of Baogang, have substantial technical weaknesses in high value-added steels. The Chinese government recently announced a major package of assistance through low interest loans to upgrade the technical quality of some of the key enterprises. Under the terms of China's entry to the WTO this would be illegal. Several of them have already established or are trying to establish major joint ventures with the multinational leaders. A major purpose is to upgrade technology through required technical transfer. Such requirements would be illegal. Several of the leading multinational firms have had protracted and often unsatisfactory negotiations to establish joint ventures in order to gain access to the Chinese market. They would now be legally entitled to establish independent, wholly-owned production facilities in China if they wished. They would also be able legally to take over Chinese steel firms, replicating the extensive takeovers of the most productive facilities in Eastern Europe by the world's leading steel producers. Chinese steel producers would no longer be able legally to prevent the multinational steel producers establishing their own distribution systems and making direct contact with their customers.

We have already seen that in the telecommunications and financial services service sectors, there will be rapid and large-scale opening of the Chinese market. In addition, the following important market access arrangements are contained in the US-China Agreement.

## Information technology

China's decision to enter the WTO will have profound consequences for China's IT industry. Both the US and the EU devoted enormous efforts to press the Chinese side to make large concessions on market access for its IT firms. The reason for this is simple. The advanced economies in general, and the US in particular, contain all the major players in the sector. This sector possesses immense opportunities for increased profits for the large corporations that occupy the leading positions in the industry. A central reason for the explosion in the stock price of the companies in this sector is the investors' belief that the leading firms in this sector will dominate the market across the world.

As we have seen, US-based IT firms are, by far, the most powerful. The US negotiators in the WTO talks put intense pressure on the Chinese side to make concessions in the IT sector. The outcome was an agreement to open up dramatically the Chinese industry to foreign competition. The White House's web site, which published the details of the US-China WTO agreement in April 2000, contained the following headline 'The US-China WTO accession deal: a clear win for US high technology, greater openness and US interests'(*The White House*).

The White House argues that access to the potentially vast China market for IT is 'vital to maintaining US global leadership in Information Technology'. Despite low levels of income, China's vast population and rapid economic growth is producing a market that is of great importance for the globally dominant US information technology firms. China is the world's fastest growing telecommunications market. Each year China installs enough phone lines to replace a network the size of Pacific Bell. By the end of 1999, China had around 40m cellular subscribers. Only the US market is expected to be larger by the end of the year 2000. The US government believes that China will be the world's second largest personal computer market by the end of the year 2000, and third largest semi-conductor market by 2001. It is predicted that there will be over 20m Internet users by the end of 2000.

US-based IT firms have already benefited greatly from rapidly growing Chinese demand for IT goods and services. Between 1990 and 1998, US high technology exports to China increased more than fivefold, and exports of communications equipment grew over ninefold. These large increases were achieved despite substantial restrictions on access to the China market. The terms of accession to which China has agreed open the possibility for far faster growth of US (and other foreign) business interests in the Chinese IT market than were achieved in the past. China's information technology tariffs in 1999 averaged 13 per cent. This added around $200 to the price of a $1500 computer, providing significant protection for indigenous manufacturers. After China's entry to the WTO, two thirds of the tariffs will be eliminated by 2003 and the remainder by 2005. Immediately on entry to the WTO China's quotas on information technology products will be eliminated.

Up until 2000, the right to import and export, or to engage in distribution services, including wholesaling, retailing, repairing, warehousing or servicing, was restricted to a small number of firms with government authorization. After entry to the WTO, foreign firms will be allowed to import high technology products into any part of the country. Foreign firms will be allowed to establish, own and operate distribution services within three years of admission to the WTO. The US Government commented: 'This will allow our businesses to export to China from here at home, and to have their own distribution network in China, rather than being forced to set up factories there to sell products through Chinese partners' (*The White House*). After accession to the WTO, foreign IT firms will be able to distribute directly to customers, enabling them to tailor products to specific markets, and to provide direct, quality after-sales service and support.

Up until the year 2000, foreign investment in telecommunications was strictly prohibited. China's accession to the WTO will allow foreign investment in all telecommunication services. For value-added services (including, for example, electronic mail, voice mail, Internet, on-line information and database retrieval, and enhanced value-added facsimile services), China has agreed immediately on accession to allow 30 per cent foreign participation, rising to 49 per cent after one year and 50 per cent after two years. Foreign service suppliers may provide services in the key markets of Beijing, Guangzhou and Shanghai immediately upon accession, followed by 14 other major cities after one year, and nationwide after two years. For mobile voice and data services (including all analogue/digital cellular and personal communication services), under the China-US Agreement, China agreed to allow a 25 per cent foreign equity share one year after accession, rising to 49 per cent five years after accession. Immediately on accession, foreign suppliers were to be allowed to provide services in the key cities of Beijing, Guangzhou and Shanghai, extending to 14 other major cities after three years and nationwide after five years. The EU-China agreement of May 2000 produced further concessions from the Chinese side. China agreed that immediately upon accession, multinational mobile phone companies would be allowed to take a 25 per cent stake in joint ventures, rising to 35 per cent after one year and 49 per cent after just two years. These were major advances compared to the US-China Agreement, of great importance to the 'European champions' in the mobile phone sector. For domestic and international services (including, for example, voice, facsimile, intra-company e-mail, voice and data services) foreign service suppliers will be allowed to hold a 25 per cent equity share three years after accession, 35 per cent after five years and 49 per cent after six years. Foreign service suppliers will have access to the Beijing, Guangzhou and Shanghai markets after three years, 14 other major cities after five years, and nationwide after six years.

On accession to the WTO, China will adopt WTO norms for telecoms regulation. China has agreed to implement 'the pro-competitive regulatory principles embodied in the WTO Basic Telecommunications Agreement' (*The White House*). These include 'access to the public telecom networks of incumbent suppliers (that is, interconnection rights) under non-discriminatory terms and at cost-oriented rates, as well as an independent regulatory authority'. This means that foreign telecom firms 'cannot be discriminated against in seeking to provide their services over the existing infrastructure of Chinese telecommunications providers'. China has also committed to technology-neutral scheduling, which means that any basic service may be provided through any means of technology (for example, cable, wireless, satellites).

China has agreed to 'eliminate practices that cost American jobs and technology'. Foreign IT firms that export to or invest in China will no longer be required to transfer their technology to China: 'This will better protect US competitiveness and the results of US research and development' (*The White House*). IT imports into China will no longer be conditional on performance criteria of any kind, including offset and technology requirements or the existence of a competing domestic producer: 'All this will make it significantly easier for American companies to export to China from the United States rather than having to set up in China in order to sell products there'.

China's state-owned electronics firms will be required to make purchases and sales 'solely on commercial terms' and 'will provide US firms the opportunity to compete on non-discriminatory terms' (*The White House*).

In sum, the conditions on which China has agreed to enter the WTO constitute a dissolution of China's right to implement an industrial policy in this sector. Immediately upon entry, if the terms to which China has signed are implemented, then the capacity of the Chinese state to support the domestic IT industry will be dramatically weakened. The agreement means that within only a few years, there will be greatly reduced capability to protect and support domestic firms in these sectors. Moreover, there is every incentive for multinational giants in these sectors to advance their actual behaviour beyond the formal regulations, in the expectation that these 'illegal' activities will be validated retrospectively, such as took place on a large scale under the China-China-Foreign arrangement (see below).

## Financial services

Under the terms of the China-US Agreement of November 1999 on the terms of China's entry to the WTO, China agreed to liberalize drastically the environment in which its financial institutions would operate. Under the terms of the Agreement the 'global level playing field' will soon arrive at the door of the Chinese financial services industry.

Currently, foreign banks are not allowed to undertake local currency business in China. Only a small number are allowed to engage in local currency business with their foreign clients. China also imposes strict geographical limitations on the establishment of foreign banks. China has agreed to allow full market access for foreign banks within five years. It has agreed to allow foreign banks to undertake local currency business with Chinese enterprises within two years of accession, and to allow local currency business with individuals from five years after accession. All geographic and customer restrictions will be removed within five years.

Currently, only four foreign insurance firms have been permitted to operate in China. These have been required to join a joint venture with a government-approved partner and their activities have been restricted to a narrow range of operations. Under the China-US WTO Agreement, China has agreed to award licences on a 'prudential' basis, with no economic needs test or quantitative limits on the number of licences issued. It has agreed to progressively eliminate geographical limitations within three years and permit internal branching consistent with the elimination of these restrictions. It has agreed to allow expansion over five years of the scope of activities for foreign insurers to include group, health, and pension lines of insurance. For non-life insurance, branch and joint-ventures at 51 per cent equity share for foreign firms are permitted on accession, and wholly-owned subsidiaries permitted within two years from date of accession. For life insurance, joint ventures are permitted with the partner of choice at 50 per cent equity share immediately upon accession.

## Other sectors

### *Agriculture*

China has agreed to reduce its agricultural tariffs from 31 per cent to 14 per cent for priority US farm exports over a maximum of four years. These include beef (falling from 45 per cent to 12 per cent), citrus fruits (40 per cent to 12 per cent), apples (30 per cent to 10 per cent), cheese (50 per cent to 12 per cent), wine (65 per cent to 20 per cent) and beer (70 per cent to 0 per cent). For grains, China has agreed to increase the import quotas for corn, wheat and rice together, from 2.6m tons to 22m tons in 2004. For imports within the quota, tariffs will be only around 1–2 per cent. China has agreed to eliminate export subsidies entirely.

### *Audiovisual*

Under current regulations, the distribution of books, magazines, movies, sound recordings, and videos is highly restricted. For example, foreign firms are not allowed to participate at all in the sound recordings industry. Under the China-US Agreement, China has agreed to allow 49 per cent foreign equity for the distribution of video and sound recordings. It has agreed to allow majority ownership within three years for the construction and ownership and operation of cinemas. It will allow 20 films per year to be imported on a revenue-sharing basis immediately upon accession.

### Travel and tourism
Currently, the activities of foreign firms are highly restricted in this sector. China has agreed to allow unrestricted access to the China market for foreign hotel operators. Majority foreign ownership will be permitted immediately upon accession, and 100 per cent foreign ownership will be phased in within three years.

### Retailing services
Under the US-China Agreement, the retail sector was opened up to greater foreign participation. Within three years of accession, there were to be no limitations at all on the equity share of the multinational companies, or on their geographical location. However, the Agreement did limit multinationals to minority participation in stores of greater than 20 000 square metres, or where the multinational operated more than 30 stores in China. Under the EU-China Agreement, China agreed to lift the equity restriction on multinational retail chains and to remove the limitations on floor space, allowing them to establish wholly-owned retail chains throughout the country, 'representing unprecedented opportunities to department stores and chain stores in the world's most populous country' (*Financial Times*).

## Implementation of the Agreement

The integration of China into the full application of WTO rules will be rapid: 'On accession to the WTO, China will begin opening its market from day one in virtually every sector. The phase-in of further concessions will be limited to five years in almost all cases, and in many cases one to three years' (Barshefsky). Even a leading US economist, who is generally strongly supportive of the Agreement, Harvard University's Richard Cooper, cautioned that he was 'very uncomfortable' with the high speed of implementation required under the Agreement.

The Agreement that China has signed is going to be taken very seriously indeed by the advanced economies and the businesses based in those countries. In early May 2000, the US initiated a series of enforcement proceedings at the WTO against five countries for violations of WTO rules. These included Brazil for alleged violations on textiles and patents, Romania on clothing, poultry and distilled spirits, India on requirements for the automotive industry, the Philippines on local content requirements for motorcycles, cars and commercial vehicles, and Argentina on patents.

The seriousness with which the US takes the Agreement on China's entry to the WTO is indicated by the fact that the US President has requested special resources from the national budget to support what will be 'the largest monitoring and enforcement effort for any agreement ever' (Barshefsky). In April 2000 it was reported that the administration was asking Congress to provide $22m for new enforcement resources for the Commerce, Agriculture, and State Departments, as well as the US trade representative's office. This would represent a tripling of resources dedicated to China's trade compliance. There is no doubt that the US will be in the lead in attempting to enforce the WTO Agreement.

The fact that China will be within the WTO means that the full weight of international pressure can be brought to bear on it to observe the Agreement which it has signed, rather than individual countries contending with China: 'Within the WTO, [the US] will be able to work with 134 other members, many of whom will be concerned about the same issues we raise and all of whom will have the legal right to enforce China's commitments' (Barshefsky). The capability to enforce the Agreement is greatly increased by the fact that it is highly detailed, with 'highly specific commitments in all areas, clear time-tables for implementation, and firm end-dates for full compliance'. These will allow the US to 'carefully monitor China's compliance and present evidence of failure to comply' (Barshefsky).

## Non-economic objectives of the Agreement

### Chinese side

It has long been recognized that state-directed industrial policy provides wide opportunities for corruption permitted by the existence of economic rents derived from control over non-market methods of resource allocation. Indeed, Adam Smith's *Wealth of Nations*, written at the end of the eighteenth century, contained a sustained critique of the corrupt British state that intervened heavily in controlling imports and subsidizing exports. There is a large modern literature on rent-seeking associated with state intervention.

China's highly-developed system of 'connections' is closely related to the huge web of state interventions in the economy. This system closely parallels that found in many developing countries with extensive state interventions to support industrial policies, such as the 'licence Raj' that is slowly being unwound in India. The extent of corruption associated with the Chinese system of state intervention in the economy is enormous, and impossible to measure. One-party rule combined with extensive channels for state intervention in the economy provides an environment in which corruption can flourish. Most observers believe that the extent of corruption increased in the 1990s. There are innumerable channels available for officials to benefit from corrupt practices in the gradually-reforming economy.

Large-scale purchases by state-owned enterprises provide wide opportunities for bribery to steer contracts in particular directions. Large-scale state allocation of financial resources through state-owned banks and other quasi-state financial institutions such as the International Trust and Investment Companies ('ITICs') provides large opportunities for corrupt allocation of loans. The collapse of one 'ITIC' and the near collapse of a major 'Red Chip' company registered in Hong Kong in 1998–99, resulted in close involvement of international auditors. They revealed fraud and straightforward theft on a huge scale. State-owned enterprises, with little monitoring from shareholders, have developed hugely complex investments in 'children', 'grandchildren', and 'great-grandchildren' companies, with a cascade of virtually unmonitored investments. Local protectionism provides a huge arena for further official corruption. A mass of local official licence and unofficial approvals are required before investment by other Chinese entities is permitted in a given locality. A wide array of local 'non-tariff barriers' operates. All of these provide opportunities for bribery of officials.

Foreign exchange controls provide a wide range of possibilities of benefiting from bribing corrupt officials. Continued state involvement in the distribution system, including the remaining price controls, provides extensive opportunities for officials to benefit from their privileged access to allocative rights. Extensive state intervention in international trade provides large opportunities for smuggling. Huge profits can be earned from smuggling goods in the most highly protected sectors such as vehicles and tobacco. Many officials in powerful institutions, especially the People's Liberation Army, have been proved to be heavily involved in smuggling. Granting foreign trade rights to a small number of state-approved entities provides a large incentive to seek personal profit from using these rights.

The channels available for official corruption in dealing with foreign business in the 1990s included extraction of payments for the right to import goods, for the right to set up a business or establish a joint venture in China, for the right to have access to distribution channels from which foreign businesses were officially excluded, or for support in hastening a bureaucratic decision. The more important the deal, the higher the level of official involved.

A deep problem for China, as for other developing countries, is the relatively slow growth of the technical capability and ethical standards of the supervisory and legal system. Corruption of the police force has been a major source of public resentment. Those who are entrusted with the task of enforcing the regular anti-corruption drives are themselves often corrupt. In one such nationwide drive in 1998, 756 prosecutors were themselves punished for corruption and mishandling of cases.

There has been huge and growing public anger at the deep extent of corruption associated with the 'network' society. One recent evaluation of the extent of corruption in China concluded: 'Corruption in China to-day has reached dangerous proportions, and involves collusion among officials, legal professionals, businessmen and even state institutions such as government agencies and banks. This trend of institutional corruption has undermined the integrity and reliability of the state apparatus and, if unchecked, may trigger serious and disruptive political repercussions.'

China's leaders have repeatedly warned of the growing dangers to the fabric of China's society of the large extent of corruption. A major anti-corruption drive in 1999/2000 resulted in some high-profile public prosecutions. In March 2000, the former deputy governor of Jiangxi province was executed for corruption. Just a few months later, Cheng Kejie, one of nineteen deputy chairmen of the National People's Congress, was sentenced to death for corruption. He was accused of amassing millions of dollars in kickbacks from land deals and in return for granting development contracts. One analyst commented on the recent death sentences: 'The problem can't be solved by just punishing some people, because this system itself breeds corruption'. Many people within China believe that fundamental reform of the economic system is necessary in order to end corruption. They believe that the application of WTO rules will greatly help to achieve this result, by reducing both international and domestic state interventions through which officials can derive rents.

## US side

The US negotiators were explicit about their non-economic objectives. The language and objectives are strongly reminiscent of the US government discussions of their policy goals in the former Soviet Union in the late 1980s and early 1990s. A key part of this is the characterization of the debate within China in black and white terms. The US public is informed that there are only two groups, 'reformers', who are 'good', and 'hardliners', who are 'bad'. The goal of US policy is to support the people who are 'good' and seek for the overthrow of the people who are 'bad': 'These commitments are a remarkable victory for the economic reformers in China ... Altogether, this will give China's people more access to information, and weaken the ability of hardliners to isolate China's public from outside influence and ideas'(Barshefsky). There is, indeed, an extreme group of 'hardliners', the 'new left wing', which is deeply suspicious of further integration with the world economy. At the other extreme, there is a significant group of people, the extreme free marketeers, who favour high-speed liberalization and immediate 'close' integration with the world economic system. However, in between is a broad spectrum of opinion. This includes a wide range of people who support the move towards a market economy and closer integration with the world economic system, but who believe that China needs to proceed cautiously. They are deeply concerned at the potential destabilizing effect of ultra-rapid integration, given the immense power of the global oligopolies, and the weakness of China's domestic 'national champions'.

The US policymakers have made a strong linkage between the Agreement and the transformation of China's political system. The US government regards China's accession to the WTO under the agreed terms as having 'potential beyond economics and trade' (Barshefsky) . It is viewed as 'a means to advance the rule of law in China', and 'a precedent for willingness to accept international standards of behaviour in other fields': 'That is why many Hong Kong and Chinese activists for democracy and human rights – Martin Lee, the leader of the Hong Kong Democratic Party; Ren Wanding, a dissident who has spent twenty years of his life in prison – see WTO accession as China's most important step toward reform in twenty years.' (Barshefsky). The US government's support for the WTO 'rests on a long-term commitment to human rights and freedoms, as well as new opportunities and strengthened guarantees of fairness for Americans' (Barshefsky).

The US government explicitly links the destruction of China's large state enterprises with transformation of China's political system: 'Opening markets will put enormous competitive pressures on China's beleaguered state-owned industries – bulwarks of political conservatism and socialist economics. In contrast a WTO Agreement will unleash China's entrepreneurial sector, which supports increased economic and political freedom.' (*The White House*).

The determination of the US (and EU) negotiators to push China towards rapid liberalization of its IT industry was not only motivated by economic considerations. A major explicit consideration also was the desire to overturn the Communist Party and achieve the same political result in China as US policy under Reagan helped to achieve in the former USSR. A further factor of great importance in evaluating the impact of the terms under which China's IT industry will be required to operate after China's entry to the WTO is the ideological purpose and consequences of the US and EU governments. As well as a business interest, there is also an explicit ideological objective to the China–US WTO agreement. A major objective is to greatly accelerate political change through undermining the control of the Chinese Communist Party: 'Opening China's Information Technology market will…increase the flow of information among Chinese and between China and the outside world, in ways and in such volumes that no amount of censorship or monitoring can totally control. *This cannot but promote the right kind of change in China.*' (emphasis added) (*The White House*).

# 3.4   Prospects: (i) The 'optimistic' view

## Structural change

The Chinese leadership has been consistently extremely positive in its evaluation of the capabilities of China's large enterprises to restructure and compete with the world's leading firms inside the WTO. In May 1999, China's Premier, Zhu Rongji commented: 'If China wants to join the WTO, and wants to be integrated into the international community, it must play by the rules of the game. China cannot do that without making concessions ... Backed by the achievements of the past two decades' reform and opening, Chinese enterprises will be able to withstand any impact.' Some foreign commentators have emphasized that large Chinese enterprises can quickly become globally competitive. For example, at a meeting of international businessmen and policy- makers in Beijing in 2000, a US business leader suggested that under the impact of international competition, China's large enterprises could rapidly improve their international competitiveness, 'just as the US auto industry did in the face of Japanese competition in the 1980s and early 1990s'.

However, the concensus view outside China is that the terms under which China has agreed to enter the WTO will produce great difficulties for China's large enterprises. The former Prime Minister of Singapore, Lee Kuan Yew, believes that China joining the WTO will lead to the 'creative destruction of outdated industrial plants'. Almost all commentators outside China, and many inside the country, welcome this likelihood. They believe that through joining the WTO, the destruction of China's 'value-destroying' large enterprises will liberate capital to infuse the small and medium-sized enterprise sector. Through this process, they believe that China will become 'one of the most important players in the global exchange of goods, services, capital, talent and ideas in the 21st century' (Lee Kuan Yew).

Many commentators and policymakers outside China, including the US president, as well as many within it, explicitly welcome the possibility of political turmoil stemming from China's entry to the WTO. They hope that through the resulting turbulence, the Chinese Communist Party will be overthrown, promoting the 'right kind of political change'. They hope that China will experience the kind of dramatic system change that the former USSR went through in the late 1980s and early 1990s. They believe that only through system collapse can a 'clean sheet' be established for thoroughgoing system reform, including mass privatization. This approach has strong resonances with the debate about reform in the former USSR in the late 1980s and early 1990s. The tone is similarly populist in its promise of huge gains for the mass of the country's citizens from the proposed system change.

In the late 1980s and early 1990s it was axiomatic among commentators to talk of the desirability of compressing the 'pain' of transition in the former USSR and Eastern Europe into a short period. Janos Kornai recommended: 'If the only cure for a person is to cut off his leg, it is more humane to perform *a single amputation* with the necessary anesthesia than to schedule a long-lasting operation and cut off a thin slice every week or month'. Another argued: 'The Polish economy clearly needs *a surgical operation* to remove the outdated and inefficient industries' (Stanlislav Gomulka). The same tone of approval for the destructive effects of international competition dominated the language of many of those involved in the debate on China in the year 2000: 'It is better to suffer pain for a short period than to drag the pain out over a long period of time' (Laurence Lau, Stanford University).

A major part of the intense debate about the impact of the WTO on China focused on the effect new information technology will have on the economy. At high-level meetings held in China in 2000 to evaluate the impact of joining the WTO, there was immense optimism from non-Chinese participants about the positive impact of the WTO through the rapid penetration of new information technology into China. A wide range of commentators argued that the IT revolution will result in the democratization of economic life and hugely enhanced global opportunities for small firms. The promise is of everyone in China becoming rich through the internet which will expand at high speed after China enters the WTO. There will be a happy marriage of US business interests in information technology with the interests of the mass of Chinese people.

Klaus Schwab, President of the World Economic Forum, argued: 'we are witnessing the democratizing [effect] of the information revolution'. Capabilities that 'in the past were possessed only by large and powerful organizations' can now be 'obtained by individuals and small organizations in all walks of life'. These technologies and services 'can generate many new and rewarding employment opportunities for every nation's citizens'. Experience around the world 'demonstrates beyond any doubt that over time, new information and communications technologies increase the overall level and quality of employment'. Laurence Lau (Stanford University) argued that the IT revolution will lead to 'existing demands for goods and services being increasingly supplied by new entrants, most of them small and medium-sized start-up firms'. He believes that the IT revolution will cause widespread 'creative destruction' in which 'new firms take away business from the old firms'. In developing countries such as China, there will be 'creation without destruction': 'Developing countries have the ability to leapfrog. There are no vested interests to protect; no existing businesses to be cannibalized; there can be creation without destruction.' (Laurence Lau).

In this view, given its massive labour force, with a high level of literacy compared to other developing countries, China can become 'sub-contractor to the world'. There are argued to be huge opportunities for Chinese SMEs to become outsourced suppliers to the world's leading systems integrators in almost every sector. Until now, the fastest-growing activities have been in 'old industries', such as garments, plastic products, luggage, sports goods, assembly of electrical goods, and furniture. However, there are opportunities for Chinese SMEs to provide subcontracting for global systems integrators in a wide range of 'new technology industries', including components and sub-systems for aircraft, heavy electrical equipment, IT hardware and auto components firms, biotechnology research and drugs testing for global pharmaceutical firms, software services for software firms, and local music, TV programmes, advertising and movies for global media companies.

As this process evolves, so China's myriad SME firms may form a steadily expanding part of the global corporation's 'external firm'. Over time, Chinese people may form a growing proportion of the managers, scientists, engineers and senior officials of globalizing systems integrator firms. Chinese financial institutions may gradually increase their ownership of 'Western' corporations as Chinese income levels rise and pension funds expand. In the long-term, China's weight of population, the high and rising quality of its human resources, and the growing fraction of global output that is produced in China, may cause the gradual 'Sinification' of the world's business system. As China gradually re-assumes its position at the core of the world economy Chinese businesses and employees may transform global capitalism from the 'inside', within the global corporation, and within the 'external firm' that is co-ordinated by the global corporation. In time China may well return to the position at the heart of the global business system that it occupied for one thousand years.

In fact, the difficulties of adjustment to the WTO under the terms agreed, are likely to be much greater than such 'optimistic' views, with their populist undertones, suggest. Moreover, the impact on the sociopolitical environment could be destabilizing with a potential negative impact on the entire economy.

## Trade and foreign investment

Most analysts have emphasized the trade-enhancing impact of China joining the WTO. Prior to the WTO Agreement, China already had relatively open access to the US and EU economies. It is not clear that the only way to maintain this access was to enter the WTO at all, let alone under the terms that were agreed. Under the existing conditions of market access, China was able to increase its exports more rapidly than virtually any other developing country. Its exports increased from $24bn in 1980 to over $207bn in 1997, and its share of world exports tripled from 1.03 per cent in 1980 to 3.01 per cent in 1997. Its average annual export growth rate from 1980 to 1990 was 11.5 per cent compared with 2.7 per cent for all low income countries (excluding India and China) and in 1990–98 its export growth rate was 14.9 per cent per annum compared with 7.0 per cent for low income countries (excluding India and China). Under the existing trade rules, China already produced one-third of the world's export of suitcases and handbags, a quarter of the world's toys, and one-eighth of the clothing. China is 'hard to beat in low margin, quick-to-market manufactures'.

Despite rapid growth of its exports, the base from which China's export growth started was very small. Consequently, by 1997, its export total was smaller than that of the Netherlands, and far behind that of the eight richest countries in the world. China's exports in 1997 were only one-fifth of those of the US. The possibility of widespread restrictions on China's exports to the advanced economies was small.

In sum, the main impact of the WTO on China's trade is likely to be a large increase in China's imports rather than an increase in exports, reducing China's large current account surplus, especially that with the US. The US made no market-opening concessions at all to China in the Agreement. The increased market access was entirely on the Chinese side. The US will be the principal beneficiary from the opening of China's markets through the Agreement. China is the US's fifth largest trading partner and growing fast. The World Bank estimates that China needs over $750bn in new infrastructure over the next decade, including power generation, transportation equipment, aircraft, environmental controls, and telecommunications networks. The US is in the prime position to be the major beneficiary from the opening of the China market through selling large quantities of these goods and services to China in the coming period. In addition to industrial products, the US will be the main beneficiary from the opening of the Chinese market for farm products:

> The American Farm Bureau has called China the 'most important growth market for American agriculture into the 21st century'. It is already our sixth largest agricultural export market and a major purchaser of US wheat, grains, meat, chicken, pork, cotton and soybeans. By 2030 it is forecast that China's annual wheat imports could reach 90 million tons, half of to-day's total world grain exports. In the 21st century, USDA projects that Asia will account for 75 per cent of the growth of US farm exports, of which 50 per cent will be in China (US-China Trade Council).

A major objective for the US in negotiating the WTO Agreement is to reduce the trade deficit with China through high-speed growth of US exports:

> WTO membership would result in an unprecedented opening of China's market, creating opportunities for US companies and driving down the deficit in a beneficial way. Whatever happens in bilateral trade flows, China's WTO market-opening can only help the overall US trade balance. The US stands to gain unprecedented access to China's markets. *We are giving up nothing*, since the US market is already open. Getting rid of Chinese barriers will open markets for leading US exports, such as high technology, capital goods, services and agriculture (US-China Trade Council).

The Congressional Research Service estimates that the WTO agreement would boost US exports to China by $13–14bn per annum by the year 2005.

China's membership of the WTO is likely to provide a stimulus to foreign direct investment, by ensuring a much more secure framework of international law within which multinationals' investment can be conducted. The elimination of the severe controls on distribution within China is likely to have a substantial impact on the incentive to conduct business in China. Southeast Asian countries are nervous that China will experience a surge of FDI at their expense. However, the long-term effects are complex.

China's entry to the WTO may have a substantial impact on the incentive structure that confronts multinational companies. We have already seen that it will eliminate the requirement for multinationals to establish production bases within China in order to supply the Chinese market, enabling them instead to import from other production locations. The Agreement may even reduce the incentive to invest in China for many types of business. New options will become available, such as exporting cars to China from close at hand production sites, such as Thailand and South Korea in preference to production facilities in China. The incentive to export from close at hand rather than to produce within China will be increased to the degree that the multinationals have doubts about China's political stability.

A further major consequence of the liberalization of investment requirements, taken together with the liberalization of marketing channels, is a great reduction in the incentive to establish joint ventures. India's liberalization process is progressing more slowly than China's. However, even India's much slower liberalization has had major effects on the incentive structure facing multinational firms. One commentator concluded recently: 'I can see the writing on the wall. Joint ventures are gone. They are history.' The landmark decision that woke India up was that of Honda to set up a wholly-owned subsidiary to produce scooters and bikes in direct competition with its joint venture, Hero Honda. Greater transparency and reduced state intervention in the distribution process has diminished the value of having a local partner. Foreign companies are becoming keen to nurture their intellectual property and brands rather than piggy-back on a local name: 'After a decade of reform, multinationals may at last be prepared to invest more in India, in high-value activities, more closely related to their global goals. However, local investors may not see many of the gains.' (*Financial Times*).

## 3.5  Prospects: (ii) The shock of defeat

### Large structural change will be necessary

When China enters the WTO, there will be intense pressure from the high-income countries to apply the rules to which it has agreed. The US is already strongly pursuing other countries, including Japan, Brazil, India and Mexico, to apply the WTO rules fully, and has made clear its intention forcefully to push China to apply them to the full. China's leaders and negotiators have repeatedly emphasized that they intend carefully to observe the rules by which they have agreed to play. If China did, indeed, apply the rules to which it has signed up, then it is likely that a considerable fraction of its large-scale industry would not survive the resulting intense competition. This is readily acknowledged, and typically welcomed, by US policymakers:

> In the short-term, WTO membership means painful short-term adjustments. Decrepit
> state-owned enterprises need massive overhaul to become internationally competitive.
> They will be forced to restructure by cutting costs, adopting modern production

methods, and eliminating excess employment and overheads. Some will fail or go bankrupt. Such adjustments explain why state-owned enterprises and political conservatives oppose a WTO Agreement. The future of continued economic reform may ride on the WTO (US-China Trade Council).

In the advanced economies, a succession of under-performing state-owned enterprises dramatically turned around their performance, and 'released enormous amounts of shareholder value'. However, privatization would do little, if anything, to improve the competitive capability of China's 'national champions' in direct competition with the world's leading corporations. China's aspiring 'national champions' face a very different situation from that of the leading European state-owned firms at the time of their privatization. Even under state ownership, companies like Volkswagen, Repsol, Telefonica, Renault, France Telecom, Elf Aquitaine, Aerospatiale, Usinor, Alcatel, Finnemecanica, ENI, BP, Rolls-Royce, British Aerospace, and British Steel, were far more powerful, with much greater technical capabilities, a much more sophisticated portfolio of products, and much greater management skills, than are possessed by the commanding heights of the Chinese economy today. Their capability to be rapidly turned into global leaders through radically changed management methods was far greater than is the case for China's 'national champions'. The challenges they had to face in the early stages of globalization were far less severe than those that confront Chinese firms now that the global business revolution is well under way. China's large state-owned enterprises are far behind the global first movers in the privatization and globalization race. Former state-owned companies and powerful private firms have already established powerful positions in sector after sector. China's potential global giants corporations are now entering the globalization race with the best positions already occupied by incumbent giant corporations.

The revolution in the nature of the global corporation is not only radically changing the nature of the opportunities for Chinese firms, but also the challenges they face. Across a wide range of sectors, from aerospace, complex engineering, pharmaceuticals, oil and petrochemicals, automobiles, IT hardware and software, and telecoms services through to production and retail of the simplest consumer goods, it has become almost impossible to compete directly on the 'global level playing field' with the world's leading 'systems integrators' based in the advanced economies. Moreover, it is extremely difficult to compete head-on even with the leading globalizing first-tier supplier companies, including such diverse goods and services as aero-engines, avionics systems, auto brake, exhaust and heating systems, metal cans, plastic bottles, investment banks, insurance, hotels, and advertising agencies. On the 'global level playing field', not only China's 'commanding heights' of large state-owned firms, but a wide range of first-tier suppliers of goods and services would also find it impossible to compete.

There is no question that China's large state-owned enterprises would be required to undergo massive 'restructuring'. However, it is impossible to imagine that many, if any, of China's 'commanding heights' businesses would be able to build themselves into global leaders on the 'global level playing field' that is likely shortly to be introduced at high speed, under the close surveillance of the US government. Their only hope would be a renovated and much more effective industrial policy.

Instead of being turned into global leaders, like most of the powerful privatized state-owned enterprises in Europe in the 1980s and 1990s, a large fraction of China's 'national champions' face the prospect of, at best, takeover by the multinationals, followed by drastic downsizing and absorption into the production system of the global firm. Many of them will face bankruptcy. There are almost ninety million people employed in China's state-owned enterprises. It is an open question how many of these will lose their jobs if China's state-owned enterprises are forced to compete rapidly on the 'global level playing field'. It is hard to imagine that the number will be small. We have seen also that there are great uncertainties about the rate at which employment will grow outside the state sector, as well as problems concerning the location and nature of new employment. Moreover, large-scale structural adjustment will certainly be required also in the SME sector as well as in agriculture. Coping with these huge structural adjustment issues simultaneously will be extremely difficult. Already, in the late 1990s there were numerous reports of strikes and violence as China's state-owned enterprises begin to downsize.

To some degree, the poorly developed state of China's infrastructure may insulate inland areas from the full impact of structural adjustment, especially in the light industrial sectors. However, in most branches of the capital goods industries, including telecoms equipment, aerospace, automobiles and components, oil and petrochemicals, and power generating equipment, poorly developed infrastructure will provide no relief from intensified competition. Moreover, even in 'basic' capital goods such as steel, as well as in food and fast-moving consumer goods, in services, such as the mass media, retailing, financial services, and hotels, there will be sharply intensified competition in the high value-added parts of the industry. This competition will be greatest in the more highly developed coastal areas, where the bulk of China's higher income earners live. The low value-added 'commodity' parts of these businesses in the hinterland are of little interest to the global giants. They do not provide the basis on which Chinese indigenous firms could generate high profits and challenge the global giants.

## The problem of finding employment for displaced workers

A key issue for the restructuring effort that will be necessary is the pace at which alternative employment opportunities will grow for the large number of employees who are likely to lose their jobs if China fully observes the terms of the Agreement to which it is signatory. There are several interconnected issues that affect the answer to this issue.

The first issue is the pace at which employment opportunities in the SME sector can grow, in order to soak up the employment which is lost from the massive restructuring of the large state enterprise sector. We have already noted that even before the Agreement, China enjoyed rapid export growth, and its exports to the US in particular grew at high speed. A large fraction of these exports came from small and medium enterprises, generating rapidly increased employment. It is hard to see how the Agreement could do much to accelerate this already rapid growth of exports from the SME sector. In addition the SME sector is itself likely to undergo a sharp increase in competitive pressure due to the opening of China's markets, due to a reduction in subsidies available to the sector from local governments, and due to intense pressures to operate more efficiently on the global level playing field through advances in the use of information technology. In other words, it is difficult to be optimistic that employment absorption in this sector will increase rapidly beyond the already high level of around 120m people, even if output in the sector continues to advance rapidly. Indeed, employment might easily decline in this sector alongside rising sales revenue.

Secondly, the issue of availability of alternative employment for workers in the disintegrating large enterprises has to be considered in relation to the potential growth of other new entrants to the labour market in the non-farm sector. China's population and workforce are still growing at a significant, if much-reduced, pace compared to the 1970s. Between 1980 and 1998, the total working age population rose by no less than 286m, at an annual average rate of 2.9 per cent. In the 1990s, the growth rate dropped considerably, as a result of the impact of the one-child policy. However, there still was an increase of almost 70m in the working age population between 1990 and 1998, with a growth rate of 1.2 per cent per annum. China is predicted to add more than 140m people to the working age population by the year 2020.

Thirdly, China's farm sector employs around 330m people. There is no agreed estimate of rural 'surplus' labour, indeed it is empirically elusive, but all estimates agree that the proportion is large. Recent Chinese estimates suggest that the number grew from 95m in 1984 to 170m in 1990, rising to 200m in 1994. Most predictions suggest that, independently of China joining the WTO, the absolute number will continue to rise for some years. The farm sector has already felt considerable pressure from changes in farm technology and concentration of holdings that have led to increasing output per worker. It is thought that around 100–120m semi-permanent migrants already work outside the farm sector. This issue has caused immense socioeconomic problems. Coping with these has been a major headache for the leadership. The WTO Agreement is likely to have an independent and large impact on the demand for labour in the farm sector. Importing significant and steadily increasing quantities of farm produce from the US and other advanced economies is likely to have a substantial effect on the demand for labour in China's farm sector. It can be expected to substantially increase the flow of labour to the cities looking for employment in the non-farm sector, and competing for jobs with the displaced workers from the state-owned enterprises.

Finally, there is the issue of the regional distribution of employment opportunities. A large fraction of the decline in employment in state enterprises is likely to occur in North and Northeast China. A large fraction of any increase in employment in the non-farm sector is likely to occur in South China (including Shanghai). Inter-regional migration is a highly disruptive process, causing great stresses on public transport, public infrastructure, welfare demands and housing stock, let alone the personal stresses on family life.

If the Agreement allowed a long period of transition, then many of these stresses might be dealt with adequately, albeit that they amount to a massive structural change. However, it will be extremely difficult to cope with them at the high speed of integration that is envisaged by the US-China Agreement. China's welfare system is still in its infancy. It is impossible to imagine how the Chinese state can provide suitable welfare provisions for the large number of people who may need assistance. One consequence of the magnitude of the task that may face the Chinese government, is accelerated pressure to privatize the most valuable assets in the state's portfolio. These include, most obviously, China's telecoms assets and urban land and public housing. It is thought that these could raise as much as $300–400bn and $200–250bn respectively for the Chinese government which 'appear to be sufficient for dealing with the pain of restructuring' (Andy Xie, MSDW). These numbers are, however, highly speculative and need to be treated with great caution.

## Information technology and the adjustment process

Several cautionary points need to be made about the highly optimistic views concerning the impact of the IT revolution on China in the period immediately ahead. First, the IT revolution is already taking place in China. It is fallacious to directly associate this with the terms under which China has agreed to enter the WTO. For example, China had already become the world's largest market for mobile phones, with huge associated infrastructure needs, independently of whether and under what terms China joined the WTO. Joining the WTO on the terms agreed could even slow down the rate of progress of the IT revolution in China, since it reduces the incentive for multinationals to manufacture IT products within China as opposed to importing them. Secondly, a major consequence of the IT revolution in China is to provide a potentially vast new frontier for the world's leading IT hardware, software and service firms, almost all of which are headquartered in the advanced economies. The potential benefits to US- and EU-based corporations from the Chinese IT revolution are enormous, with major implications for the stock price, wealth and pensions of US and EU citizens.

Thirdly, the IT revolution is inseparable from the revolution in the global media industry. There is no doubt that the WTO Agreement has major implications for the telecoms and media industry in China. Dominance by US-based firms of the global media revolution has enormous implications for the way in which a global culture is being produced, dominated by US values and language. If China applies fully the terms of the WTO Agreement, then the combined impact of these two revolutions upon China's society and politics would be profound. Fourthly, infrastructure over much of China is still too poorly developed to easily allow SMEs to integrate with the global value chain. An apocryphal story was circulating in China in the year 2000 about an old man who grew garlic in a remote part of China. In this story the old man passes an internet café (*sic*) and goes inside to investigate. The owner of the café helps him to surf the net and find a buyer for his garlic in the US. The moral of the story is that even Chinese farmers can get rich on the internet, and that there is just one big interconnected, win-win world in the internet age. The story does not explain how the farmer was able to transport his garlic to the supermarket in the US from a remote part of China.

Fifthly, as we have seen, China's exports from SMEs have been the fastest-growing part of the Chinese economy during the reform period. It is questionable whether China's entry to the WTO and possible increased access to B2B business could significantly raise the growth rate of output value from China's SME sector much beyond the very high rates of growth already achieved. Thus, the rate of growth of new jobs in the SME sector, consequent upon increased exports of goods from Chinese-based SMEs connected by new information technology to the global value chain of large corporations, is highly uncertain. Sixthly, a major countervailing impact of the IT revolution is the dramatic reduction in administrative work undertaken directly by people that is made possible by the new technologies. The Chinese economy is ripe for large-scale replacement of the huge number of employees in SOEs who are engaged in routine administrative tasks. A sector in which employment levels are likely to be especially heavily affected by the rapid growth of information technology is the distribution system. At the end of the 1990s there were over 50m people working in China's wholesale, retail and distribution systems. As global businesses and their 'external firms' expand in China, so they will increasingly replace the vast labour-intensive structure with a more reliable, modern logistics system co-ordinated by state-of-the-art information technology. This will have large implications for employment levels in the distribution sector.

Finally, as we have seen, an important part of the change in the nature of the global firm in the business revolution has involved the 'cascade' effect, flowing down from global systems integrators to first-, second- and third-tier suppliers. This places great pressure for consolidation and associated cost reduction and technical progress upon the whole supply chain. It is highly uncertain how far the IT revolution will lead to the emergence of local production among relatively large, capital-intensive firms in China as opposed to myriads of SME firms. The associated impact on employment is, correspondingly, highly uncertain. It cannot be assumed to be positive.

## Socio-political consequences of the shock

If China strictly observes the terms of the WTO Agreement, as well as the conventional structural adjustment problems, it will face large-scale psychological and political adjustment difficulties. In almost all cases, successful late-industrializing countries established a group of indigenous large corporations that could compete on the global level playing field. This was true even for small countries like Sweden, Holland and Switzerland, and latterly, Taiwan, Korea and Hong Kong. If China were to continue to grow rapidly in the coming decades, then it would develop a unique form of capitalism among successful latecomer countries. This would be one that had few internationally competitive large corporations, and the commanding heights of whose business system were controlled mainly by international corporations based in the advanced countries.

Even for advanced European countries, it has been difficult to accept that 'national champions' may be unable to compete on the global level playing field as individual players. However, whereas individual European countries may have to accept the demise of their national champions, the continent as a whole is breeding a group of regional champions and transatlantic champions. For China, the absence of a 'national team' to compare with the 'European team' would present far greater political-psychological difficulties than was caused by the demise of old-style 'national champions' in individual European countries.

This result would cause intense difficulties for the Chinese national psyche. China has a long and proud economic history, combined with an acute sensitivity to its international humiliations from the 1840s onwards. The difficulties of accepting that the catch-up process is dominated by foreign corporations would be made all the more challenging by the fact that these corporations would be perceived as the instrument causing massive disruption within the state-owned sector. The challenge would be made even greater by the fact that the most powerful force of businesses within this process will be US-based large firms. It would undoubtedly be argued by many in China that Chinese jobs were being sacrificed in the interests of American shareholders. Moreover, almost everyone recognizes that the gains from joining the WTO within China are likely to be highly unevenly distributed. Many highly educated Chinese people would find employment within the global corporations or within the 'external firm' working indirectly for the global corporations. However, this number would be dwarfed by the number who were excluded from this magic circle. Indeed, China is entering the WTO at the time of the most intense pressure on employment within the global corporation and its surrounding 'external firm'. This pressure is being greatly intensified by the potentially large labour-displacing effects of new information technology.

The shock arising from the destruction of China's 'national champions' might not be confined to China. It might well have a deep impact on international relations. The most potent source of potential international conflict is in relations with the US. I have already analysed the US's dominance of the global business revolution. This dominance is most marked in the most sensitive of sectors, information technology, which is laying the foundation for the global economy of the twenty-first century. Already, there is powerful anti-US sentiment in China. Many people who are totally supportive of China's move towards a market economy feel dismayed by the potential dominance of US-based multinational firms within the Chinese economy after China enters the WTO. For them, it represents a further national humiliation after more than one hundred years of humiliation.

As a result of the recent revolutionary process of international merger and acquisition within the advanced capitalist economies, former 'national champions' have become truly international corporations. However, they still remain headquartered within the advanced economies. The vast bulk of their shareholders are institutions or citizens based within the advanced economies. There is, consequently, still a strong possibility that the impending acceleration in the rate of growth in investment within China by multinational firms will be perceived as a highly unequal relationship of dominance by advanced cultures, within which the US is pre-eminent, over the ancient culture of China. It is certain that many people in China will raise the cry of a 'Second Opium War'.

The forthcoming changes in the Chinese mass media will be a major element in the process of structural adjustment that awaits China within the WTO. It is highly uncertain how far the Chinese government will be able to control access to the global mass media once global corporations start to play an increased role in Chinese telecoms and mass media systems. There will be tremendous pressure to provide ubiquity of access to the global mass media. This pressure will arise from Chinese consumers, from Chinese equity partners, from Chinese firms in the industry, and from within the government itself to raise revenue from telecoms and media services. There will be constant pressure to push back the frontiers of access.

This will have at least two important and contradictory effects. On the one hand, the potential explosive increase in access to the global mass media will tend to lead to the fast growth of 'internet opium'. For private consumers of the global mass media, far from being a personally liberating, interactive, learning medium, the evidence so far is that the principal activities that the global internet is used for by private consumers are pornography, sports and cartoons. To some degree this might tend to reinforce, not reduce, political stability. However, rapid penetration of China by the global media might make it much more difficult for the Chinese government to control political dissent. Moreover, much of the content of the global mass media, while not being explicitly political, could have a socially destabilizing effect through its corrosive impact on China's value system, especially among young people.

It is possible that the political and social instability that might result from full implementation of the WTO Agreement in China might increase the degree of central political control rather than reduce it. Only in this way might China be able to survive the coming period politically and avoid the nightmare of a Soviet-style collapse of the state. The current ferocious campaign against corruption symbolises the central leadership's intense determination to maintain socio-political order. Its rapidly escalating nature illustrates the fragility of the current state of China's institutional evolution. In January 2001, Vice-Premier Li Lanqing warned that unless current trends in corruption were reversed it would 'ruin the party and the state'. High-speed entry to the WTO under these conditions carries large risks.

# 3.6   Prospects: (iii) an alternative outcome?

If China does, indeed, stick closely to the agreed terms of entry to the WTO, then China's leaders would have to deal simultaneously with several shocks. These include the shock of 'normal' restructuring due to intensified high-speed competition consequent upon the terms under which China has entered the WTO; the shock of having to compete on the 'global level playing field' with a global business system that has never been so concentrated; the shock of the impact of the IT revolution upon employment; the shock of the drastic impact of the global media revolution upon Chinese culture; the shock for Chinese people's self-esteem of the country's failure to establish a group of powerful indigenous corporations; and the shock of dealing with the dominance of US-based corporations. It is possible that the very prospect of such shocks might lead to intense pressure to reinvigorate China's industrial policy. A number of factors could facilitate such a development.

## Deep-seated Chinese ambitions

A persistent theme of this book has been the intense ambitions within Chinese politics and society at large to construct large, globally competitive businesses that can take their place on the global stage alongside the world's leading corporations. These intense national ambitions are reflected in daily discussion with Chinese people, from ordinary citizens to leading business people and politicians. These powerful nationalist sentiments are reflected in forms such as the best-selling book, *China Can Say No* (Song Qiang *et al.*, 1996) as well as other popular books, such as *The Foreign Army Grabs China* (Chen Fang, 1999) and *Robbing China* (Cun Fu, 1998). They are reflected also in the passionate and deeply-researched onslaught on China's decision to join the WTO in Han Deqiang's book, *The Globalisation Trap and China's Present Choice*:

Even though the competitive strength of China's banking, insurance, automobile, communications, chemical industry, textiles and agriculture are still very weak, and even though these sectors have a fundamental importance to the Chinese economy, and although they could become completely controlled by foreign companies, China, with a thick head still wants free market competition, calling itself a fervent disciple of the free market economy.

China's decision to join the WTO under the terms agreed with the US and EU respectively has prompted intense debate within the country about China's development path. Unsurprisingly, the degree of explicit public discussion among senior policymakers is limited. Beneath the surface there is deep, passionate argument. In wider circles, unconstrained by the burdens of political leadership, there is open public debate. These forces combine to produce intense pressure on China's leaders to demonstrate that they are defending China's perceived national interests. The intensity of the policy debate is reflected in the fact that negotiations over the final details of China's entry to the WTO had still not been completed by March 20001. Foreign Trade Minister Shi Guangsheng did not believe that China would enter the WTO before late 2001, three years after the initial deal was struck with the US.

## High quality, ambitious Chinese large enterprise managers

Throughout this book we have encountered many examples of the deeply-felt ambitions of the managers of China's large enterprises. These entrepreneurs are now far more aware of the nature of the competition that awaits them on the global level playing field. Despite high levels of corruption, there are also deeply-held ambitions among China's bureaucrats to build a powerful 'national team' of large corporations. The China Big Business Programme itself, which formed the basis of this book, was initiated precisely by such a combination of bureaucrats and business leaders, who hoped through the Programme to advance their understanding of how China could construct globally competitive large firms. China has no shortage of entrepreneurs who are able to lead the growth of China's large firms if they are given the appropriate environment in which to do so. There is deep ambition within the Chinese large-scale enterprises to become genuine global players, despite the enormous difficulties that they face.

## Increased East Asian co-operation in response to the Asian crisis

There are strong feelings of resentment within the East Asian nations at the way in which the Asian crisis was perceived to be primarily an 'internal' problem of poor governance and lack of transparency in business institutions. There is also deep resentment in the region at the perceived crudeness of the IMF response, and the subsequent failure of the international financial institutions to implement substantial reforms that could prevent such a crisis occurring again. In June 2000 in Beijing, the Chinese People's Political Consultative Conference organized a high level meeting on globalization, with leaders of many of the world's multinational firms, several former national leaders, including Lee Kuan Yew, and a few scholars. At this meeting, the former Deputy Prime Minister of Thailand commented on the impact of the Asian crisis:

> In the 1990s capital flowed into the emerging economies like water into the lower basin after the floodgates are lifted. After a while, the whole basin becomes heavily flooded. All the farms, buildings and cattle are submerged under water. When everything is destroyed, the water is quickly drained out, and the whole area dries up completely. Then we are blamed that we are cronies, imprudent, inefficient, over-investors, have weak financial institutions, a poor supervision system, the wrong exchange rate regime, and a poor auditing system. After accepting the IMF's bail-out funds, we were forced to accept a ready-made formula prescription that forced our economies to contract drastically so that the lenders could recover their money as rapidly as possible. There has been a demand from the emerging countries that the world financial order should be reviewed. Globalization of capital movements can be destructive and destabilize the world economy. In the long-run it may not benefit anyone except the speculators, financial brokers, investment bankers and fund managers. The short-term gains of these groups of people will be a great obstacle in allowing the world to reach a high level of welfare. The gains will be concentrated only in a group of the world's financial centres. The credibility of the IMF has completely gone, at least in East Asia. They listen but they never hear.

By the time Dr. Ramangkura came to deliver his speech on the final day of the 21st Century Forum, most of the representatives of the multinational companies and many of those from the international institutions, had left the Forum for more important tasks.

The widespread feelings of resentment and humiliation among the East Asian countries began to take a concrete form later in the year 2000. In July the annual meeting of the ten Asean (Association of Southeast Asian Nations) countries was marked by the first formal meeting of the foreign ministers from Asean with those of China, Japan and Korea, 'in a further manifestation of their intensifying co-operation' (*Financial Times*). The meeting attracted special interest because some people believe that 'this group could eventually transform Asia's relationship with the rest of the world and alter the balance of global economic policy-making by creating a new regional bloc' (*Financial Times*). The new group has been nicknamed 'Asean plus three' since it started to have regular meetings during the Asian crisis. For outsiders the new spirit of Asian co-operation is 'unnerving', since it seems to 'hark back to the East Asian Economic Caucus (EAEC) proposed in the mid-1990s by Mahatir Mohammad, Malaysia's Prime Minister'. That upset the US, because it was specifically excluded from the arrangement.

It was the Asian economic crisis that drove the group towards closer economic co-operation. This includes an agreement in May 2000 to set up a network of bilateral currency swaps to help protect them against currency speculation. A key factor has been China's willingness to participate. The new institutional forum is important as a sign of improvement in China's 'prickly relationship with Japan' (*Financial Times*). Asean is putting the finishing touches to its own free trade area and bilateral free trade negotiations are starting to proliferate, for example, between Japan and South Korea and Japan and Singapore. If these developments were the signal for more extended co-operation on matters of industrial and financial policy, including significant cross-border mergers and acquisitions within the region, then it could herald a substantial shift in the balance of power in global business. A more deeply integrated East Asia, with regionally-based large corporations that spanned boundaries within the East Asia region, including both Japan and China, would be the basis for a powerful challenge to the emergence of large corporations based within the EU and the US.

In August 2000 a highly significant development in East Asian business was announced. This was the agreement to deepen the partnership between Posco and Nippon Steel, to form 'one of the most high-profile alliances between a Japanese and a Korean company in decades' (*Financial Times*). These were already the world's two largest steel producers. Their combined output totals around 50m tons. They have a joint global market share of around 7 per cent, and significantly above this in high value-added steels. The groups agreed to broaden a strategic alliance to cut costs and increase their defences against a hostile takeover. The groups agreed to deepen their cross-ownership to around 3 per cent in each direction. They agreed to pool their resources in research and development, in information technology and to co-operate in overseas joint ventures. They are discussing the possibility of pooling their procurement and distribution.

## Uncertainties over the US economy

Despite the seeming invulnerability of the US economy and US large corporations, there are important uncertainties surrounding the US economy. Most obviously, it is still uncertain how the long boom of the US stockmarket will develop. In 1999, the 'old economy' stocks marked time. The year 2000 saw a large downturn in the value of the high technology sector. It remains to be seen if the US economy will achieve a 'soft landing' from the long stockmarket boom of the 1990s. Much of the US economic and stockmarket boom depended on the perception of the unlimited opportunities offered to US big business by the liberalization of the global economy. However, the future of the WTO is far from certain. The institution is dominated numerically by members from the developing countries. There is tremendous pressure from them to resist the US's wish to impose global standards on investment rules, on labour regulations and environmental conditions. If China and the main developing country members were to work together to attempt to push the institution to serve their own ends rather than those of the advanced economies, it could have profound results, with substantial implications for US business. Even the very survival of the WTO is uncertain.

## Central role for East Asian people in US high technology

A further important uncertainty in the development of the US business structure is the long-term role played by Chinese and Indian scientists and engineers in the growth of the 'brain' of the US economy, in the shape of the leading edge of research in the high technology industries. We have seen that there is a severe shortage of capable indigenous US citizens able to meet the technical challenges of these occupations. Consequently, a large and fast-growing fraction of the leading edge of US technological progress is being undertaken by Asian people. It is uncertain what the implications of this will be. A highly important issue surrounds the degree to which these people will return to their native lands, either physically or in terms of business development. The scarcest resource by far in the information revolution is high quality human resources. In this sense, the Asian nations already are moving into the driving seat of the world economy in the early 21st century.

## Intense competition produces opportunities as well as challenges

The very intensity of global competition is producing many opportunities for Chinese firms to catch up. In every sector in the advanced economies there are powerful players that cannot maintain the pace of competition with the leading players. They may possess strong technologies, global markets and global brands. If they were given the choice, they might prefer, in the long-run interests of their shareholders, to join forces with a major Chinese player, rather than being merged with another large corporation based in the advanced economies. This may be especially true within East Asia and in developing countries generally. The automobile, oil and petrochemical, steel, aerospace, telecoms services, IT hardware, media and fast-moving consumer goods sectors, all have obvious examples that spring to mind.

## Renewed East Asian business confidence

Despite the great severity of the East Asian crisis, and the deep problems it revealed in the institutional structure of the East Asian conglomerate, the region quickly began to regain its confidence. The number of Japanese companies in the

*Fortune 500* (ranked by sales) sharply dropped from 126 in 1997 to 100 in 1999, before starting to rise again to reach 107 in the year 2000. The number of companies from Japan in the *FT 500* (ranked by market capitalization) collapsed from 110 in 1996 to just 46 in 1998, but in 1999, the number recovered quickly to reached 77. The number from the Four Little Tigers in the *FT 500* collapsed from 21 in 1996 to just 11 in 1997, but had recovered to 20 in 1999. Despite radical restructuring in Asian-based large firms, the Asian model of using state industrial policy to support the growth of indigenous big business was far from dead. The state itself was playing an important role in the region's restructuring process.

## The role model of global oligopoly

The global business revolution made it more and more clear to Chinese policy-makers that the neoclassical interpretation of capitalism was based on a deep misrepresentation of the real nature of that system. Chinese popular newspapers, for example, were at least as interested in the global merger and acquisition boom as the Western media. China's agreement with the US in 1999 on entry to the WTO coincided with the value of global mergers and acquisitions considerably exceeding $US3 trillion, of which the US alone accounted for $1.9 trillion and Europe for $1.5 trillion. By comparison, mergers and acquisition within Non-Japan Asia were just $150bn. In Greater China they stood at only $41bn. The total of mergers and acquisitions in China in 1999 stood at a mere $15 bn.

It has become abundantly clear that the barriers to entry for Chinese firms were getting larger and larger. On the one hand, this produced feelings of despair at the possibility of industrial policy in China allowing Chinese firms to catch up. On the other hand it made it increasingly clear that if Chinese firms wished to catch up with the global leaders they could only do so on the basis of powerful large corporations. This meant that large internal mergers and acquisitions were crucial, whether they were through the market mechanism or were state-led. It meant also, that Chinese firms needed to think even more carefully than before about the need to realistically benchmark themselves against the global giant corporations, and allow modern corporate managers the autonomy to run their business in a competitive fashion. It meant that Chinese firms needed to think even more realistically about the need to expand into global markets for both products and for businesses. No globally competitive player can rely purely on the 'home market' any longer, even if that market is the US or the EU, let alone China.

## Re-invigorated industrial policy?

These factors combine to produce many dynamic possibilities. They provide an environment in which it is possible to imagine a combination of forces that could produce a different response from Chinese policymakers than simply administering the WTO rules as agreed with the US and the EU. Indeed, as China enters the 21st century there are already contradictory signs in respect to industrial policy. On the one hand, the giant AVIC aerospace corporation was broken into two separate pieces. Separately they stood even less chance of global success than as a united entity. In the financial sector, China's policymakers were enacting the very polices which the US had so recently rejected, of strictly separating the different sectors of business in order to maintain 'greater competition' among domestic financial institutions and help to prevent financial system instability. In sector after sector, as we have seen, there was a complete failure to achieve mergers across regions due to local protectionism.

On the other hand, there were signs that the prospect of intense competition within a very short period of time from the global giants, was focusing the minds of China's policymakers. There was a quickly-growing awareness of the great weakness of China's large firms, as the need to benchmark them realistically against the global giants greatly intensified. It was no longer possible to think vaguely about the possible competition from ill-defined future competitors. The benchmark now had suddenly become the world's leading firms in each sector. There were some indications that this was leading to a shift in central policy-makers' view of the degree of urgency of the task of creating genuinely competitive large firms. Faced with the extreme severity of the challenge, it is possible that the bureaucratic forces that previously prevented the necessary mergers and acquisitions, and the necessary appointment of high-quality managers with the authority to manage and improve enterprise performance, might be overcome. There were several indications that this might be the case.

Between 1998 and 2000 the central government led the massive restructuring and international flotation of CNPC (PetroChina) and Sinopec. This process was widely criticized as an example of 'bureaucratic-led restructuring' as opposed to 'restructuring through the market'. Despite these criticisms, the state-led restructuring and international flotation of CNPC and Sinopec were basically successful. They signalled a very different pattern of advance for Chinese industrial policy faced with the challenge of globalization. These were highly significant events for China as it entered the 21st century. They provided a very different signal from the break-up of AVIC into two separate 'competitive' firms.

In 1998 China Telecom (Hong Kong) merged with the Jiangsu Mobile Phone Company in a $2.9bn deal, and in 1999, it merged again with Fujian and Henan Mobile Phone companies in a deal worth $6.9bn. This increased the number of subscribers from 9m to almost 16m. By April 2000, the market capitalization of China Telecom (Hong Kong) had risen to $99bn, so that the company was now a serious player in international markets. At that point, their-named China Mobile (Hong Kong) had a market capitalization almost equal to that of British Telecom and WorldCom MCI, and considerably greater even than that of Telefonica (Spain). This could form the basis for significant expansion outside China. A further indication of the capital-raising possibilities of China's potential global giants was provided by the IPO of the state-backed China Unicom,

China's second-largest telecoms company, in June 2000. The listing raised almost $5bn.

In July 2000, two important announcements provided a further signal that there might be a significant shift in policy under way. The first was the announcement that Chinese airlines were to be reorganized into three big groups, based around China Southern Airlines, China Eastern Airlines and Air China. A few days later it was announced that Huaneng Power International and Shandong Huaneng Power Development Company were to merge. This was much the largest merger of two foreign-listed Chinese companies. The merged companies will have a total installed capacity of 11 000mW. The new entity will be China's largest independent power producer. One enthusiastic analyst commented: 'It is the biggest meanest fish in the pond. It will be the McDonald's of power in China'.

It is still far from certain that such a strategic shift has been made. However, should it indeed prove to be the case, then it is highly likely that the capital markets would respond to provide the needed capital for the radically restructured large Chinese firms. Despite rapid growth since the 1980s, China's domestic stock markets are still very immature and highly speculative. By 1998 China had almost 800 domestically-listed companies. Their total stock market capitalization was $231bn, amounting to around one-quarter of China's national product. This ratio was not much above the average for low income countries and far below that of the mature, stockmarket based economies (Table 3.14). China's overseas listings in 1999 had a market capitalization of only around $60 billion, far below the total domestic listings. Around 70 per cent of the total equity of China's enterprises was held by the Chinese state.

**Table 3.14 *Stock market development in China and other countries/regions, 1998***

| Country/region | Stock market capitalization | GNP | |
|---|---|---|---|
| | $bn | $bn | % |
| China | 231 | 929 | 24.9 |
| Hong Kong | 413 | 158 | 261.4 |
| US | 11 309 | 7921 | 142.8 |
| Low income countries | 387 | 1 844 | 21.0 |
| Middle income countries | 1 405 | 4 420 | 31.8 |
| High income countries | 21 749 | 22 599 | 96.2 |

However, there is a relatively large volume of savings held by Chinese people. In 1998, funds held in Chinese savings deposits totalled over $640bn. Therefore, even within China, there is considerable scope for China's potential global giant corporations to raise capital through the stock market and through the commercial banking system. This possibility is dwarfed by the potential of global financial markets. If China were to establish a credible industrial policy for building globally powerful commercially-oriented large firms, then there are almost unlimited opportunities to raise capital from international markets, through stock and bond markets and/or from bank loans. Passive privatization of China's large enterprises in the face of the impending challenge from global giants, would not produce this outcome since it is becoming increasingly obvious that on the 'global level playing field' few of China's large firms could survive in direct competition with the global giants. In order to raise capital in a sustained and large-scale fashion for China's large enterprises, China's government would need to demonstrate that it had entered a new era of industrial restructuring. This would involve demonstrating that strong domestic firms were able to merge with other strong domestic firms, whether through the market or through the bureaucracy, that they had genuinely independent and strong management, that they were able to pursue international mergers and acquisitions, and that they were supported by a coherent set of government industrial policies.

## Conclusion

It is conceivable that China's industrial policies might be given fresh life with a renewed focus and sense of urgency due to the impending shock of joining the WTO under the terms agreed. Despite the enormous challenges presented by the global business revolution, it is possible to imagine a strategy that might lead to the growth of competitive large firms based in China. In this case, China's large corporations might assume an important place among the world's giant corporations and Chinese-based firms might themselves begin to directly assume the functions of 'global systems integrators'. Such a large shift in industrial policy would involve tense and complicated issues in China's international relations, especially in relation to the US, since it would involve a *de facto* re-negotiation of the terms under which China enters the WTO.

The US government put enormous effort into convincing the US public that the Agreement is in the interest of the US people. It had to cope with great opposition from human rights groups and from organized labour, convinced that US jobs will be lost by an even faster growth of Chinese imports than in the past two decades. The US people, and especially the relevant lobby groups, were barraged with arguments about the 'fairness' and ethical desirability of China joining the WTO. They were reassured at great length that China could be trusted and would, indeed, observe the rules to which it had signed agreement. We have seen that the US has put into place more comprehensive monitoring arrangements than exist for any other member of the WTO. It is significant that one of the major speeches delivered by Ambassador Barshefsky on the implications of the Agreement was delivered at the United States Military Academy, where she explicitly linked the issue of the Agreement with the US's national security interest: 'Trade and American National Security: The Case of China's WTO Accession'. She commented: 'This Spring as Congress considers China's accession to the World Trade Organization and permanent normal trade relations, we face a decision which illustrates, as clearly as any in the past fifty years, the links between trade policy and national security'.

Within China, there are powerful forces that are dismayed by the Agreement. They will do all they can to slow down the implementation of the Agreement. It is unknown either in what ways the composition of the Chinese leadership might alter. China's three leaders, Jiang Zemin, Zhu Rongji and Li Peng, are all scheduled to retire within the next two years. A variety of possible factors could lead to a significant shift in the leadership's position towards foot-dragging on the Agreement. Among the most obvious such factors might be if the impact on China's large enterprises was greater than the leadership had anticipated. If there is widespread flouting of the terms of the Agreement, then there will be great difficulties for international relations, especially between the US and China. US business and public opinion will be united in their indignation that the long-negotiated Agreement had not been treated seriously. There will be widespread feelings of anger at the 'unfairness' and 'non-ethical' nature of such behaviour. These feelings are likely to be intensified if the US economy enters a period of serious economic downturn. Such a background provides a fertile soil for escalation of conflict in ways that cannot today be predicted.

History is far from dead. The uncertainties are great. The prospects are highly dynamic.

# Recommended Reading

Amsden, A. A., *Asia's Next Giant: South Korea and Late Industrialization* (New York and Oxford: Oxford University Press, 1989).

Aoki, M. and Dore, R. (eds), *The Japanese Firm: the Sources of Competitive Advantage* (London: Oxford University Press, 1994).

Bernstein R. and Munro, R. H., *The Coming Conflict with China* (New York: Random House, 1998).

Chandler, A., *Scale and Scope: the Dynamics of Industrial Capitalism* (Cambridge, MA: Harvard University Press, 1990).

Chandler, A., Amatori, F. and Hikino, T. (eds), *Big Business and the Wealth of Nations* (Cambridge: Cambridge University Press, 1997).

Chang, H. J., *The Political Economy of Industrial Policy* (New York: St Martin's Press, 1994).

Dicken, P., *Global Shift* (London: Paul Chapman, 2nd edn, 1998).

Groomridge, M. A. and Barfield, C. E., *Tiger by the Tail: China and the World Trade Organization* (Washington, DC: American Enterprise Institute,1999).

Hirst, P. and Thompson, G., *Globalization in Question* (London: Routledge, 1995).

Huntington, S. P., *The Clash of Civilisations and the Remaking of the World Order* (New York: Simon and Schuster, 1996).

Janelli, R., *Making Capitalism* (Stanford, CA: Stanford University Press, 1993).

Johnson, C., *MITI and the Japanese Miracle* (Stanford, CA: Stanford University Press, 1982).

Kornai, J., *The Road to a Free Economy* (New York: Norton, 1990).

Lake, D. A., *Power, Protection and Free Trade* (Ithaca, NY: Cornell University Press, 1988).

Lardy, N., *China's Unfinished Revolution* (Washington: Brookings Institution, 1998).

Lin, J. Y. F., Cai, F. and Li, Z., *The China Miracle* (Hong Kong: Chinese University Press, 1996).

Lloyd, J., *Rebirth of a Nation: The Anatomy of Russia* (London: Michael Joseph, 1998).

Lo, D., *Market and Institutional Regulation in Chinese Industrialization, 1978–94* (Basingstoke, UK: Macmillan, 1997).

Miller, J., *Mikhael Gorbachev and the End of Soviet Power* (Basingstoke, UK: Macmillan, 1993).

Naughton, B., *Growing out of the Plan: Chinese Economic Reform, 1978–1993* (Cambridge: Cambridge University Press, 1995).

Nolan, P., *State and Market in the Chinese Economy* (Basingstoke, UK: Macmillan, 1993).

Nolan, P., *China's Rise, Russia's Fall* (Basingstoke, UK: Macmillan, 1995).

Nolan, P., *Indigenous Large Firms in China's Economic Reforms: The Case of Shougang Iron and Steel Corporation* (London: Contemporary China Institute, 1998).

Nolan, P., *Coca-Cola and the Global Business Revolution: A Study with Special Reference to the EU* (Cambridge: Polity Press, 1999).

Ohmae, K. (ed.), *The Evolving Global Economy: Making Sense of the New World Order* (Boston, MA: Harvard Business School Publishing, 1995).

Penrose, E., *The Theory of the Growth of the Firm* (Oxford: Oxford University Press, 1995).

Porter, M., *The Competitive Advantage of Nations* (London: Macmillan, 2000).

Ruigrok, W. and van Tulder, R., *The Logic of International Restructuring* (London and New York: Routledge, 1995).

Steinfeld, E., *Forging Reform in China* (Cambridge: Cambridge University Press, 1998).

Vogel, E., *The Four Little Dragons* (Cambridge, MA: Harvard University Press, 1991).

Wade, R., *Governing the Market: Economic Theory and the Role of Government in East Asian Industrialization* (Princeton, NJ: Princeton University Press, 1990).

Wang, X., *China's Price and Ownership Reform* (Basingstoke, UK: Macmillan, 1998).

Wang, X. and Nolan, P., *Strategic Restructuring* (*Zhanlue chongzu*). Shanghai: Wenhui chubanshe, 1998.

Xu, D., and Wu, C., in C. Curwen (ed.), *Capitalism in China 1644–1840* (Basingstoke, UK: Macmillan, 2000).

# Index